MW01254200

FAR FROM THE CHURCH BELLS

This book is an historical and anthropological study of Locorotondo in the Province of Bari in Southeastern Italy. It focuses on the unusual nature of peasant society in the region and attempts to explain how it came about. What distinguishes Locorotondo and the neighbouring towns, is that peasants live dispersed in the countryside rather than in densely populated rural towns, the pattern more typical for Southern Italy. The people are mainly small proprietor grape growers, and have traditionally been better off than other southern Italian peasants. The book traces the development of this settlement pattern from the eighteenth century. Interweaving anthropological understanding with historical data, the author assesses its effects on family life, social structure, and the relationship between the town and country.

Stone wall and *trullo*

FAR FROM THE CHURCH BELLS

Settlement and society in an Apulian town

ANTHONY H. GALT

Professor of Social Change and Development
and Anthropology, University of Wisconsin – Green Bay

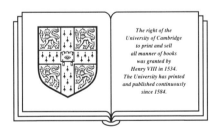

The right of the
University of Cambridge
to print and sell
all manner of books
was granted by
Henry VIII in 1534.
The University has printed
and published continuously
since 1584.

CAMBRIDGE UNIVERSITY PRESS

Cambridge
New York   Port Chester
Melbourne   Sydney

Published by the Press Syndicate of the University of Cambridge
The Pitt Building, Trumpington Street, Cambridge CB2 1RP
40 West 20th Street, New York, NY 10011, USA
10 Stamford Road, Oakleigh, Melbourne 3166, Australia

First published 1991

Printed in Great Britain at the University Press, Cambridge

British Library cataloguing in publication data
Galt, Anthony H.
Far from the church bells: settlement and society in an Apulian town.
1. Italy. Locorotondo. Rural communities. Social conditions, history
I. Title
307.720945751

Library of Congress cataloguing in publication data
Galt, Anthony H.
Far from the church bells: settlement and society in an Apulian town/Anthony H. Galt.
    p.   cm.
Includes bibliographical references and index.
ISBN 0-521-39444-9
1. Ethnology – Italy – Locorotondo. 2. Land settlement patterns – Italy – Locorotondo.
3. Peasantry – Italy – Locorotondo. 4. Locorotondo (Italy) – History. 5. Locorotondo
(Italy) – Social life and customs. I. Title.
GN585.I8G34   1991
306'.0945'751 – dc20   90–1897 CIP

ISBN 0521 39444 9   hardback

GE

This book is dedicated to the memory of
Antonia Parisi Galt,
my mother, who passed away during its writing.

Contents

Plates

All photographs were taken by the author.

Figures

Tables

Acknowledgments

There are a number of people and institutions which must be acknowledged for having facilitated this work. First, the initial research in 1981–1982 was supported by a grant from the Anthropology Program of the National Science Foundation (NSF Grant BNS-8023297), in conjunction with minor funding from the University of Wisconsin–Green Bay. A small amount of money from the university's Research Council also helped facilitate return to Italy in 1986 to continue archive research in Bari.

In 1985 I attended Richard Herr's National Endowment for the Humanities Summer Seminar at the University of California at Berkeley and want to acknowledge that agency's support, and thank Richard Herr for putting together a most stimulating seminar in which some of the early phases of my analysis could be developed, and for his interest in the work then and since. By the time this book is published, a shorter version of Chapter 7 will appear in the collection compiled from that seminar (Galt, forthcoming).

I owe debts of gratitude to many people in Locorotondo. There are many informants who I would like to thank by name, but I conducted most interviews with guarantees of anonymity. I would like to extend thanks to the then mayor of Locorotondo, Michele Gianfrate, whose interest and early support of my fieldwork, and help solving some practical problems having to do with settling in, facilitated the initiation of the project. Two local scholars and intellectual entrepreneurs, Giuseppe Guarella and Franco Basile, also deserve my gratitude for their initiative, with the help of others, in extending knowledge of things Locorotondese through the founding of a lovingly published local journal, *Locorotondo*, in which they have graciously included popular versions, written in Italian, of some of the material in this book.

Above all I must express my gratitude to Giorgio Cardone, initially my field assistant, and soon after good friend, key informant, and colleague. Giorgio and I worked hard as a team. His intelligent conversation and comments on the project constantly stimulated my thoughts and helped direct the research in fruitful directions. The field work would have been completed only with difficulty without him, and not within the space of a year. His help was also invaluable during my return visit in 1986 when he called to my attention a crucial document, the 1811 Napoleonic census, upon which he had already performed some preliminary analysis. Locorotondo is fortunate indeed to be able to boast of his citizenship.

At the University of Bari I made the acquaintance of several individuals with whom I could interact professionally, and upon whom I could call for help later. These include Patrizia Resta, Anna Maria Rivera, and Antonino Colajanni, all then at the Institute of Ethnology, and Angelo Massafra, historian. I am especially grateful to the latter for pointing me in some important directions in the archives, reading and commenting upon a preliminary article manuscript, and for keeping me informed of important publications I would have discovered only years later in the United States.

At the Archivio di Stato di Bari I would like to acknowledge Giuseppe Dibenedetto, Director, and Domenico Pansini for their help during the first phases of archive work, and especially the diligent and knowledgeable Grazia Maiorana, who served as Virgil to me during my descent into the mysteries of the police and judicial records during 1986. Gregorio Angelini, now director of the Archivio di Stato di Potenza, and Giuseppe Carlone, two historians also showed me several important documentary sources and made welcome suggestions about how I might best use them.

At my university Roxanne Dornaus and Carol Bacon helped with the arduous task of making survey and archive data machine readable. Paula Allen, graduate assistant, provided expertise and practical help in mainframe computer analyses. Kathleen McDonough graciously found, xeroxed, and sent me some material from the National Library in Florence which I could not retrieve in American libraries. Colleagues Craig Lockard, Harvey Kaye, and Bela Baker provided moral support during the book's long gestation period, as did George Saunders at Lawrence University. Larry Smith visited my family and me at our field site, and provided help coding survey data and many useful suggestions.

The four reviewers for Cambridge University Press to whom my book manuscript was sent, one of whom voluntarily identified himself as Donald Pitkin, provided invaluable (although sometimes contradictory) comments. At the Press Jessica Kuper, Wendy Guise, Jayne Matthews and Gillian Maude, have been of enormous help in putting the book into its final form.

All of the people mentioned facilitated my work, but, of course, I alone am responsible for whatever errors of fact or interpretation I may have made.

Finally, there is no way to repay the gratitude I feel toward Janice Galt and Alexander Galt, my wife and son, for their moral and tangible support during the two experiences in Locorotondo and during the years in between and afterwards. There is no substitute for having a family which believes in one's work.

Chapter 1

INTRODUCTION

BACKGROUND

In Locorotondo, in the heel of Southern Italy, the rural folk repeat a proverb: "If you want to eat bread, stay far from the church bells."[1] This book is about the meaning of that proverb. It explores the history, causes, and sociocultural ramifications of the unusual settlement pattern found in Locorotondo and in other towns located in a zone of Apulia in Southern Italy known as the Murgia dei Trulli (the Plateau of the Trulli). *Trulli* are peasant dwellings characterized by cone-shaped domes surmounted by whitewashed finial ornaments, and are found only in this zone of Italy. Here a high proportion of residence in the countryside accompanies a moderate degree of peasant prosperity in what one turn-of-the-century geographer called "an oasis of small property in a zone of large estates" (Maranelli, 1946). The settlement pattern of Locorotondo originated at least as far back as the early eighteenth century, consolidated during the nineteenth, and has endured through the upheavals of the twentieth into the present. A little over 50 percent of the town's population continues to live in the countryside, and relative prosperity, based upon the building trades adopted by the sons of generations of peasant small proprietors, persists in the countryside.

After a day's visit in 1974 during a journey home from the Island of Pantelleria, my other field site, and after much library research, I chose the Murgia dei Trulli for concentrated study. The area, its Locorotondese heartland in particular, contrasted sharply with the south of the *latifondo*, agrotown, and rural proletarian. I felt that in unraveling the history and culture of such a place I could not only gain an understanding of why a dispersed settlement pattern and small holder agriculture had developed, but also of how these facts related to social structure and values.

Peasants, settlement, and the Murgia dei Trulli

I made my choice from a concern that the historical and ethnographic portrayal of rural South Italy be made more complex and complete. Both within the Italian tradition of writing about the south (called *meridionalismo*) and the "southern problem," and within the English-language anthropological, sociological, and journalistic literatures on the area, there emerges an emphasis on the agrotown with its poverty stricken rural proletariat. However, as Arlacchi has recently reiterated in his analysis of Calabria, there are and have been many southern Italies (Arlacchi, 1983). To be sure much, even most, of the south has a history of agrotown settlement and endemic poverty, and the thorough descriptions of Cornelisen (1969, 1976), Davis (1973), Lopreato (1967), Blok (1974), and Schneider and Schneider (1976), among others, constitute essential contributions which portray with accuracy and insight the realities those authors experienced. But so far there has been little ethnographic or ethnohistorical work which is comparable in thoroughness to those works and which focuses on small proprietor peasant settings in the south, or on the zones which contain dispersed settlement.[2]

Of course the concentration and dispersal of settlement among European peasantries is a topic which has generated considerable literature. Dovring, in his classic work on twentieth-century European agricultural systems, reviews some of this literature and broadly maps the degree of dispersion and concentration in settlement patterns throughout Europe. Apulia as a whole fits into his category of very highest concentration into agrotowns (1965: fig. 1). This underlines the suspicion that something remarkable accounts for the strong development of the opposite pattern in the sub-zone of Apulia where Locorotondo lies.

Anthropologists and others have now dealt at length with dispersed peasant settlement patterns and their social organizational implications in Central and North Italy. Notable among these studies are Silverman's study of an Umbrian town (1975), Kertzer's historical study of coresidence among peasants living near the city of Bologna (1984), and Barbagli's discussion of Northern and Central Italian peasant family patterns (1984: 113–121). All three works devote attention to the *mezzadria* (long-term sharecropping) pattern typical for peasants in those areas. Although the classic upper Italian *mezzadria* pattern certainly involved dispersed residence, the histori-

cal, economic, and social circumstances under which it developed are
completely different from those of the deep south where such
long-term, tightly controlled, sharecropping and family coresidence
patterns were rare.

There have been several efforts to map and describe dispersed
settlement areas specifically in the Italian South (Biasutti, 1932;
Dickinson, 1956), but these studies adopt a spatial approach lacking
an anthropologically holistic view of society and a concern with
understanding specific cases in depth. Attention to the concentration
and dispersion of peasant populations in the post-Second World War
literature particularly relates to agrarian reform efforts in the *mezzogiorno* which in part consisted of trying to move peasants into the
countryside to settle on redistributed land. Although done with the
conviction that peasant small proprietorship and rural residence
would promote development and greater working efficiencies, these
engineered efforts met with mixed success (Dickenson, 1956: 297;
Blok, 1966). It is therefore important to understand an area such as
the Murgia dei Trulli where dispersed settlement developed indige-
nously in seeming contradiction to the normal southern agrotown
pattern.

In a short article Blok attempted to explain the existence and
persistence of the agrotown pattern in Southern Italy and in the same
breath addressed the opposite phenomenon, dispersed settlement
(1969). Through a review of previous literature, and his own field
experience in Sicily, he invoked some of the variables which were
likely to lead toward agglomeration and toward dispersion. His
conclusion about the latter was that it accompanied intensive agriculture and made sense "only if the peasant is either owner of a more or
less united plot, or if as a tenant he enjoys a certain degree of
independence regarding a similar piece of land" (1969: 132). While
united land does not prove to be crucial to dispersed settlement on the
Murgia dei Trulli, the factor of long-term control over land is
important for understanding it in Apulia and will be considered in
later chapters.

More recently Arlacchi provided an analysis of three agricultural
regimes in Calabria which he asserts differ strikingly in terms of their
agricultural exploitation, their economic conditions, and their social
structures (Arlacchi, 1980). The areas Arlacchi describes include a
zone of rural proletarians and great estates; a zone of constantly
shifting entrepreneurial activity, and a zone of dispersed small

proprietorship. He argues that these three peasant economic situations produced three distinctive types of social and family relations. His analysis introduces a greater expectation of holism into the analysis of the connection between settlement, land tenure, and social organization in South Italy and begs for amplification and verification. One of the areas he describes recalls the characteristics of Locorotondo and surrounding communities. The generalizations Arlacchi makes about the small proprietor regime there serve to define a South Italian small proprietor type, and as such they will deserve discussion in the last chapter of this work.

Through the years several Italian scholars have written about the Murgia dei Trulli, describing its major characteristics and correctly attributing differences between it and surrounding *latifondo* zones to perpetual lease (emphyteusis) contracts (Calella, 1941; Maranelli, 1946; Presutti, 1909; Ricchioni, 1958, 1959). However, these writers based their analyses upon contemporary observation of varying quality, not thorough archival research, and they do not provide an understanding of the ramifications of small proprietorship and dispersed settlement in the social settings of the towns in the zone. Their writings are especially valuable, however, as first hand reports of conditions during the times in which they were published.

Themes and organization

This book is meant, then, as a case study of a town on the Murgia dei Trulli which will broaden scholarly understanding of small proprietor and rurally settled peasant lifeways in the *mezzogiorno*. Part I describes the present of Locorotondo as I came to know it during my first field season in 1981–1982. It focuses on the theme of work and values about work, and compares town and country. Part of my task in the rest of the book is to describe the collective historical experience which produced those values. My approach to the present is diachronic. The "present" of a population is really the accumulation of the "pasts," the experiences, of the individuals who make it up. A profound sense of having been born into a "traditional" world which has been transformed into a "modern" one typifies the experiences of adults in Locorotondo. I do not mean to suggest by this use of a "traditional" and "modern" dichotomy that I subscribe to a variant of "modernization theory," which proposes change from some kind of static "classic peasant" situation toward an inevitable urban one. In fact, as I will show, the past described as traditional and little changing by my informants was full of change, and the unusual directions Locorotondo and neighboring locales have taken in the twentieth century put any notion of inevitable kinds of "modernization" to the lie. Rather, most of my informants grew up, learned to work, and formulated a set of values in a society *they saw* as linked generationally to a peasant past, and then in the late 1950s and early 1960s felt the jolt of a variety of changes which produced a strong sense of discontinuity with that past.

I have therefore adopted a shorthand terminology to refer to this sense. In this book the term "peasant" will refer to those families whose values and aspirations centered around carrying out full-time, but small-scale agriculture, but who often needed to supplement income by engaging family members in agricultural wage labor for purposes such as trousseau and marriage savings, or to provide a better living. During 1981–1982 there were still such families, but with few exceptions aging patriarchs headed them. The 1950s was the last decade in which it is safe to conclude that most rural families fell into this category. Aside from long distance migration, which would soon become an important factor, there were few other possibilities. The term "postpeasant" will refer to the individuals and families who came into adulthood during the decades after and including the 1960s, many of whose experiences include migration to the north and to other European countries or significant work experience outside agriculture in Apulia. Some of these individuals could be labeled "worker-peasants" – indeed some of them work in the Italsider steel mill in Taranto – but others have also been small-scale construction entrepreneurs with a high degree of autonomy. Also, while men have often been "part-time peasants," their wives have given full-time to agriculture and the household. Therefore, I have preferred the less restrictive term "postpeasant."

Part II of this book traces the historical development of settlement patterns in Locorotondo and the development of its peasant society in detail. Of course, social historical analysis in anthropology needs no special justification at this juncture in the development of the field, especially among scholars who concentrate upon Europe, but Anton Blok's introductory words in *The Mafia of a Sicilian Village, 1860–1960* are worth recalling.[3]

However invaluable and indispensable, the field work experience alone is insufficient to cope with the events of change in complex societies. To grasp the relationship between peasants and the larger society, data from field work must be supplemented with historical information. (1974: xxx–xxxi)

Insofar as I know, my book is the first anthropological history of a South Italian town to push detailed historical analysis back into the eighteenth century. For the eighteenth and nineteenth centuries I rely, wherever possible, upon archival documentation, and the research brought to light many documents which were unknown even to local scholars in Locorotondo. To move from the recent present into the past, particularly to cast light on poorly documented dim areas, such as peasant family structure, I have had to rely upon oral history.

The words of an important eighteenth-century Neapolitan liberal thinker, Antonio Genovesi, suggested a central theme for the analysis of Locorotondo's development. In 1769 Genovesi, deploring the state of agriculture in the kingdom, and comparing it unfavorably with that of other parts of Europe (particularly England), asserted that ideally agriculture ought to fall into the hands of gentlemen and scientists, and wrote of the discouragement of its development in the following terms:

It is too well known how much difference there is between the cultivation of one's own field and that of another. The desire for wealth, for the hope of being better off ourselves, and for leaving our children in a better state, is a great motive to animate us toward work, and to make us think about and work upon our business with more skill, diligence, and spirit. So those peasants who have their own lands are always the wisest, most judicious, and most industrious. They think not only of earning for the present, but they push their thoughts toward the future and therefore use ingenuity to better and to perpetuate their holdings. This does not happen among those who work in the fields of others. What is it to them if all is ruined within a few years? Instead, the insult of seeing others fatten on their fatigue will make them rascally and so instead of improving things they will make them worse so as to be destructive. They also become sneaks, thieves, and assassins. And when it does not seem to them that they will succeed well at this life, they will live as thoughtless lazy beggars, or they will go populate certain cloisters to live off the backs of those few who continue to work. (Genovesi, 1978: 7–8)[4]

Genovesi underlined the problem of absentee and unconcerned landlordism, particularly among churchmen, raised the spector of class conflict and peasant rebellion by referring to "those excitations and steam vents, to which every so often the people are subject," and suggested the remedy that lands held by "those who either will not or cannot cultivate them," be "bestowed in perpetuity." He continued:

I know many wise and prudent gentlemen, once retired to the capital and being unable to supervise their estates, who have immediately sold or given their lands in perpetual lease. And I do not believe they have given it a second thought afterwards. One who gives his land in emphyteusis, even if he earns less income, can be sure of two points in accordance with human behavior: (1) that the income will be certain and constant; and (2) that the farm will not finish in ruin. If there were more who ceded their land in emphyteusis, they would be surer of their incomes because in that way population increase would not be lacking, and this is always a secure guarantee of a market for produce and consequently of income for proprietors. Therefore the true economy for lay proprietors who cannot oversee their properties or cultivate them, would be to lease them out in perpetuity. They would be looking after their own good and that of the community. But the clerics cannot and (as things now stand) must not farm for themselves. To say that St. Paul took pride in having worked with his hands to live and that among the rules of the first religious orders agriculture was a requirement, is not to realize that from the 18th century standpoint one is speaking of men of the 1st and 4th centuries. Therefore so that their lands do not become degraded, one cannot give them better counsel than, 'Divide, divide, but in small portions!' and I know that the most prudent think in this way. (1978: 9–10)

In these passages Genovesi suggested an *adaptive strategy* for landowners which was not, as he noted, original to his thinking but which he was among the first of the *Meridionalisti* ('Southernists') to formally espouse. That strategy was to divide unproductive estates among the peasantry through emphyteusis, or perpetual lease, with the stipulation of improvement of the land by the peasant tenant. Genovesi noted that this would produce a strong incentive to work hard, cultivate well and make the land productive, and, he thought, would guarantee a secure income to the landlord. Genovesi neglected to mention the landlord's other advantage in following such a strategy. This was that under the laws of the Kingdom of Naples, the tax burden of the land held under emphyteusis fell on the shoulders of the tenant. He also erroneously believed that the population of the kingdom was diminishing when, instead, during the eighteenth century it doubled in most zones. Understandably he failed to foresee the inflation which would erode emphyteutical rents over the coming decades.

I have chosen John Bennett's key concept of "adaptive strategy" for its usefulness in the study of complex societies such as that of the Murgia dei Trulli (Bennett, 1976: 271–272). As Bennett defines the concept it refers to the idea of purposive behavior – what Bennett calls "doing something about" – on the part of individual social actors. It can be expanded, as Bennett does in his account of the adaptive strategies of various subgroups on the Canadian plains, to speak of the purposive behavior of social groups (1969). The concept reminds us of something most people realize about their own social realities, but which has often been lost in the common attempt by social scientists to impose overly neat structures upon societies. This is that social reality is composed of individuals acting in groups and sometimes alone, who through their cultures (which in complex societies are "messy" in that they contain degrees of confusion and contradiction) attempt to make sense of the world around them, and using that sense of understanding attempt to do something about their situations. Out of these anything but smooth processes we may as social scientists be able to observe emergent patterns. Indeed, social groups may "pickle" successful emergent patterns as values and associated symbolic representations which help enculturate succeeding generations with the strategies. The "church bell" proverb, this book's title comes from, is a folkloric statement of the long-term peasant adaptive strategy in Locorotondo.

Further, the adaptive strategy concept moves the notion of adaptation away from a simplistic dichotomy between environment which must be adapted to and society which must do the adapting. Clearly groups must adopt adaptive strategies with respect to other groups, both near and distant (to the bureaucracies of nation states, for instance), as much as they must adapt to physical environmental conditions and changes in them. Particular adaptive strategies, as historian William Cronon has shown, may change environments in such a way as to require further changing strategies (1983). The notion opens the way for a connection between environmental anthropology, from which it comes, and the consideration of relationships between local places and broader, even global, political economic systems.

The concept is especially useful for analyzing social settings in which class and power relationships are central to social process. In such cases it can be used dialectically to analyze the purposive strategies of those groups who have power, taking into consideration their interests (which may be culturally or situationally defined). It can then be used to analyze how those with less power adapt or react to the actions of more powerful groups or to external factors. The broad concept of "strategy" allows us to deal both with higher class attempts at manipulation and exploitation and with subordinate actions mounted to cope with them, evade them, or reverse them. The concept does not assume that groups with differing interests end up in symbiotic relationships. The concept differs from the functionalist approach to adaptation which focuses too much on the notion of supposed equilibria reached through the process of adaptation in a system, and too little on the process itself. In fact, adaptive strategies may be unsuccessful after very little time or short sighted over the long run. They are also likely to have unexpected consequences for those who adopt them. I have kept these considerations in mind in my description of the historical development of settlement and agricultural patterns in Locorotondo.

The concept of adaptive strategy also unlocks the scholar from the assumption that ethnographers during their seasons in the field must somehow represent a describable structure instead of a process of change. Although anthropologists who have studied Italy are no strangers to historical methods and analysis, and those who have adopted such approaches have arrived at them from other theoretical directions, the adaptive strategy concept virtually demands a diachronic approach.

Emphyteusis was an adaptive strategy adopted at various times and in various places by landowners during the long history of Southern Italy and this book chronicles the case of the town of Locorotondo and its environs. Both lay and ecclesiastical landholders adopted emphyteusis at several moments in the area's history, but most particularly from the late eighteenth century through the beginning decades of the twentieth. It cannot be said that those landholders directly followed Genovesi's advice (although it is entirely possible that some were aware of it), because emphyteusis had been adopted as a strategy locally before he wrote, particularly by ecclesiastical institutions.

Moreover, Locorotondo and surrounding municipalities provide an interesting situation in which to observe the consequences of landowners and peasants following such a strategy. A thesis of this book will be, therefore, that the settlement pattern and development characteristic of this part of the Murgia dei Trulli are the result of a local landowning class strategy to realize income from a landscape which was agriculturally marginal, and which could only be made productive through massive amounts of intensive peasant labor, which was unaffordable directly, but capturable through emphyteusis and the incentives for peasant investment it offered. The adaptive strategies of landowners, however, called forth peasant counterstrategies, and the unique landscape and peasant culture of Locorotondo must be seen as dynamically related to such strategies, and have been created by them. Indeed, "to eat a piece of bread," the peasants of Locorotondo decided to *live* "far from the church bells," not merely commute to the fields as did their counterparts in most other towns. Unlike the upper Italian "classic" *mezzadria* pattern, nothing in the contracts directly compelled them to do so.

Part III of this book concerns the social, cultural, and political implications of the dispersed small proprietor peasant adaptive strategy. For the most part, this section relies upon oral historical material to reach into the past from the present. Documentary evidence tells little about peasant social structure in the deeper past, with the exception of information about marriage settlement. Decisions, made initially at the individual household level, but eventually made by the whole of the town's peasantry, were economic. However, as more and more families followed, and as the dispersed settlement pattern grew into a cultural expectation and was no longer a conscious individual strategy, certain characteristics of peasant social structure, with specific rules about inheritance, welfare of family members, authority, and relationships with neighbors, evolved to fit. Furthermore, the move of the peasantry of this small Apulian center to rural dwellings had certain implications with respect to the nature of power in local social organization. As I will show, in the early nineteenth century, as the local bourgeoisie became aware of the change underway, it reacted by trying to move the peasantry back within the town walls forcibly, probably in an attempt to recoup lost house rents. Later, particularly in the post-Second World War era, peasant suffrage meant that would-be political leaders needed to capture the rural vote, and that they needed to evolve specific political strategies for attracting or coercing rural folk into their party camps.

Lastly, the discussion will turn to some comparative matters. I will consider the significance of the Locorotondese case in the context of trying to define some kinds of peasantries in the *mezzogiorno*, and discuss the degree to which Locorotondo's peasantry shaped its countryside by comparing their experience with that of several other peasantries sharing potentially similar characteristics.

Unfortunately undertaking field and archival research forces certain decisions about what matters can be investigated thoroughly and what must be more lightly probed. Similarly, conveying the results of a research project becomes subject to certain practical and thematic limits about what can be included. In this book I have focused upon settlement pattern, agriculture, social organization, and peasant/town relationships, particularly those of a political nature. Space limits have forced me to give too little attention to matters of religious and magical belief, to migration, and to the description of the fascinating and sometimes colorful history of the elite and artisan classes of Locorotondo. Future publications will bring these topics to light.

RESEARCH IN AND AROUND LOCOROTONDO

I carried out the field research upon which this book is based during the academic year of 1981–1982. Ethnographic generalizations concerning present conditions refer to the early 1980s. My family and I made a second trip to Locorotondo during the summer of 1986, during which I carried out further research with nineteenth- and twentieth-century documents in Bari.

My wife, Janice, my son Alex (then 7), and I took up residence in the field during September of 1981 in the rural hamlet of Lamie di Olimpia on the northern border of the municipality of Locorotondo with that of Fasano. I hired a fine field assistant – really colleague – named Giorgio Cardone who helped with arranging and carrying out formal interviews, designing and conducting a sample survey of rural households, inculcating in me a smattering of the local dialect, and generally facilitating the completion of the field phase of the project. Cardone has a degree in sociology from the University of Bari, has written and published on local historical and ethnographic matters, and took an extremely active interest in the project from the beginning.

Alongside the participant observation which comes to the anthropologist as a natural consequence of residing in a new place, I placed much emphasis on conducting formal interviews. The reasons for this are several. First, the short amount of field time available and the large amount of data to be gathered dictated a more systematic approach than waiting about for things to happen. Secondly, the Municipality of Locorotondo contains roughly 12,000 people and has an area of 47.5 square kilometers, over much of which about half of its population is distributed. It would have been impossible to establish the kind of rapport necessary to carry out participant observation in a wide variety of scattered local environments, and I relied upon lengthy interviews to sample various social and geographical situations. Third, the design of the project contained from the inception a strong diachronic orientation, and this called for the collection of oral historical data in formal interviewing situations.

Where possible, I taped interviews for further elaboration into notes and for use as direct documentation. I carried out interviews in Italian. Cardone came to the rescue when questions or concepts needed expression in the local dialect. Locorotondese, a central Apulian dialect, is largely unintelligible with Italian. My comprehension of the spoken dialect developed and improved as fieldwork continued, although I never really acquired a thorough speaking knowledge. Therefore field work was carried out in a mixture of Italian and dialect, and I used my graduate school linguistics training to develop a serviceable writing system for transcribing local speech. Both Cardone and I attempted to assure informants that they were welcome to express themselves in dialect if they wished. The taping of a large mass of interview material, much of it in dialect, helped preserve narrations from the early days of the field experience, when dialect comprehension was nonexistent, for a later stage when I could deal with them more competently. Further, the acquisition of some local dialect helped immensely with the interpretation of 200 years' worth of historical documents which often contained Italian transliterations of strictly local terms.

Alongside the participant observation and the formal interviewing which comprised much of the ethnographic side of the field research, Cardone and I carried out a sample survey among 127 rural households meant to provide basic socio-economic and demographic data. The sample was drawn randomly from the records of the municipality's population kept in the *Ufficio Anagrafo* (Records Office) of the town hall.

The sample survey was not easy to administer because the rural population of Locorotondo is wary of strangers asking questions. The most successful strategy was to make a first contact leaving a calling card and an oral explanation of the project with an invitation to contact any one of several important and widely trusted local leaders, such as the Mayor, the Archpriest, and the union secretaries of various political colors, for a reference. This tactic tended to alleviate the fears of informants. With Cardone's help and intimate knowledge of the social territory I became confident of the accuracy of most of the figures collected, and aware of which questionnaire items were likely to have stimulated exaggerated or distorted responses. The sample survey was carried out during the winter months of 1982, and from now on will be called the 1982 Locorotondo Sample Survey.

In addition to the ethnographic field investigations and the sample survey, I spent considerable time in archives and libraries in an attempt to uncover primary sources which would allow the reconstruction of the history of the local landscape, settlement pattern, and the division of the social structure into such distinct urban and rural segments. I carried out most archival work in the *Archivio di Stato di Bari* (National Archives of Bari) where documents relating to the administration of the Province of Bari, both when it was part of the Kingdom of Two Sicilies, and after Italian Unification, are preserved. I also made a trip to Naples to consult preparatory papers for the *catasto onciario* (a massive tax register) of 1749 conserved there in the National Archives. Unfortunately, it was not possible to visit the ecclesiastical archives in Ostuni.

I conceived the approach and methods used in this project from an interdisciplinary perspective, and the mixture of ethnographic and historical work carried out in the field produced much cross-fertilization. Four or five hours in the archive in Bari would often precede four or five hours' worth of interviewing in the evening. Past and present were naturally and automatically juxtaposed in my mind. Many hours were spent talking over new documentary discoveries in the archives with Giorgio Cardone, who relished the conversations and added to them the richness of his local experience and speculative abilities. The mildewed documents took on greater life in the context of living in the landscape described in them. Obscure dialect words encountered in the documents could be explored with the help of informants who sometimes had dim recollections of such words being used by their fathers or grandfathers. Place names, which would otherwise have been abstract, took on the contours of reality, and it was possible to visualize past versions of the landscape.

Lastly, as the reader will have noted by now, I have chosen not to follow the common social scientific convention of disguising the identity of the community I have analyzed. First of all, this would be futile because it is one of a handful of highly distinctive towns which make up the Murgia dei Trulli and any local person would be able to identify it from my descriptions. Second, I feel it is important to reveal the identities of field localities to provide other scholars, both international and local, with accurate information, and to allow the process of scholarly scrutiny to sharpen understandings in the future. However, where necessary I have disguised the identity of individuals, and I sincerely hope that what I have written offends no one in Locorotondo.

Part I

THE REMEMBERED PRESENT

Chapter 2

WORK AND THE CROWDED COUNTRYSIDE

A good place to begin is with the countryside and country folk of the present and the recent past. Although there is definite continuity to the Locorotondese settlement pattern, and to many institutions belonging to its rural population, much change has taken place over the last several decades. In keeping with the observation that the present equals the cumulation of living experiences, in this description of contemporary rural Locorotondo "recent past" will mean "within the lifetimes of living people," and therefore roughly pertaining to the period between the First World War and the present, and incorporating both terminal peasant and postpeasant phases of rural life. For the peasant population of Locorotondo, work and associated values form the center of life. Therefore labor is the theme of this chapter.

THE PHYSICAL AND CULTURAL SETTING

The environment

Apulia is a big region which includes the "heel" and the "spur" of Italy and a vast territory to the interior. Coastal plains characterize the Adriatic edge and the lower part of the Salentine Peninsula, and in the interior three plateaus, or *murgie*, the Northern Murgia, the Murgia dei Trulli, and the Salentine Murgia, descend step-like from northwest to southeast. The Murgia dei Trulli covers the area of juncture between the "heel" and the "boot," and contains communes belonging to three Provinces: Bari, Brindisi, and Taranto. Unlearned local inhabitants, who identify most with their own towns, do not give this geographical designation much thought, and scholars have given it slightly differing definitions since Carlo Maranelli first suggested the name "Murgia dei Trulli" in 1908 (1946: 76; see also Liuzzi, 1981; Ricchioni, 1958; Garofalo, 1974; and Massafra, 1983). This zone is commonly defined as comprising territory partially

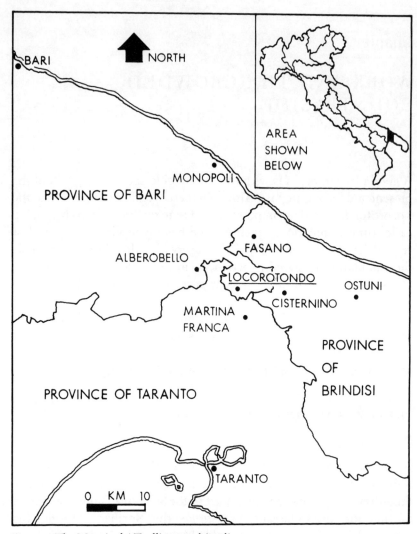

Fig. 2.1. The Murgia dei Trulli zone of Apulia

within the boundaries of the Communes of Conversano, Polignano a Mare, Monopoli, Castellana Grotte, Putignano, Noci, Alberobello, Fasano, Locorotondo, Martina Franca, Cisternino, Ostuni, and Ceglie Messapico (see Figure 2.1). These communes all have *trulli* within at least portions of their territories and have, relative to the rest of Apulia, higher proportions of their populations permanently residing in the countryside (see Table 2.1). The area of the zone exceeds 100,000 hectares.

Table 2.1. *Resident population, rural population, and percentage of rural population for the principal Murgia dei Trulli municipalities in 1971 (Modified from: Liuzzi, 1981: 150).*

Murgia Dei Trulli towns and cities	Total population	Rural population	Percent rural
Alberobello	9.40×1000	1.80×1000	19.15
Castellana Grotte	14.80	2.60	17.57
Ceglie Messapico	20.60	2.20	10.68
Cisternino	10.70	4.20	39.25
Conversano	18.60	1.60	8.60
Fasano	33.20	2.80	8.43
Locorotondo	*11.70*	*6.10*	*52.14*
Martina Franca	39.20	7.40	18.88
Monopoli	40.50	8.80	21.73
Noci	17.00	3.20	18.82
Ostuni	31.00	3.50	11.29
Polignano	13.70	1.40	10.22
Putignano	22.30	3.00	13.45

The heart of the area — the zone most characterized by *trullo* dwelling small holders — includes the high parts of the Commune of Fasano, the entirety of the Communes of Alberobello, Locorotondo, and Cisternino, and the northern half of the Commune of Martina Franca. Between the latter four communes, in a valley called the Valle d'Itria, the patterns typical of the Murgia dei Trulli are most pronounced and have the most historical depth.

The plateau is part of the Apulian karst. In most places the red soil is thin and rocky, but fertile upon first clearing. Winter rains drain through the soil into fissures in the strata of limestone bedrock, and flow through underground watercourses into the Adriatic. There is no permanent surface water, and water for living purposes must be trapped in catchment basins and cisterns. Underground water is far too deep for economical exploitation. The great limestone cavern at Castellana Grotte formed by underground water action is a major tourist attraction on the Murgia dei Trulli, and there are many other caves. The surface forms a landscape of rolling hills and ridges punctuated now and again with dolines and other forms of enclosed depressions characteristic of karsts. The soil depth in such depressions is much greater than on the slopes, and such features have long been used as sources of imported soil for hillside fields under transformation. The swallow holes in the depressions are generally clogged with soil and slow drainage results in temporary sink-hole ponds during the wet months. Sometimes, however, a standing pond will drain suddenly, like a bathtub, causing a memorable event for country dwellers.

The altitude of the Murgia dei Trulli averages about 420 meters above sea level. The plateau drops abruptly to the coastal plain in the direction of the Adriatic Sea, and slopes more gradually toward the gulf of Taranto. Because of altitude and exposure, the climate differs from that of the coastal plains. During the winter there is more precipitation and even an occasional snowstorm. Frost is also a greater danger and this makes tending olive trees, which blanket the warmer coastal plain below, risky. Cooler climate on the *murgia*, however, attracts coast dwellers during the hot summer months, and some of the *trullo* hamlets of the plateau's Adriatic edge, Selva di Fasano and Laureto in particular, have long been Fasanese summer retreats as well as peasant communities.

For Locorotondo there is an extraordinary series of rainfall measurements beginning in 1830 and ending in 1951 (Mennella, 1957: 469). The long-term yearly mean is 816.7 millimeters, with a minimum of 387 and a maximum of 1,356. Three years have been marked by what Mennella called exceptional drought (less than 450 millimeters) and fifteen by dryness (less than 570 millimeters). On the other hand, four years have been exceptionally rainy (more than 1,250 millimeters) and twelve have been wet (more than 1,100 millimeters). He considers ordinary years to range between 650 and 1,000 millimeters. Monthly rains have averaged 68 millimeters but, as in other climates characterized as Mediterranean, maximum rainfall occurs in the autumn and winter, brought by damp Atlantic winds during November and December in particular (means are 108.3 millimeters and 104.7 millimeters, respectively). The driest month is July with a mean of only 16.2 millimeters. Locorotondo has a mean of 7.4 days of snow a year, with a maximum in February, followed by January and March (Liuzzi, 1983: 84). Small amounts of snow on the ground cause school cancellations and paralyze activity.

Temperatures in the area range from between 23 and 24 degrees Celsius in July to an average low of 6 degrees Celsius in January (Liuzzi, 1983: 78). During the year an average of 53 percent of days must be considered windy with a maximum in fall and a minimum in spring. The prevailing winds blow from the north and northeast (44 percent of windy days) and from the south and southwest (39 percent). One-hundred-and-forty-five days of the year are sunny, 76 are partly cloudy, and 144 are overcast (Liuzzi, 1983: 81).

The seasons on the Murgia dei Trulli are well marked and the winter can be uncomfortably cold, forcing country dwellers to huddle around their hearths. Few country houses have any other form of heating and the hearth remains a central focus of country life both for warmth and cooking. Traditional furnishings included stools and small folding tables designed to draw up around it. Some older *trulli* have small rooms which are themselves hearths in which people sit by a fire built on a stone platform on the floor – the chimney rises from the center of the conical dome. Braziers to keep feet warm under the dining table, and bedwarmers in which coals from the hearth glow, were standard equipment in the peasant household and still are in some.

The hot summer days of July and August are peak harvest periods, and working in the open fields exposed to the sun and heat is arduous. Only with the recent introduction of the automobile have plateau dwellers sought escape at the nearby seashore. Some refuge can be found inside the thick insulating walls of whitewashed *trulli*, but even these heat up with the oppressive July sun, and postpeasant country dwellers enjoy owning refrigerators in which they can make ice and chill beer and soda pop. Placed here and there about the landscape of the *murgia* are *neviere* – stone-lined pits into which rural children in pre-refrigeration times were paid to deposit snow layered with straw. Snow pit owners sold this snow to cafés in town for making sherbets to cool gentlemanly customers.

In a zone like the Murgia dei Trulli, which has been subjected to human exploitation since prehistoric times, it is difficult to talk of "natural" flora and fauna. As late as the early nineteenth century, parts of this area were heavily forested, but the ravages of pastoralism, clearing for agriculture, lumbering, and woodcutting for fuel greatly reduced the forest cover. There are still occasional woods, and solitary oaks punctuate fields and hills. The most common oak is called the *fragno* (*Quercus troyana* Webb.), a species which occurs only in Apulia on the Italian peninsula, and otherwise in the Balkans. The holm oak (*Quercus ilex* L.), also punctuates the *murgia's* rolling hills. Other common tree species include the terebinth (*Pistacia terebinthus* L.), *Rhamnus alaternus* L., *Phillyrea latifolia* L., the carob (*Ceratonia siliqua* L.), *Pyrus amygdaliformis* Vill., and the arbutus

(*Arbutus unedo* L.). Lentisk (*Pistacia lentiscus* L.), briar (*Rubus fruticosus* L.), broom (*Calycotome spinosa* L.), and in areas of sparser cover, myrtle (*Myrtus communis* L.), and various species of cistus grow in the woods and in macchia areas (Leone and Vita, 1983).

The wild animal population has shrunk to include only small mammals such as rabbits and hedgehogs, various lizards and snakes, and birds. Larger fauna have been absent for at least two hundred years. There are indications of the presence of herds of deer in the sixteenth century, but by the middle of the eighteenth a document from Martina Franca noted that professional wolf hunters could not find adequate work in the area, indicating the lack of prey for these carnivores (Aleffi, 1983).

Settlement pattern and rural architecture today

The Commune of Locorotondo, which belongs to the Province of Bari and extends like a peninsula from its southeastern border between the Provinces of Brindisi and Taranto (see Figure 2.1), measures 47.5 square kilometers; with its longest east–west axis reaching about 19 kilometers and the longest north–south axis about 15 kilometers. With a total resident population of 12,211 at the 1981 census (ISTAT, 1983), this means a population density of 257.1 inhabitants per square kilometer, which is near the provincial mean. Locorotondo's population is divided into rural and urban segments, and according to 1981 data supplied by the communal offices, 6,292 people (or 51.53 percent) reside in the countryside and 5,919 people (or 48.47 percent) reside in town. Data for other *murgia* communes are not available for 1981, but according to Liuzzi (1981: 150), in 1971 Locorotondo had 52.1 percent of its population residing in the countryside and this was by far the highest proportion for any *murgia* town (the next was neighboring Cisternino at 39.2 percent). Locorotondo has held this record since the distinction between urban and rural population began to be reported in the 1871 census, when almost 65 percent of its inhabitants resided in the countryside (Liuzzi, 1981: 99). Again, only Cisternino approached this level.

Expectably then, Locorotondo has a crowded countryside (Plate 2.1). Looking out in any direction from the town center one sees the dark cones and gleaming white finials of *trullo* homesteads and hamlets. This contrasts starkly with landscapes only 25 kilometers away, as one moves toward the higher *murgie* of Apulia, where the fields lack peasant dwellings of any kind. On the coastal plain the headquarters of a large estate pokes its roofs above the gray-green mantle of olive trees here and there, but far fewer small proprietors live in the countryside.

Locorotondo, town, is the hub of a series of roads which lead toward various destinations internal to the commune and to neighboring towns. Along these roads, most of which date to at least the middle of the eighteenth century, lie the major *trullo* villages, or *jazzèlere* (singular, *jazzeile*). The largest of these is San Marco, a village of around 500 people with a few small stores, a post office, a newly built *trullo*-domed church serviced by its own priest, and an upper and a lower *jazzeile*. Trito is another large *trullo* village – also a small center with a school, post office, and stores. Other *jazzèlere* contain smaller clusters of houses; a few have elementary schools and a church, and bear such names as Sant'Elia, Tagaro, Lamie Olimpie, Mancini, and Tumbinno. Here and there on the main radiating roads there are small general stores which service the daily needs of country dwellers, and even a few café bars.

A *jazzeile* is a special kind of residential situation in which neighbors own the space between dwellings in common and recognize a set of traditional communal use rights which have to do with cistern water, threshing floors, and open space. Decisions about use of space in a *jazzeile* must be unanimously agreed upon among all neighbors. Frequently this leads to trouble and it is common to find feuds in Locorotondo's *jazzèlere*. Not all country dwellers live in a *jazzeile*. Many live in *trulli*, or newer houses built of reinforced concrete or cement block, constructed along the roads and not clustered together in hamlets. Such people consider themselves neighbors but do not recognize the set of special relationships which adhere to residence in a *jazzeile*.

Each *trullo* house consists of a cluster of corbel-domed rooms.[1] A typical *trullo* had a central room, often occupied by a table and chairs used only on ceremonial occasions, off which opened bedrooms and alcoves, and the kitchen with its hearth. *Trullo* cones covered rooms which were plastered and whitewashed on the inside. The central room's cone was often closed by a platform used as a storage loft called the *orie*. In this room there was usually an overhead shelf used to store ripening cheeses. To either side of the fire the hearth room contained wall niches used for storing small utensils and cooking staples. Shelves held bigger cooking utensils and crockery. The bedrooms also had storage niches and narrow windowed openings to the outside. Traditionally floors were sheathed in limestone slabs, and walls plastered and whitewashed.

External spaces immediately around the *trullo* were paved with limestone slabs, and builders often provided the wide main door arch with small stone benches to either side of the opening. On hot days, this still provides a shady place for women to sit and work at tasks like shelling fava beans. Most typically, the outsides of currently inhabited *trulli* are whitewashed and owners frequently renew the coating, often just before religious holidays (Plate 2.2). Some old *trulli* were not plastered and whitewashed on their outside walls. Attached to the habitation there are often *trullo* covered stalls and storage rooms, and sometimes a bread oven or an outdoor hearth for summer cooking. Bread ovens are a recent addition to many houses, however, and a sign of mid-twentieth-century prosperity. Before, there were communal ovens in the countryside where women went to bake. In the countryside of Locorotondo; standards of cleanliness are high and peasants do not keep animals in the house, which is a practice commonly encountered elsewhere in Southern Italy, especially in Sicily. Many *trulli* still have symbols – some of them clearly religious, others probably zodiacal – whitewashed on their roofs. Some inhabitants vaguely explain their roof symbols as having the power to ward off the evil eye or the devil. Most just re-whitewash the symbol without having much sense of its meaning or function.[2]

Local people no longer build *trulli* because the spaces which can be spanned by this technique are restricted and inadequate for the newer material wants of postpeasant country families. *Trulli* with fake domes made of concrete applied to flat roofs are still built for vacationers. The artisans who built *trulli* are fast disappearing and only a few men remain active who can maintain those which are still inhabited. Many abandoned *trulli* punctuate the landscape. New houses are built in the countryside by the sons and grandsons of *trullo* dwellers, but they are only rarely stone built because of the prohibitive costs of quarrying and transportation, and are usually flat-roofed cement block constructions. The new generations of men in the rural areas of Locorotondo are part-time peasants who gain most of their income from skills such as tile setting and plastering. Most of these men have considerable building skill, and before they marry, construct large and comfortable houses using their own labor, and that of brothers and friends, on inherited land. They also enjoy discounts on materials because of connections in the building trades. This results in the construction of sometimes startlingly luxurious houses in the countryside. It is surprising to discover, for instance, that a particular house which looks like a rich man's villa, complete with a balustraded grand stairway on the facade and polished granite floors, belongs to a steel worker employed at Italsider in Taranto, who does plastering as a second job, and who cultivates inherited fields with his own, and particularly his wife's labor.

Gentle probing during interviews reveals that there is no small element of revenge in these preferences. The model now followed is either the town apartment of the middle-class professional, or, as in the case of the house above, the country villa of the old figure of the landowning gentleman. The lot of the latter class has declined precipitously in the post-Second World War years, and the fortunes of country dwellers improved. Conversations with the sons and daughters of peasants elicit the sentiment that it is now their turn to flaunt prosperity, and they make no secret about the pleasure of doing so in the face of families who used to lord it over their parents from the second story balconies of estate buildings.

Here and there in the countryside one finds a *masseria* – headquarters of a large old estate. A *masseria* is typically a multi-storied stone building covered with the pitched roofs typical of the historic center of Locorotondo. Such roofs really cover corbeled vaults, not true barrel vaults. In Locorotondo people strongly associate this kind of roof with urbanites and only gentlemen constructed them in the countryside (Plate 2.3). Peasants built *trulli*. A gentleman's estate overseer, his *massaro*, usually lived at the estate headquarters, but almost always in a *trullo*; the massive pitched-roofed building was reserved for the gentleman and his family during their summer and autumn weeks in the country. Aside from the *massaro*'s *trullo*, a *masseria* typically includes *trullo* outbuildings which serve as stalls, storage areas, and hay lofts. *Trullo* hay lofts lack the decorative finial found on dwellings; instead they have a trap door in the apex of the roof cone into which the owner stuffs hay. Most *masserie* also had small chapels in which the landowners worshiped during summer sojourns. Sometimes laborers were also expected to worship in them during the harvest so that time would not be lost from work by going into town. The gentlemen's country residences often date to the eighteenth century or before, and are well-appointed, even frescoed, inside. The walls were built massively and the buildings were fortress-like to protect the grain and other foodstuffs stored on the upper floor under the vaults. The countryside of Locorotondo was plagued by thieves and cattle rustlers until the 1950s, and in the nineteenth century by bandits, and the gentleman's country fortress afforded him and his family protection from such marauders.

Some *masseria* owners have sold their buildings and peasant families now inhabit them, but a few descendants of the local gentry still use their *masserie*. Most of the large estates of the past are now much reduced in area because of the long history of division and cession under perpetual lease, or sale to peasant small proprietors. Several of the large estates do, however, remain intact, especially on the eastern side of the communal territory, and in that area the dispersed settlement pattern typical of the rest of the countryside is patchy. Typically, landowners have not transformed their large estate land into vineyards and have farmed cereals in areas of deeper soil and left the land to pasture in others. Only in the immediate vicinity of the estate headquarters are there a few fruit trees or small vineyards.

The poor quality of *masseria* land and the demise of a market for animals of traction have made larger estates uneconomical enterprises and reduced the value of the land to virtually zero. One older landowner reported that he was seriously considering allowing what remained of his family patrimony in Locorotondo to return to woods to create a nature preserve. Several small *masserie* were for sale during the early 1980s, but no buyers seemed to be on the horizon. Similarly, few men want to become sharecropping or salaried *massari* because this means accepting the accommodations available on the *masseria*, usually an unimproved *trullo*. The construction trades are far more attractive and lucrative opportunities for younger men, and allow far more comfortable housing. This is a change from the more traditional peasant past in which the figure of the *massaro* was enviable. Taking on a *masseria* provided an opportunity to farm on a larger scale than the ordinary small proprietor worker peasant could, but such opportunities were rare because there was a preference among landowners for hiring *massari* from large estate towns, such as Martina Franca or Gioia del Colle.

The landowners and peasants of Locorotondo set buildings such as *trullo* and *masserie* in a patchwork of fields and terraces neatly delineated by stone walls. Most of these walls are about a meter in height and built without mortar. They serve primarily to separate fields and retain soil, and in the past, to prevent the passage of grazing animals. Near *masserie* there are often orchards, vineyards, and gardens with high walls sometimes surmounted by a row of broken glass set into mortar. Walls border almost all country roads on either side. Artisan specialists build and repair them, although most small holders have done their own wall construction and maintenance as well. The walls of the Murgia dei Trulli inspired Tommaso Fiore, the Apulian essayist, to write in a locally famous passage:

I asked myself how these people were able to excavate and line up so much rock. I think that this would have frightened a population of giants. This is the harshest and rockiest of the plateaus; to reduce it to cultivation, making terraces, as they tell me has been done in the area of Genoa, on the hills of San Giuliano between Pisa and Lucca, on Lake Garda, and in the Cinque Terre beyond La Spezia as in a few other places, no less was necessary than the industriousness of a population of ants. (Fiore, 1978: 8)

The communal roads radiate spoke-like from the historical center. The main arteries have many branches and cross-cutting roads link them almost concentrically. The high percentage of small property and residence in the countryside explain the density of the road network, and road paving and maintenance programs place a special strain on the municipal budget not felt by other more centralized municipalities, as do demands from postpeasant country dwellers for rural electrification, Apulian aqueduct water, school busing, and garbage collection. By 1982 most major road paving projects had just been completed in response to the demand generated by the wholesale diffusion since the 1960s of automobiles, scooters, and mechanized means of traction. The use of animals for traction or transportation had been a thing of the past since the early 1960s. Before, the soil was turned either by manual labor with the large local hoe (Plate 2.4) or plowed with horses or oxen. Most country families had a buggy for transportation, and some had a cart for hauling large loads, although this was also a specialized occupation taken care of by carters.

LAND AND AGRICULTURE IN THE TWENTIETH CENTURY

Land and production

The distribution of landed property in Locorotondo is distinctly uniform. This distribution can be measured and compared using techniques such as the Lorenz curve and accompanying Gini coefficient (G), for which a figure of 0 denotes perfectly uniform distribu-

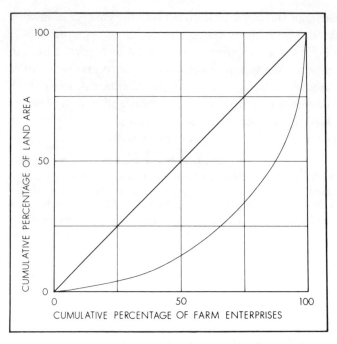

Fig. 2.2. Lorenz curve showing distribution of land among farm enterprises,
Locorotondo in 1971. (Source: calculated from ISTAT, 1972.)

tion of wealth, and a figure approaching 1.0 indicates maximum concentration of wealth. The 1970 Agricultural census data yields a Gini coefficient of 0.55 (ISTAT, 1972: Table 18). Mean farm size equals 2.34 hectares and there are 2,110 agricultural enterprises recorded in the census. (The accompanying Lorenz curve is found in Figure 2.2.) Gini coefficients for the province calculated from the same source range from 0.41 to 0.80 with a median and mean around 0.62. Table 2.2 shows the distribution of G for surrounding communes generally associated with the Murgia dei Trulli zone (which belong to Provinces of Bari, Brindisi, and Taranto) and only neighboring Cisternino has a lower coefficient than Locorotondo. Comparable data referring to agricultural enterprises reported in Calella (1941, 112) allows computation of a Gini coefficient only fractionally higher (G = 0.56) for the late 1920s. Therefore, Locorotondo's current distribution of property reflects no post-Second World War land reform, as would that of many other Apulian towns. However the number of farm enterprises has increased over the period between the 20s and 1970 by 592 indicating a degree of fragmentation.

Table 2.2. *Land distribution statistics for Locorotondo and nearby municipalities of the Murgia dei Trulli (Calculated from: ISTAT, 1972, Fasc. 74–76, Tav. 18).*

Towns	Total agricultural land surface (hectares)	Mean farm enterprise size (hectares)	Gini coefficient
Alberobello	4145.16	2.63	0.63
Castellana Grotte	6390.90	2.60	0.64
Ceglie Messapico	11799.00	2.80	0.59
Cisternino	6011.05	2.10	0.52
Conversano	11592.50	2.16	0.57
Fasano	12224.40	4.91	0.68
Locorotondo	4943.86	2.34	0.55
Martina Franca	28000.70	3.51	0.68
Monopoli	14766.00	4.24	0.65
Noci	13933.30	6.72	0.71
Ostuni	19959.80	3.18	0.67
Polignano	5324.38	2.94	0.59
Putignano	9524.21	4.62	0.69

Although during the twentieth century there have been larger estates within the municipal boundaries, these were only large in the eyes of local small proprietors. No Locorotondese property reported by Calella (1941: 112) for the late 20s exceeded 100 hectares, and only 9 fell into the range between that size and 50 hectares. The wealthiest landowning families diversified their holdings by acquiring estates in a variety of other zones through purchase and marriage, and several of them owned estates in neighboring communes. The vast *latifundia* typical of other areas of Apulia (cf. Snowden, 1986), and of several other regions in Southern Italy, are neither typical of the Locorotondese countryside now, nor have they ever been.

According to the 1970 agricultural census the "utilized agricultural surface area" of 4,763.17 hectares was 58.4 percent cereal fields and 32.4 percent tree crops. The other 9.2 percent was in pastures and meadows. Another 51.4 hectares remained in woods and the census classified 129.3 hectares as "other surface area" (ISTAT, 1972: Vol. 2, Fasc. 74, Table 19). Vineyards account for 23.8 percent of the total, and for about 72 percent of the surface planted to tree crops. The rest of the tree-crop areas are planted to olives, and rarely to fruit orchards (Table 21). The proportion of tree crops and therefore of vineyards has dropped from figures reported earlier in the century. The 1929 cadaster, for instance, shows that about 53 percent of cultivated lands were planted in tree crops and 37.3 percent were in cereals. The amount in pastures and meadows has remained constant and low since then (Calella, 1941: 113).

The distinct change in the proportion of cereal fields to vineyards and orchards reflects the expense involved in replanting vineyards and the low prices grapes have fetched in recent decades because of competition with more irrigable areas. Vineyards must be replaced every fifty or sixty years, and many of those now existing are old. There is little incentive to reinvest money in vineyards because of low prices paid for grapes by the local cooperative and other wineries. Viticulture is threatened. Few younger men seriously consider themselves full-time grape growers; only old men still do. Instead, young men seek their fortunes in building trades, in the Italsider steel mill at Taranto, or in occupations such as trucking. Most, however, continue to cultivate their fields as best they can, and the rural landscape of Locorotondo retains its well-husbanded appearance, although there are now fewer vineyards than in times recently past.

The pattern of part-time work on family land supplemented by wage labor elsewhere is not really new. The small proprietor peasant of rural Locorotondo has always been a worker peasant. Few families in the past really achieved total agricultural autonomy and some members of each family (usually unmarried) worked as *braccianti agricoli*, or agricultural day laborers for at least part of their careers. However, even if not always attained, the goal was autonomy, most especially, autonomy from the town culture as reflected in the church-bell proverb which sets the theme for this book, and part of the strategy used to achieve this autonomy was to produce for subsistence as well as for market. The novelty of the new postpeasant division of labor comes in the differentiation of work life between industry and agriculture.

For the small proprietors of Locorotondo the cash crop has long been grapes; they grew other crops – cereals, olives, fava beans, and fodder – to provide for family needs. Animals were raised for the milk, and therefore cheese, and the meat they provided, not so much for market. Remnants of this pattern continue even in the families of country dwelling industrial and construction workers who farm to produce some wheat to be ground into flour at local mills to make an annual supply of wine from a portion of the grapes produced, and to produce milk and cheese from a family cow. Rural postpeasant families obtain cash income from grapes, and frequently from selling milk and raising a calf each year. Husbands contribute labor for these subsistence and cash agricultural activities after work, and their wives do farm chores during the day.

The variety of grape grown in the Locorotondese countryside is called Verdeca and is suited for the production of dry white wine, which, because of cool conditions around Locorotondo, is low in alcohol content. The wine produced in Locorotondo from this variety is called Bianco di Locorotondo, and in 1965 it earned the right to the important legal designation *"denominazione di origine controllata,"* (denomination of controlled origin) as an indicator of quality. (Interestingly, one hears the abbreviation of this designation, "DOC," used figuratively in conversations to denote quality in other things besides wine.) Since that time the local cooperative winery has made successful attempts to bottle the wine directly and market it, although in the early 1980s the market for this wine was still largely within the region of Apulia. Local wine is also especially suited for making white dry vermouth, and until the 1970s the cooperative sold most of its product to local representatives of such internationally known vermouth producers as Cinzano and Martini and Rossi, who shipped it to the north by train and processed it into their products. (Martini drinkers will have imbibed the product of the vineyards of Locorotondo and surrounding municipalities.)

Part of the motivation for producing locally bottled DOC wine is to escape economic dependency upon these companies, and to reap profits from a finished product which can be marketed directly. The hope of the cooperative's administration is that through local production it will be possible to pay a better price to the members and in turn entice some younger men back to the vineyards. The fear that within a few years there will no longer be a Bianco di Locorotondo is founded in the obvious fact that few of the cooperative's 900 members are below the age of forty-five. At the annual meetings of the cooperative, gray and white hair predominate.

Before the founding of the cooperative (1933), peasants sold home-produced wine to country dwelling middle men who in turn sold it to the vermouth firms, or to wine merchants on the coastal plain. To bring up the alcohol content, and therefore to prevent spoilage during hot weather, grape producers fortified wine destined for the hotter lowland market with juice boiled down into a syrup.

This is a pattern which dates at least as far back as the early eighteenth century. The founding of the cooperative and the implantation of industrial level wine making brought an end to home wine production for market. Most grape-producing households continue to produce wine for home consumption, however, and fortify a portion of it for the hot months.

The yearly cycle of family production

Rhythms determined by the cycle of tasks comprising the agricultural year structure and punctuate the life of an agricultural community. The foundations of this rhythm in Locorotondo were, and still are, the subsistence crops, grain, and fava beans, and the principal cash crop, grapes. Before the massive changes which took place in the 1960s and 1970s, Locorotondese peasant society nourished itself on all days but Sunday and Thursday with mush made from fava beans. Men working away from home took balls of mashed favas with them to the fields, and those who ate at home, consumed them with their families from a large common bowl. Eaten with olive oil, bread, and some greens, this was an adequate, if monotonous diet. Favas are rich in calories, and if eaten with bread, provide the necessary amino acids. On Sundays and Thursdays, families had pasta for their major meal, most often in the common Apulian form called *orecchiette*, "little ears." This too was accompanied by bread, and typically a large bowl of stalk vegetables such as celery, romaine lettuce, or chicory which people say "lighten" the pasta. Until after the Second World War, and the introduction of refined white flour, women made both pasta and bread from whole wheat flour, and they were richer in fiber than the kinds currently consumed. Households consumed meat only on Christmas and Easter.

Except for oats, planted early in September, local farmers sow grains and fodder crops during the second half of October and the first half of November. They plant both wheat and barley, as well as vetch. Weeding of cereal fields takes place during April, and during May, fodder crops are harvested. Family members reap grain, tie it into sheaves and stack them in shocks to dry, and then thresh from the middle of June through the middle of July. After this they burn the stubble and plow the fields for the new year.

Currently cereal-field owners hire a mechanized reaper-tier and operator for the harvest. On the *masserie* sickles and scythes disappeared during the 1930s in favor of horse-drawn McCormick-style reapers which required a crew of two. However, among small proprietors their use persisted until well after the Second World War. The tied sheaves are gathered and piled into two kinds of shocks for drying, depending on whether wheat or barley is being harvested. Proprietors allow the crop to dry for ten days in the fields and then take it to the *jazzeile* or *masseria* threshing floor for threshing, which was done traditionally by walking animals dragging a heavy stone slab over the grain and then using the wind to separate grain from chaff. The fields of Locorotondo are much too small for the use of combines, which are now used in other areas of Apulia.

Ideally peasants rotated crops between grain and fallow, or between grain and a legume, particularly fava or lupino beans. However, one old *massaro* claimed that it did not matter what was rotated as long as the crop was changed, and that he had rotated wheat and oats or barley. He also claimed that wheat might be grown in successive years on land in dolines. Neither practice would have been wise. Until the beginning decades of this century peasants sometimes planted grain on the ridges which bordered the square depressions hoed around grape vines. This was a poor practice because it robbed the soil of nutrients, although Presutti (1909: 140) reports that at his writing peasants bought chemical fertilizers and dusted them on the ridges as a supplement. Informants remember that this system followed a kind of fallowing, opposite sides of depressions being planted in alternating years. After this practice was given up, through the influence of production-conscious landlords and the increasing commercial market for grapes and wine, small proprietor viticulturalists continued to use the ridges to plant a few vegetables or some favas.[3]

Favas are also a winter crop. Households sow them during the second half of October, and the first half of November at the same time they sow grain, and harvest them in two stages – fresh in May, and dried on the bean stalk in July. Families relish fresh favas raw, or make them into soup. Growers rotate favas with grain crops. When peasant families subsisted on them, the proper daily supply of favas was about one half kilogram per individual, and their production was a primary activity.

In the past, and this is a pattern documentable as far back as the eighteenth century, peasant families without enough land to sow this important subsistence crop took land in informal sharecropping arrangements with landowners and their *massari* in the territory of the neighboring municipality of Martina Franca. These arrangements varied in favorability to the peasant depending upon the demand for land. During the Second World War, when times were lean (a percentage of the grain and fava crop had to be turned over to the government) and its aftermath, families from Locorotondo cooperated with one another and took on uncleared sharecropping land for growing staple food crops. The families had to clear the land by October 15th. This, of course, was a great benefit to the landowner, who, aside from his share of the crop, reaped cleared arable land from the agreement. His investment consisted of little more than allowing the sharecroppers the use of animals for plowing and several pair of oxen for threshing. He would also provide a barn in which to sleep during the harvest season. Generally by October 15th families who had to participate in such agreements had little seed left and would have some advanced to them by the owner against the next summer's harvest. The crop was divided in half by alternating measures full of beans, one for the owner, one for the sharecropper. The owner always got the first measure.

Growing grapes follows a different rhythm. The yearly harvest finishes by the second half of October, and just after, grape producers cultivate their vineyards, nowadays with a rototiller, but before about 1960 with the heavy local hoe, or with animal drawn plows. During the winter (from about mid-December through the beginning of February) proprietors carry out pruning chores. Women gather the pruned shoots for use in the bread oven and the hearth. Depending on the system being used in the vineyard, men tie the fruit bearing shoots to taut wires or support them with forked sticks.

Locorotondese grape growers use three systems for supporting the vines in the vineyards. Under the traditional system each vine stands alone without wire supports. In the past, before the widespread adoption of the rototiller, each vine grew in a square depression hoed around it in the winter, giving the vineyard surface the look of a waffle (Plate 2.5). The depression funneled water to the plant roots and contained erosion by preventing water from washing across the face of sloping fields. The worker formed this depression with a couple of well-calculated motions as he reached out with his hoe to bite into the soil and carried it back toward his body, at the same time turning the tool so the load would fall neatly from it to form the rim. A forked stick supported the heavy fruit-bearing shoot of the vine.

Almost no grower continues to hoe vineyards in this way because labor and time are at a premium, and rototillers do the work of turning the soil in a fraction of the time previously required. With the traditional system the peasant performed three hoeings each year – the first and heaviest, which formed the depressions, between December and the middle of March. For the other two the grower used a lighter hoe and worked between April 20th and May 20th, and June 1st and July 15th, respectively.

The system growers now most commonly use consists of pruning the vines so that they can be attached to wires strung tautly between cast concrete poles (Plate 2.6). With this system the vines bear fruit at chest height, and the soil between rows can be turned with a rototiller. Rototilling fields loses the anti-erosional feature of the older system, but since vineyards are now more commonly grown on flat or bottom land, and this way of turning the soil is more thorough than hoeing, that disadvantage is minimized. The third system is confined to large flat vineyards in only a few locations. By this system the vine trunks grow up to an overhead latticework of wires, and the bunches hang at a convenient height for harvesting. The bunches grow far from the ground and therefore from dangers of spoilage and disease.

A rototilling accompanies the tasks of pruning and preparing the vine for fruit bearing. Growers spread fertilizer, manure early in the century, chemical fertilizer later, during March, which is also the month for grafting year-old new plants. Just after, it is time to dust the plants with copper sulfate to prevent downy mildew, a fungus disease. In May another tilling introduces air into the soil and promotes growth. At the same time women carry out "green pruning," designed to remove leaves and the ends of growing shoots so that more nutrients are concentrated in the growing fruit. This also allows more sunlight to reach the grapes. During June growers dust again with copper sulfate and in July perform another rototilling. The rototiller has allowed more frequent and more thorough turning of the soil and increased production. During August producers who are developing new vineyards start new vines, but, because of the expense and low return on growing grapes, this is now a rare sight. The grape harvest takes the first half of October, and families mobilize all possible labor in the vineyards to get the crop off the vines and to the cooperative, or other wineries. Women cut grapes and men transport them in large plastic tubs (traditionally baskets) to the road to be picked up by a truck (traditionally cart). Householders then make wine from the proportion of the crop held back for home use (Plate 2.7).

Another major household crop is olives. Locorotondese country people grow olives for pressing an annual supply of oil. They prune the trees in May and September and harvest during the second half of November and December. Olives and olive oil are not usually a commercial crop for the *murgia* dwellers because there is too much risk of frost damage for commercial production, given the altitude and temperature. Producers press harvested olives at one of two cooperative olive-oil mills located in the municipal territory.

Most families also possess several fruit and nut trees which help supplement the daily diet. People refer to dried figs as the "candy of the past," and recognize them as an important high-calorie energy food. One informant described how his mother would give him and his brother a few figs to eat as they went to work on foot before dawn. The two boys would compete with each other to see who could make his figs last until they reached the worksite. They were also a primary target of marauding town artisan boys who would descend into the country to pluck them off the trees. Figs are now a low prestige food, largely replaced by purchased cookies and candies, and drop from many trees unharvested. Families commonly eat almonds and walnuts as a major part of the small evening meal. Neighboring municipalities produce cherries which grow well in the thin soil of the karst landscape, require less care and cultivation than grapes, need little fertilizer, and are more cheaply harvested. Only a few innovators have planted cherry orchards in the Locorotondo area. Probably this can be ascribed to the conservatism of older growers and to the disinterest of younger men who have given up full-time agriculture. Cherry orchards are, however, almost six times less expensive to plant than new vineyards, and as the latter age and become unproductive, cherries may be seen as a more economical solution to the problem of what to do with family land.

After the Second World War, raising cows for milk and for veal production began to replace small-scale raising of sheep and goats. Costs of feed and the opportunity costs of labor have begun to lessen small-scale dairy production. Tending goats and sheep takes almost as much labor as keeping a cow and, of course, produces much less income. Also there is no longer any local market for wool. Some households keep goats and sheep to milk for home cheese production. In the past they were more important as a source of meat consumed on Christmas and Easter, and women spun and wove wool in the household. Also carters and animal drivers used whole goat hides sewn into vessels to carry oil and wine.

Country households raise cattle in stalls instead of pasturing them because few own enough pasture land. Therefore they must grow as much fodder as possible, but most have to buy some feed as well. Cow owners currently follow the strategy of finding a relative or neighbor who has a field with fruit or olive trees on it and offering to cultivate the soil for the purpose of putting in a crop of vetch or alfalfa. The livestock raiser's cultivation of the soil allows the owner to keep his trees productive by reducing the cost of labor he would otherwise need to meet to keep the land surface plowed and clear. Sometimes livestock raisers pay a token rent, but for all intents they obtain free use of the land in this symbiotic relationship. Dairies centered in Bari and the nearby town of Noci pick the milk up early in the morning. Milk producing households also produce their own cheeses.

Currently, households with cows produce what is called in Italian, *vitellone*, which might best be translated as "older veal" – it is slaughtered at eighteen months. The demand for milk-fed veal is low, and because of meat production shortages in Italy there are government subsidies paid for raising animals beyond the age of six months. Now, veterinarians breed cattle by artificial insemination, but fifteen to twenty years ago larger landowners kept breeding bulls on the *masserie* and this contributed to the income of those larger agricultural units.

At present, agricultural workers are mostly adolescent girls and older men. Rural young men gravitate toward more lucrative and prestigious ways of earning a living and accumulating savings toward their marriages. Older men who do not have enough land to be full-time agriculturalists work as agricultural hands for others, but labor is scarce and expensive for those on the *murgia* who must hire it. Proprietors, both small and large, complain about finding adequate and skilled workers. Trends toward the aging and feminization of agriculture, so often discussed in the general Italian press, are well advanced in the hamlets of the Murgia dei Trulli.

Just after finishing elementary school between the ages of eight and ten, the work lives of most adults who are now middle aged began with the task of carrying soil and stones during the transformation of fields into vineyards. This process is central to the development of the characteristics of the Murgia dei Trulli and will be described in detail in a later chapter, but here suffice it to say that it consisted of breaking up the strata of bedrock to a depth of about a meter and importing soil from dolines. Grape producers hired children at four and five pre-war lire a day to carry soil up the slopes from the quarry in baskets, and bring them down full of stones to backfill the empty pit. This was seasonal work as proprietors transformed vineyards during the hot months of June, July, and August. It was extremely hard for small bodies and people talk of it as important to them as the experience during which they learned how to work.

After this initiation into work, girls began a phase of their lives characterized by labor on local and distant *masserie* undertaken to earn money for their dowries. Alongside working the olive harvest in Fasano which still employs Locorotondese girls, many middle-aged women have vivid memories of traveling by cart to work the grain harvest, first in the Province of Brindisi to the southeast, and just after in Martina Franca. This was hard labor in hot fields working with the sickle, tying sheaves, and piling shocks. The workers ate a thin soup made of favas, except on Thursdays and Sundays when they received pasta without much cheese on it; the proprietors also gave them hard onions grown on the farm especially to feed workers. They slept in the barns on these large estates. The harvest was especially tiring work, and they spent their evenings resting. In work gangs in which both sexes were present, girls slept with their legs in empty flour sacks to deter any suspicion of advances during the night.

Before the diffusion of automobile travel, Locorotondese women, especially unmarried girls, descended to the coastal plains around Fasano and Monopoli for the olive harvest which lasted from three-and-a-half to four months during the winter. Once a month they were carted back to Locorotondo to visit their families and get bread which had been baked for them in ring shaped loaves which could be stored on a pole high off the ground to keep it away from vermin and mildew. The work was tedious and girls were driven to fill their five kilogram baskets with olives by a female boss who would shout at them, *pensièr o panaridde!* – "Keep your minds on your baskets!" It was lightened, however, by singing, and shouting jokes to other picking squads in other trees. Olive-picking girls spent their evenings dancing the *tarantella* to music played by men at the *masseria* who would hang around. Sometimes the fiancés of the workers would steal in to visit against the wishes of the *massaro*, who was held responsible for watching over his workers.

Most currently middle-aged and older men followed their childhood work experiences at transporting soil and stones by becoming *braccianti*, and continued to work for others as they accumulated savings toward a house and other marriage necessities. Often work for others continued after marriage. Proprietors always contracted male labor in Locorotondo directly with individual laborers, seeking them out at their homes. This contrasts sharply with the more common Southern Italian early morning labor market in a major town *piazza*, and strongly reflects the Locorotondese scattered settlement pattern. Instead, in neighboring Martina Franca, laborers assembled before dawn in a square below the main church, and proprietors, or their *massari*, chose some of them for a day's work.

The most common agricultural worker's speciality in the area was that of *zappatore* – hoer. The rapid expansion of vineyards in Locorotondo and neighboring communes during the late nineteenth century created a high demand for this speciality, and workers from Locorotondo hoed in the zones surrounding the commune. Hoers formed teams of four or five men which proprietors hired as units. One of the men in a team played the part of leader and negotiated jobs and pay. Most informants testify that they took pride in this work, especially if working for peasant employers, but that they took less care with the vineyards of larger proprietors. A life of work with the heavy short handled hoe typical of the area has left many old men with severe back problems.

Some Locorotondese men have made a specialty of pruning vines for hire. This is more exacting work than hoeing and those who currently do it for a living often have some training from the agricultural vocational school in Locorotondo. Traditionally, men who pruned used a locally made tool, the large razor-sharp pruning hook known as the *ruciddione*, but this has given way to industrially produced pruning shears. They drew the pruning hook across the branch being pruned while bracing the vine's trunk against a boot. Many men have nasty scars on their thighs as a result of slipping with this tool. Before a passerby found him unconscious in a vineyard, one informant almost bled to death from such a cut. Specialized pruners from Locorotondo now find work in neighboring communes and in the lowland vineyards of the Province of Brindisi. Most local small proprietors do their own pruning. Pruning specialists also graft European varieties onto disease resistant American root stock, an operation necessitated since the disastrous attacks of phylloxera, which early in this century destroyed grapes all over Italy after having wiped out French vineyards. Before the phylloxera disaster grape growers propagated vines from suckers.

Unlike certain other areas of Southern Italy, western Sicily in particular, women in Apulia work in the fields alongside their husbands (cf. Blok, 1974: 49). Most family agricultural tasks are defined such that a husband and wife work together. One informant stressed that the team he and his wife formed was so important to him that he would not go to the fields to work if she did not come along. During pruning, for instance, men cut the vines and wives and daughters gather the cut shoots for use as fuel at home. Women cut grapes and men transport them to the roadside for transport. Women are responsible for weeding fields and for the work of "green" pruning in vineyards. Men wielded the sickle or scythe and women gathered and tied sheaves and made shocks. Generally women do not wield heavy implements like plows or the full-sized hoe, or nowadays the rototiller, but informants testified that during the Second World War when men were away, women did all agricultural tasks, and that many, in fact, knew how to use men's tools. Traditional rules prevented menstruating women from climbing trees to pick cherries, or from baking bread or making tomato sauce. Not all families continue to observe these prohibitions, however.

Values about work and land

In the Locorotondese countryside strong values emphasizing hard work and a real concern for the fields, the hard won patrimony of rural families, contrast with the dislike of agriculture and the soil expressed by Southern Italian peasants elsewhere and reported by other scholars (Lopreato, 1967: 60–61; Moss and Cappannari, 1960: 28–29). For instance, Blok's experience with peasants who would not allow themselves to be photographed working in the fields is alien to Locorotondo (Blok, 1974: 48). In Locorotondo the general Southern Italian liking for being photographed extended to the vineyards, although subjects who knew they were going to be photographed sometimes dressed in better than their normal work togs. Work well done is a central value of the peasant and postpeasant generations of Locorotondo. When squads of men hoed vineyards they held competitions to see who could hoe a row of depressions around the vines most quickly, taking pride in the weight of hoe a man could handle.

When asked whether work in itself was a satisfaction, an old man, smiling wistfully, replied:

By Bacchus, it was a great satisfaction! If you could see the men of before – when I was a young man . . . you could see certain old men, of my age, they could make soil quarries in the ground so squarely that not even an engineer could do it! *U Boss* was like a professor at cutting earth! He would work smoking a cigar; every blow and fifty quintals of soil would go down![4]

This kind of pride in agricultural work – in all manual work – even that done for others, especially other small proprietor peasants, is commonplace in Locorotondo and has made the transition to the current generation of part-time peasants. For the new generation of building tradesmen who farm in their off hours, pride in work translates into a widespread demand for Locorotondese contractors and workers because they have a reputation for working hard.

One should contrast this attitude to that of a certain Francesco, a Sicilian peasant, quoted as typical by Anton Blok:

Caro Antonio, you should understand one thing: work is a necessity, not a pleasure. People have to work in order not to die. Blessed is he who does not need to work. The man who lacks brains or luck has to work with his hands. He is a *disgraziato* who will never become rich or even respected. Manual work has been made by the devil. (Blok, 1974: 48)

Because of the importance of grape growing to the historical development of the local settlement pattern, values about life and work, and other important elements of local culture, the peasants and postpeasants of Locorotondo consider themselves specialized in tending vineyards. Peasant small proprietors have been planting and harvesting grapes in Locorotondo since before the eighteenth century and, as the historical record will show in later chapters, viticulture was inextricably intertwined in the formation and consolidation of the scattered settlement pattern typical of the zone, and the hope for small proprietorship. Therefore growing grapes has a certain symbolic loading as well as economic value. This becomes apparent in conversations with men who have spent their lives in the vineyards as they talk with pride about the hard work of hoeing the soil and the skills involved in pruning. It is easy to understand why the obsolete tools of the trade – the heavy hoe and the pruning hook – have become important mementos of deceased fathers in many families.

The sale of family land, particularly of vineyards, is a topic for gossipy criticism by neighbors and relatives. There is a sense that the labors of previous generations won land, and that it should be maintained in the family and kept productive. In part, these attitudes account for the labor that men of the current generations, whose primary occupations are not on the land, put into agriculture. Since about 1960 small-scale peasant agriculture alone has not been a viable way of life in a society characterized by rising material expectations, and in which the market price of grapes has remained low because of increasing competition, particularly from much larger growers in irrigated zones. Because of this, many younger men and women think of the possession of land as a burden. Keeping it cultivated can indeed be an economic burden, particularly if labor must be hired, or a family begins to calculate such things as the opportunity costs of their own time, or the costs of things easily forgotten, such as gasoline for transportation or for the rototiller. The practice, described above, of allowing free use of land surface to livestock raisers in fields with trees, has helped somewhat to stave off the problem of abandoning land because of economic pressures. Older parents often recognize and understand their children's mixed feelings, but bitterly feel the loss of a sense of peasant progress through the generations in winning land. One 64-year-old informant lamented:

There's no one coming behind us, but I don't blame them. We're impassioned about the land; we want to go ahead and make progress, but when you work you make no progress. There comes a day sooner or later and you tire . . . Our ambition for this our zone is to make a step ahead . . . One says to one's children, "I've made a step, you try to make a step."

Later in the same interview the informant bitterly and sadly said that he wished he had sold out when he was a younger man because now his life's work amounted to nothing. However, there is some consolation for this generation of men and women in the idea that they have inculcated respect for hard work in their children.

In the rest of this book, it will be suggested that the stark contrast between the land-hating Southern Italian peasants reported by others, and the land oriented peasants of Locorotondo and surrounding municipalities, derives from differing relations to land. It would be difficult to expect the rural proletarians of Western Sicily to have much appreciation for land when they had little or no control over its cultivation and no expectation of being able to "make a step ahead" in land ownership for the next generation. However, for reasons which will be explained historically, Locorotondese men and women could hope to build upon their inheritances to provide for their children, or if without inheritances, they could aspire to providing a patrimony for the next generation by capturing land through purchase with savings or emphyteutical leasing. The story of those hopes is the central theme of the rest of this book. First, however, it is important to round out this portrayal of Locorotondo, *circa* 1982, with a description of the world within the historical town center and nearby suburbs.

Chapter 3

INSIDE LOCOROTONDO

Town and country form separate worlds in Locorotondo. In dialect the line of demarcation is the bygone towered wall which a mid-nineteenth-century town administration razed. A peasant is, in dialect, a "man of the outside" (*l'omme de feuore*); townsmen are from "inside" (*de jinte*). People from the inside and from the outside ridicule each other's dialect and talk about drawls which a foreigner untrained in linguistics can barely perceive. There has been, and continues to be, animosity and distrust between those socialized in town and those socialized in the country, although such feelings are weaker in recent times than before. This division began in the early nineteenth century, and it is based upon social class and ways of earning a living, including the habits of work which accompany them. This chapter will describe the town, its atmosphere, and its population, and draw some contrasts with the "people of the outside," particularly around the theme of work.

THE TOWN AND ITS ATMOSPHERE

In 1982 Locorotondo's town center seemed charged with urban modernity – bustling auto traffic, a skyline sprouting construction cranes, middle-class men in blue jeans standing about in the town square, teens fondling in the park in the early afternoon, chic little shops with English names like "Man, Lady, Baby Shop," over the door, and semi-pornographic movies playing at the movie house – but a little questioning soon showed that a process of radically changing social reality had formed most adult Locorotondesi. As in the countryside, the lines of demarcation in that experience of change stand out clearly as the Second World War, and the passage from the 1950s to the 1960s, which many experienced as a time of discontinuity between the last decade of a locally felt traditional way of life, and integration into a modernity which became more national in charac-

44

ter. Therefore it is necessary to describe the town and its people in a way that constantly confronts that previous Locorotondo with the present one, and attempts to account for the changes the Locorotondesi have experienced.

People in Locorotondo live in housing which dates from the sixteenth century to the present. It is somewhat difficult to define urban neighborhoods strictly by class, because there is a mixture of kinds of people living in various areas, but one can safely generalize that the historical center, the neighborhood originally defined by the walls, and the old extramural neighborhoods immediately around it, house the town elderly and poor, as well as some descendants of the gentry and the old petty bourgeoisie. In the new apartment complexes which have sprouted up around the periphery dwell merchants, public servants, teachers, and sometimes prosperous retired peasants. According to a recent study of the conditions of life of Locorotondo's elderly population, only six percent of the random sample of old people live in the new expanding periphery (Pinto Minerva *et al.*, 1983: 14). The cramped plebeian quarters of the historical center, like the restricted spaces of country *trulli*, do not lend themselves to the exigencies of modern material life, and young people do not view them as desirable housing.

Small one- or two-room dwellings open onto the street level, and contain the shops and dwellings of the remaining members of the old artisan class. Earlier in this century (and records attest to the practice as far back as the eighteenth century) prosperous peasants would acquire one of these rooms, known to them as a *jeuse*, to rent to an artisan as a shop during the week and to use as a place to repair to and change clothes during Sunday Mass and market. Here and there cramped neighborhood grocery stores and a few specialty shops, including a cooperative bookstore run by a group of leftist students, open their doors onto the narrow alleys. By contrast to the one- or two-room ground floor dwellings, the houses of the old elite classes in this area are spacious with vaulted, sometimes frescoed, ceilings. Women of the historical center keep its narrow stone-paved streets swept and immaculately clean, and its house walls gleamingly whitewashed (Plate 3.1). Locorotondo's center is typical of urban cultural patterns in the general area, and these can also be encountered in nearby hill towns such as Cisternino, Martina Franca, Alberobello, and Ostuni.[1]

Except for several houses engulfed by the new expanding perimeter of the town, there are no *trulli* in the urban part of Locorotondo. Ceilings in town are vaulted not domed. They are built on the same principle of corbeling found in *trullo* cones, but the cantilevered stone courses extend longitudinally rather than in the round. The masons of the past covered roofs with the same sort of limestone slabs used on *trullo* domes. These weather to a charcoal-gray color and become dotted here and there with patches of a golden lichen. Before the laying of the Apulian aqueduct, town roofs performed the same water catchment function as country domes, and a shaft for bucketing water ran from the underground cistern up to the highest story. Each dwelling had a hearth as well. House facades reach three stories, but are more commonly two, and balconies and porches, sometimes decorated with elaborate stone-carved lintels, sills, and cornices, punctuate the whitewashed surfaces.

The neighborhoods beneath the town center contain nineteenth- and early twentieth-century construction, often with flat roofs. Most of the town's stores, the Bank of Naples, the central elementary school, the city hall, the cafés, and the news-stands border Via XX Settembre, more often called the "*Corso*," the main avenue of this section. Several of the stores appear unexpectedly fashionable for a town center of 5,900 people. During the morning business hours and the evening promenade the main artery fills with pedestrian traffic, cars, and scooters. It is difficult to find a parking space, and often it is necessary to pull two wheels onto the sidewalk.

On the *Corso* near the town hall, and on nearby side streets, are the section offices of the principal political parties and nearby their affiliated union organizations. Across from the municipal building, behind a small open space with a drinking fountain, an artisan's aid and burial society has its headquarters. Here retired stone masons hang around the door or play cards inside during public hours. Behind and below the municipal building, on the main road to Martina Franca, Locorotondo's locally originated bank, the *Cassa Rurale ed Artigiana*, and the barracks of the *Carabinieri* open their doors. Within a short walk of the town hall there are also two "agencies," which sell auto insurance, make photocopies, and for a fee, see that official papers are processed properly with the appropriate government bureaucracies.

Reinforced concrete apartment houses of four and five stories rise up in the newer periphery. Their bottom floors contain stores, workshops, and offices, and in this peripheral area hardware, auto parts, furniture, appliance, and construction-materials outlets predominate along with mechanics, and some neighborhood groceries, green grocers, and butchers. These neighborhoods extend to the railroad station, and beyond, nearly to the cooperative winery on the road to Alberobello. Locorotondo boasts a middle school, but, with one exception, students must go to neighboring towns to attend higher institutions of secondary education. Just at the edge of town along the road to Cisternino, on the grounds of the old Masseria Caramia, is Locorotondo's Agrarian Technical Institute. This institution specializes in viticulture and oenology and provides excellent training at the secondary level, although few from the countryside elect to send their children there.

At the railroad station one can catch a local train on the privately run line to Bari or Martina Franca. Buses, which stop in Piazza Marconi, connect Locorotondo to Martina Franca and Taranto to the south, and Fasano and the coastal cities as far as Bari to the north. There is a special bus for men who commute to the Italsider steel mill and foundry in Taranto during the week. It is therefore possible to travel from Locorotondo to the major cities of the area by public transportation to conduct daily business or attend schools such as the classic, scientific, or girls' high schools in Martina Franca, the school for hotel keepers and food service workers in Fasano, or the University of Bari. Few commute as far as Bari, a two-hour ride, for work, however.

A regular pattern of events punctuates Locorotondo's urban scene during the year. Friday is market day and to the streets of the town come many stalls run by itinerant merchants, who sell goods ranging from fresh fruits and vegetables, meat, and fish, to hardware and both new and used clothing. Markets in the region are scheduled on different days of the week, and merchants move their wares from one to the other. This is not now a peasant market; instead the fruit and vegetable stalls are run by commercial green grocers. Although there are occasional bargains, prices in the market are not markedly different from those available in stores, because the latter must compete with the itinerant vendors, and heated bargaining is considered appropriate in both contexts. However, the street market offers more variety, along with an opportunity to shop outdoors and run into friends and relatives. Country people come into town on Friday morning to go to market and take care of other business such as banking (there are special buses which circulate in the rural neighborhoods only on Fridays), and the streets are crowded. Before the Second World War market was held on Sunday and country people could combine shopping with attending Mass.

The major saints, particularly *San Rocco*, the town's protector, *San Giorgio*, the traditional town patron saint, and *San Cosimo* and *Damiano*, who are important local healing saints, are celebrated civically with processions, fireworks, rich lighting of the streets, band concerts, and stalls selling cheap goods and snack foods such as nuts and broiled sausages. These are major urban occasions during which people from all over the territory come into town and the town streets fill with people strolling up and down meeting friends and relatives and having a good time.

The Festival of San Rocco, celebrated in August, is the major such occasion. During this festival automobiles bearing license plates from the northern Italian provinces, and from Germany and Switzerland, swarm in the streets. The event draws many people who have emigrated back to their hometown, and functions as the major occasion when families reunite. There are outdoor band concerts by renowned bands hired from larger towns, fireworks competitions which pit rival pyrotechnical companies against each other, bicycle races through the main streets of town, soccer matches, foot races, an amusement park, and processions for the saint. Before the demise of animal traction in the 1950s such occasions were also marked by important livestock fairs, which were held in what is now a residential neighborhood of Locorotondo's periphery and were important aspects of agricultural commerce.[2]

The San Giorgio celebration, which comes on April 24th and 25th, is smaller than San Rocco and differs in significance. It is a public performance which highlights the town's authority structure instead of celebrating the community and its diaspora. A parade of dignitaries, including the mayor in his tri-colored sash, the executive committee of the town council, the marshal of the *Carabinieri*, the head of the town police, and the heads of veterans societies, marches from the town hall to the Church of San Giorgio (Plate 3.2). There the archpriest celebrates a mass which includes a procession inside the church, during which the dignitaries kiss a reliquary containing a relic of Saint George. The next day, shifting squads of men carry the heavy statue of Saint George and the dragon in a religious procession.

Sad strains and muffled drum-beats of dirges, played by the town band during funeral processions, take citizens of the town and country on their last journeys up the *Corso*, into the old center, and to the Church of San Giorgio. Funerals are more frequent in the winter, and weeks pass during which black-bordered announcements appear on customary walls in town and country, and there is a procession nearly every day. On Holy Thursday an elaborate procession which is, in effect, a funeral procession for Christ, mirrors the funeral processions of individuals at a cosmic level. The town band, which plays for such events and also plays brighter music for the saints' processions, is composed entirely of men of urban artisan origin, and forms the center of musical culture in Locorotondo. Town dwellers of all classes have a high interest in music, and a club called the Friends of Music sponsors, with funding from the regional level, a rich concert series which includes fine chamber-music groups, and the Bari Symphony Orchestra. There is also considerable connoisseurship devoted to other bands in the region, and to their *maestri* and virtuoso players, who are invited to play during the local saints' festivals. Around the turn of the century Locorotondo's band toured Europe and even played in front of the Kaiser in Germany (Tragni, 1985: 113–114). This piece of local lore is a point of pride for town dwellers.

THE TOWN POPULATION

Occupations

Few agriculturalists live in Locorotondo, and the town population is more occupationally varied than the country population. A random sample taken from the town-hall family records, which list occupations for heads of household (see Table 3.1), shows a small percentage (5.5 percent) declared as agricultural workers. Care must be taken when assessing this category because, under past social-welfare regimes, people sometimes fraudulently declared themselves members of it to obtain certain fringe benefits. Two townsmen in the sample (1 percent) are small proprietors, both born before 1910, and are likely to have retired into town from the countryside. Another one percent of the sample falls into the large landowner category.

Almost a quarter of household heads in the town are craftsmen of one sort or another. These can be divided into the "traditional" crafts, such as tailor, barber, carpenter, blacksmith, shoemaker, and repairer, tin smith, stone carver, and stone mason, and the newer

Table 3.1. *Occupations declared by town heads of household, Locorotondo 1981 (Random sample drawn from the municipal* schede famigliari*).*

Occupational categories	Number of household heads	Percentage of household heads
Not reported	14	7.04
Housewife	12	6.03
Agricultural worker	11	5.53
Construction worker	2	1.01
Other manual laborer	5	2.51
Waiter	1	0.50
"Traditional" artisan	27	13.57
"New" artisan	22	11.06
Independent trucker	5	2.51
Clerk, private sector	3	1.51
Industrial worker	5	2.51
Steel worker (*Italsider*)	6	3.02
Technician, private sector	1	0.50
Manager, private sector	1	0.50
Small proprietor peasant	2	1.01
Large landowner	1	0.50
Merchant	19	9.55
Contractor	2	1.01
Service entrepreneur	1	0.50
Hall porter	6	3.02
Clerk, public sector	11	5.53
Teacher	3	1.51
Manager, public sector	5	2.51
Technician, public sector	2	1.01
Self-employed professional	5	2.51
Police or military	5	2.51
Retired	22	11.06
Total	199	100.00

artisan trades, such as automobile mechanic, appliance repairman, electrician, and plumber. Independent truckers, who account for 2.5 percent of the sample of heads of household, can be classed as similar to the latter category, because they are entrepreneurs earning a living from technology diffused into the area within the post-war era. The mean birth year for traditional artisans in town is 1931 (with a standard deviation of 12.36 years), and the mean birth year for "new" artisans is 1942 (standard deviation equals 12.88 years) indicating transition between the two categories.[3] Another 6 percent can be classed as employed industrially either as workers or technicians. Of these, half work at Italsider on the outskirts of Taranto and enjoy high wages and benefits. The others work in local small industries such as the recently founded garment factories, which take work from northern firms on subcontract, or print shops. About 3.5 percent are construction workers.

Thirteen-and-a-half percent of heads of household in the sample draw a salary from the municipality or the state (this excludes the 2.5 percent employed in the military and police). The largest category (5.5 percent) consists of office clerks. Three percent of public employees are hall porters – people who run errands, carry messages, and provide general aid in the halls and offices of public institutions, especially schools. Notoriously this is a political-spoils job. Teachers account for 1.5 percent of the sample, and 2.5 percent are in executive roles such as municipal office heads.

Store operators comprise a large and variegated category (9.5 percent) which ranges from proprietorship of corner tobacco shops to the elegant boutique near the public park. Some make marginal livings, and some do well and must be classed among the town's new elite. There are in town a few contractors and developers (1 percent in the sample) who are responsible for the construction which characterizes the town periphery. Their wealth and political connections make them a center of power. Some such men, however, are solidly linked with the countryside and reside there. Lastly, 2.5 percent of the sample can be classed as self-employed professionals – lawyers, doctors, and notaries.

As in the countryside, there have been important changes in the occupational structure of the town during the decades following the Second World War, especially since about 1960. Key factors have been the demise of the artisan economy and the rise of other avenues for employment. Before the Second World War most of the population of the town exercised artisan trades. Interviews with old artisans testify that apprenticeship to a master artisan was a lower-class town boy's expected path to a livelihood. Access to education was severely limited by class expectations and economic means and other opportunities were unavailable. The parents' conventional wisdom was that enough education to be able to sign one's marriage documents would do. Apprentices learned what accounting or mathematical skills they needed on the job. Since artisans produced most locally consumed goods, retail stores were limited in number. The two local factories – one produced carts and the other organs – were family businesses which did not employ many craftsmen.

It is instructive to consider data collected in an interview with Donato, a retired tailor, about the vocational fates and whereabouts of the twenty boys and two girls who, after a few years of elementary school, had been apprenticed with him to learn the trade of tailor or pants seamstress. Of the males, only three remain tailors in Locorotondo. Another began as a tailor but, as a livelihood became more difficult to obtain, became an entrepreneur and opened a small garment factory which subcontracts work from northern firms. Such small factories proliferated during the 1970s as northern firms sought to escape higher labor costs brought about by union victories early in the decade. Expected wages were lower in the south, and southern employers used non-unionized workers. Eight emigrated and are tailors in North Italy, and in one case Argentina. Another eight, the informant's most recent apprentices, remained in Locorotondo, but changed fields entirely. Among them number a laundry owner, a telephone company worker, a municipal policeman, a municipal clerk, a bartender, a beverage distributor, and a mechanic. The two women have remained seamstresses who sew pants on consignment from Locorotondese tailors. For the majority, therefore, changing economic factors have meant either emigration or a distinct career change.

Several factors have altered the town's employment profile. The recovery and expansion of northern industry in the decades following the war and its connection to the European Common Market in 1957 was accompanied by increasing penetration of the south of Italy by cheap industrially manufactured goods. Increasing exposure to national advertising, designed to incorporate places like Locorotondo into national and international consumer markets, brought about changes in the definition of what things were necessary for a minimal lifestyle, or desirable for an elite one. Whole classes of goods which were previously available only in bigger centers such as Martina Franca, or even only in Bari, are now readily obtainable in Locorotondo in the proliferation of stores which line the *Corso* and other streets. This penetration brought about a crisis in the late 1950s and early 1960s during which industrially manufactured goods almost totally replaced locally made goods. This replacement, a factor all over the south of Italy (Martinelli, 1985: 54), meant the demise of an already precarious traditional artisan economy.

In the long run some opportunities for entrepreneurial activity and for employment have come with these changes. A few artisans have been able to make the transition between making items and selling industrially produced goods. Locorotondo's once renowned cart factory, for instance, is now a hardware store owned by the sons of the old master cart maker. Ex-artisans also operate the town's shoe stores and clothing stores. However, retailing could not absorb a large proportion of displaced craftsmen and many, like eight of Donato's apprentices, had to take their trades elsewhere, and others had to find new ways of life.

The economic recovery and "miracle" of North Italy and economic growth in Northern Europe during the 1950s and 1960s drew many who had been deprived of an artisan trade, or of a living in agriculture, into employment in the north, in Germany, and in Switzerland as industrial workers. Then economic crises through the 1970s, in the regions and nations which had absorbed workers from Southern Europe during the 1960s, forced many to return to Locorotondo. Some men and women brought back newly acquired skills which have been put to good use in Locorotondo. One man learned to be an automobile mechanic in Belgium and returned with a Belgian bride. Another learned silkscreen printing in Paris, and upon his return opened a print shop which has expanded into a small factory which now takes orders internationally for silkscreened wallpaper-sample book covers. Some, of course, left Locorotondo for good and have become part of the diaspora which returns for the Festival of San Rocco.

Around 1960 government policy toward the south shifted 180 degrees from sole concentration on the development of agriculture toward the development of heavy industry (Martinelli, 1985: 49). During the 1960s the Italsider steel mill in Taranto was founded and completed with massive infusions of public funds. This meant employment opportunities for many men from the Province of Taranto and neighboring communes in the Province of Bari. About 150 men from Locorotondo work at Italsider, and two-thirds of them are from the town as opposed to the countryside. Working at Italsider means good pay (800,000 to 900,000 lire a month for an experienced worker in 1982) and benefits brought about through attachment to national labor union movements. Such industrial and union socialization has given the Italsider workers a degree of sophistication lacking in men with less outside experience, or men involved in the more individualistic "new" trades. In town there is a 110 member after-work club for the Italsider workers which operates a cooperative grocery store for them.

Most of the town men employed at Italsider began their work careers as artisans. Because there has been little new hiring since the plant's developing years, these men form a cohort averaging about 40 years of age. This cohort effect reflects the failure of further heavy industrial development in the area which was to come about through a supposed "trickle down effect." As Martinelli notes (1985: 72–73) this has not occurred because the policies which implanted heavy industries such as Italsider, or the Montecattini Edison industrial complex in Brindisi (which employs few from Locorotondo, but many from neighboring Cisternino), have not encouraged linkage through development of supporting firms founded by local entrepreneurs. Fully mature, instead of developing, industries were transplanted to the south. Cynical jokes about the plant buying even the toilet paper for its rest rooms from northern suppliers accompany serious local discussions of the failure of industrialization in the south.

Another factor has, of course, been growth of the public sector. This has meant the expansion of welfare and public-health systems, and public education. Laws requiring compulsory education through middle school were adopted in the mid-1960s and this increased the demand for teachers trained through university level as well as for elementary school teachers. Vocational secondary schools have also expanded in the area, providing teaching jobs not present a quarter of a century ago. There are now social workers and a publicly paid consulting psychologist in Locorotondo who attempt to provide services for the poor and troubled. The municipality even employs two women as "cultural facilitators" (*operatrici culturali*) whose job is to organize festivals and other cultural opportunities such as adult-education classes. New positions have also developed in health areas. Quasi-public-sector employment opportunities also exist in the education and social service oriented local arms of the major unions.

Often the development of public sector posts has simply given the dominant political parties of southern towns more spoils to bestow during patron–client political maneuvering, and therefore amplified the possibilities of a long-established pattern (cf. Salvemini, 1955). The position of hall porter (*bidello*) is often a political plum which can be obtained through patron–client relationships. In other cases, positions, in teaching for instance, must be won through competitive civil-service examinations, sometimes with a little help from patrons, and are honestly and professionally occupied. There are not, however, adequate numbers of such positions to employ those with training. Unemployment, underemployment, and the frustration consequent to them, are endemic in Locorotondo among highly educated young men and women who take civil-service exams for teaching posts, and other public-sector jobs, and then hope to be employed. Landing a job through this strategy often means working first in some far-away locale in Italy and then transferring one's way into a position within commuting distance of Locorotondo with the help of patronage, luck, or both. The educated all over Southern Italy face such problems.

Work and the traditional artisan

The old working classes of Locorotondo – peasants and artisans – had differing ways of socializing youth into the rigors of work, and differences in social values stem from them. Artisan men had, in effect, two fathers, because a man's *maestro* had as much responsibility for his socialization as his real father, and much more responsibility for inculcating values about work and craftsmanship. Peasants, instead, learned to work from their parents, and as part of child-labor crews working at transforming land into vineyards. As one artisan informant observed while explaining that no townsperson would become a peasant, "There was no peasant apprenticeship." The artisan boy spent more time with his *maestro* than with his parents and the bonds were strong. A boy might be apprenticed as young as the age of six, although apprenticeship usually began a few years later when he would be placed in an artisan shop by his parents. The child spent his first years hanging around, watching, and carrying out small tasks – in tailor shops sitting to the side practicing sewing scraps of cloth together, or in shoemakers' shops straightening bent nails. From such a tender age until it was time, at the age of 19, to go away for military service, the boy spent his days from 7:00 a.m. to noon, and then from 1:30 p.m. until the work was done – sometimes as late as midnight if there were rush orders – at work in his *maestro's* shop. Normally he would arrive home at night in time for the evening meal and then collapse into bed. During this long period of apprenticeship the *maestro* exerted much authority over his boys, particularly concerning the way they managed their time, and the company they kept. One informant remembered stoically burning a hole through his underwear into his leg while concealing a smoldering cigarette in his pocket. His stern *maestro*, who had forbidden smoking, unexpectedly returned to the shop from an errand.

This level of intense and long specialized training led to another key difference between peasants and artisans. A town informant noted that "our peasants know how to make do." He did not say this in admiration particularly, but instead conveyed the sense that peasants, to save money and be independent from the artisans of the town, would try to make things for themselves and give each other haircuts. This is the other face of the proverb, "If you want to eat bread, stay away from the church bells." The town artisan was a skilled specialist, the peasant was (and still is) a generalist who could, if necessary, render himself almost completely independent of the workshops of the center. This led to a certain degree of envy from artisans because the peasant laborer was a small-scale food producer as well as a wage earner, and did not have to depend so much upon the grocery store. The artisan, on the other hand, learned to value specialized work for its own sake, and took an aesthetic pleasure in fine craftsmanship. For a *maestro*, an apprentice's work was always short of perfection, and the apprenticeship instilled high standards in many artisan minds. There was, then, a certain mutual respect for specialization among artisans. Shoemakers, for instance, would never attempt to cut hair or make clothing.

The trade of tailor was the most prestigious in a hierarchy of artisan occupations, which townspeople ranked according to the cleanliness of the work environment and whether they were carried out indoors or outdoors. At the bottom were masons – skilled stone carvers and cutters just above them – who were called *l'omme d'a polvere*, – "men of dust." (Note that these are distinguished from the country masons, the *caseddère*, who built *trulli*, and the *paretère*, who built field walls.) In the middle fell the barber, carpenter, blacksmith, shoemaker, and tin smith, whose trades people considered dirty in comparison to that of the tailor, who not only worked in a clean environment but gained a certain prestige because he entered the houses of the highest classes, the *galantuomini*, to take measurements and make fittings. Shoemakers took consolation in sitting down to work. Because of this their shops, which were also relatively quiet, became locales for impromptu drop-in conversations.

The barbers were also figures of some importance because they came into contact with everyone and were founts of information.

Before the craftsmen of Locorotondo succumbed to competition with northern industry in the 1950s and 1960s, there were staggering numbers of shops, particularly tailor and shoemaker shops, most of them concentrated in the historical center. One old shoemaker recalled that before the Second World War, 111 shops practiced his trade in Locorotondo. Counting apprenticed boys, around 300 people made shoes. Tailors and their apprentices were even more plentiful and shops with 25 apprentices existed. The prestige of tailors in the hierarchy made apprenticeship to them attractive to parents, and in the small-town life of Locorotondo, which before the artisan crisis was a face-to-face community concentrated in the historical center and the neighboring *borgo*, parents took offence if an artisan turned a boy away. The only reasonable excuse was lack of space in a shop, usually consisting of a single room. The production of so many tailors created competition for work and kept the prices which could be charged down, although, before the 1950s, there was no competition from ready-made clothing retailing, except from the stalls which sold used American clothing in the weekly market. It is no wonder that Locorotondo was an exporter of tailors.

Elite strata

As in other areas of Locorotondese life, the answer to the question *"Chi commanda a Locorotondo?"* ("Whose word goes in Locorotondo?") has changed with the broad social and political changes of the post Second World War era and therefore within the experiences of most mature people. Power now has its basis in complex patron–client systems which link a variety of key individuals, mostly belonging to the dominant Christian Democratic Party.[4] This party is by no means monolithic, either nationally or in Locorotondo, although the local factions, which are loosely labeled with the names of national faction leaders, do not necessarily have much to do ideologically with their national counterparts. The development of the post-war political system of Locorotondo, particularly as it touched the rural population after the Second World War when politicians found it necessary to adapt themselves to the peculiar settlement pattern of the zone, will be treated in a later chapter. Below follows a discussion of Locorotondo's higher strata.

The older pre-war power base of the large landowners, and the professional small landowner "middle-bourgeoisie" eroded considerably during the post-war era, and members of these families no longer have political importance (although some still serve on the municipal council), nor are they accorded particularly high positions among townsmen. Indeed, many townsmen take a certain pleasure in talking of their fall from power. Notably, nearly all the significant actors on the town's political stage are teachers. They base their power either on the control of patron–client ties within local and distant bureaucracies, or on ties with centers of wealth, and preferably on both. The Christian Democratic faction in power during the early 1980s is connected to construction interests in Locorotondo, and these interests form a center of power based upon wealth. One politically experienced informant expressed the opinion that self-made men in the area seek careers in politics to lend legitimacy to their rising fortunes and to their family futures, rather than for what commercial advantages might be gained from political connections. Other individuals, however, expressed suspicions about the manipulation of things like building permits and public works contracts. The vice-mayor during the time of the study, a major construction entrepreneur and employer, was not from town, however, and gained his political support from the rural neighborhoods where he grew up. His career reflected the new equalization in power between country and town in Locorotondo. Current centers of bureaucratic power include the party affiliated labor organizations (CISL, affiliated to the Christian Democrats; and CGIL affiliated to the left), key positions in hospital and health department administrations, the cooperative winery, the town hall, and the schools. Such diffusion of power makes for a political scene in which there is constant jockeying between factions within the Christian Democratic Party, the opposition parties looking on and occasionally exercising some power through voting alliances and swings in the municipal council. As one communist informant put it, there is no serious alternative to the Christian Democrats because they are well organized and have political experience.

The new urban middle class consisting of teachers, office managers, merchants, and professionals leads a comfortable life in well-furnished and spacious modern condominium housing. Members of this group often show great concern for style, in both dress and furnishings, and comprise the clientele for the few fashionable shops along the *Corso*. For teachers, and for many office workers, the day's work is over at midday and many men spend the latter part of the afternoon and the early evening along the main street, or in the squares and sidewalks near the municipal gardens, seeking conversations. There is also an elite club, located in the old main square where a card game or a conversation can be found, or the newspaper can be read.

The new middle class has varied origins. Many members grew up in artisan families in which parents concerned themselves with their children's education and achieved social mobility for them in that way. Others have belonged to the petty bourgeoisie families of the town for several generations and simply continue that tradition. This is especially true of some of the professionals whose fathers held strong values about sons continuing in the same profession. Lastly, the urban middle class includes some men and women descended from the older leisure class of gentlemen, who, because living from estate income is no longer possible in Locorotondo, have had to find professions.

Before the Second World War and during about a decade and a half afterwards, and therefore well within the experience of many Locorotondesi, a different social structure held. The gentry of Locorotondo was divided into two strata: those who exercised a profession and who had some land, and those who had enough land to live from estate income and sometimes held a position on the side (one such family ran the tax collecting office of Locorotondo, for example). The latter category consisted of a handful of families called the *signorotti* or, as noted before, the *galantuomini*. The richest of families attempted to concentrate landed wealth into the hands of the first born son to keep patrimonies intact. They dowered their daughters in cash instead of land and sometimes attempted to place a son in the priesthood. Such families often had their larger and more remunerative landholdings outside communal boundaries, as the small proprietor settlement pattern of Locorotondo and the poverty of its untransformed land surface made large-scale farming uneconomical. In awe, peasant informants told of 16 de Bernardis *masserie* which stretched from Locorotondo to the Adriatic. Don Nicola Aprile-Ximenes claimed that his father held on to the local Masseria Cardone, 60 hectares before it was divided, only to raise horses. Factors which include the high cost of agricultural labor, the low price of grapes and the costs involved in replacing old vineyards, and the demise of a demand for stud animals because of the obsolescence of animal traction along with the introduction of artificial insemination, have eroded the economic positions of the landowning gentry considerably. This group has lost its local landed power base and therefore the ability to sanction political ascendancy and prestige, or create dependencies among peasants or poorer townsmen.

Just below this handful of families ranked the professionals. Nowadays the members of this group call themselves the middle bourgeoisie (*media borghesia* – a suspiciously sociological sounding term), and concede that in the old days they ranked below the gentlemen, but decidedly above merchants and artisans. Except for the very richest families in town, clear distinctions are difficult over time because family fortunes had their ups and downs. Typically, males exercised professions requiring university educations, such as notary, lawyer, or medical doctor (which before the war meant study at the University of Naples), or at least a secondary school diploma, such as pharmacist (a profession only recently requiring a university degree). One old lawyer recalled 8 doctors, 2 pharmacists, an engineer, and 5 lawyers (to which must be added at least 1 notary) in pre-Second World War Locorotondo. Generally they were more educated than the members of the highest class which, after all, needed little education to make a living.

The number of retail merchants was limited until several decades ago, but the better off among them would have been ranked only in the low end of this "middle bourgeoisie" class. The town's elementary school teachers (who, until recently, did not need a university degree) and petty bureaucrats also ranked on the periphery of the middle bourgeoisie. An artisan informant bitterly recalled what he considered his schoolmaster's illegitimate pretension to the title "Don." Although pharmacists did not have university degrees, in Locorotondo their shops were hubs of elite male gossip because of central location and conduciveness to conversation, and they were more solidly included in the class despite their lesser educations. Their high incomes also helped.

The two ranks of elite society lived in a world apart from the rest. At least for males, associations were more cosmopolitan both socially and in business – their worlds did not stop at the borders of the municipality. Many traveled for reasons of education and before the Second World War the fascist student group organized touristic junkets to ski, or even to visit Albania across the Adriatic. Education beyond elementary school meant travel at least to Martina Franca, and for many boys a period in a boarding school far from home in a cosmopolitan center such as Naples or even Bologna.

Marriage with people of similar rank was a necessity, and would-be matchmakers often contrived and arranged it in gossip circles when the parties involved were adolescents. One informant spoke of what she called the "club" for women, which was an informal gathering of elite women who sat in the courtyards of the three most prominent families. They would do needlework as they watched people pass by through their gates, and "subject them to their scissors," that is, gossip. She said she knew of many marriages which had been arranged in those courtyards. There was, in any case, little opportunity for girls to engage in courtship on their own because their parents rigidly secluded them, and allowed them out only in the company of the family maid. Since the circle of possible candidates, particularly for the upper-elite families, was restricted in size, people often sought partners among the higher ranks of society in neighboring towns such as Fasano, Martina Franca, Alberobello, and Cisternino. This led, of course, to social and political alliances, as well as sometimes to control over dowered or inherited land holdings in other zones (not all landowner families practiced primogeniture), and therefore to the advantages of diversification of agricultural enterprises.

These were leisure classes in contrast to the eternally laboring artisans and peasants, both of which groups still express resentment because of this. Labor was not the central value of their lives. Elite men spent many afternoon hours at the gentlemen's clubs exchanging gossip, reading the newspapers, and playing cards and billiards. Hunting and gambling were favorite pastimes and gentlemen from neighboring towns would hold intense card games, particularly in Selva, the nearby summer resort for the elite families of Fasano, in which properties, sometimes including whole *masserie*, would be bet in games of poker and *zècchenètte*, the local card game. A few of the gentlemen did attempt to practice improved agriculture and may be responsible (claims from peasant informants sometimes to the contrary) for the introduction of innovations like the use of rototillers around 1960. Following their own interests, several more enlightened larger landowners had a significant hand in starting both the cooperative winery and the locally begun popular bank.

Those of the elite strata emphasized their rank in Locorotondese society in many ways. Lesser members of that society addressed and referred to them with the titles *Don* and *Donna*, and in dialect with the pronoun *signurine*, instead of the *tu*, second person form, used in all other conversation. However, the elite responded to their inferiors with *tu*. The title *Don* is now reserved for priests, and out of habit and sometimes respect, for some of the remaining members of the fallen gentlemanly class. Deference paid by artisans, especially the poverty stricken masons, was a calculated necessity. Accounts from both artisan (Lisi, n.d., 1), and upper-class sources (interview data) indicate that in hard times, especially during the winter, the urban poor circulated offering to do odd jobs for bread, or simply begged for whatever food could be spared. Archangelo Lisi's personal account of having to do this leaves the impression that certain of the rich families could generally be counted upon for generosity.

Gentlemen and their families also separated themselves from the masses with certain rules of everyday behavior. One interviewee, who married a Locorotondese professional, but who was herself from elsewhere in Italy, recalled being criticized during her early months in Locorotondo in the 1950s for carrying her own packages in public. Servants did that. The highest in society required tradesmen such as barbers and tailors to service them in their town houses instead of publicly in shops. The higher one climbed in the hierarchy of Locorotondo, the more secluded everyday activities, and even significant life events, became. The highest even married at home, served by the ranking churchman of the town, instead of in the church. The world came to them; they did not go out to seek it.

Rich families also demonstrated their rank publicly during celebrations and rites of passage for family members. In the municipal theater they organized an exclusive Carnival celebration which was well known for its sumptuous buffet – an informant claimed that some people from the town lower classes would come masked and take advantage of this. Betrothal parties, held at home, were ceremonial occasions to which both the archpriest and the town mayor were expected to come. Interviewees recounted how there was a display of conspicuous consumption in hiring the town band for the funeral procession, but ordering it to remain silent during the procession. This was to signal a distinction from peasant funerals in which much money was spent, especially upon hiring the band. Also elite funerals were marked by entry of the Church of Saint George through the large central door – a privilege which cost extra. There was an elaborate catafalque upon which the pall bearers placed the coffin, and three priests said a high mass. The processions of the poor entered through the left side door and placed the coffin on the floor with a few candles. The archpriest eliminated the distinction of doors, at least, in 1940, but many remember, and resent it as a strong marker of rank in Locorotondo. The resting place of the dead in Locorotondo well reflects the town's stratificational system. In the older parts of the cemetery elaborately carved tombs belonging to the older elite families line a grid of paths surrounded by the ossuary lined walls and the workers' association mausolea which contain the remains of ordinary people. Elite landowners and professionals occupied the center of the cemetery just as they occupied the center of town life.

The town, therefore, is and was very different from the countryside. It has long been more differentiated by class and occupation, and more tied to the outside world. Until quite recently artisans and middle-class individuals saw the world very differently from peasants and peasant workers, and some of those differences in world view persist. In the recent past, the two populations saw eye-to-eye very little, and this will be a theme discussed in a later chapter which specifically takes up the consequences of the dispersed settlement pattern of Locorotondo with respect to the town/country dimension. Now the narrative must move toward the past to provide a sense of understanding of the origins and development of the patterns described for town and country, and experienced by living adults of the early 1980s.

Plate 2.1. Coming and going from the crowded countryside to market

Plate 2.2. Woman whitewashing exterior of house

Plate 2.3. Side view of *masseria* showing pitch roofed great house and chapel, and associated *trulli*

Plate 2.4. The heavy local hoe (*a zappe*)

Plate 2.5. Old style vineyard hoed with ridges and depressions

Plate 2.6. Spreading fertilizer by hand in a newer style vineyard cultivated on wires (note stony soil)

Plate 2.7. Pouring grape must into large fermentation jars

Plate 3.1. Street in the historical center

Plate 3.2. Town pitched roofs and the Church of St. George

Plate 4.1. The oldest known *trullo* (1599)

Part II

THE DOCUMENTED PAST

Chapter 4

SETTLEMENT AND ECONOMY UNDER THE WANING OLD ORDER

The first good evidence of a developing pattern of dispersed settlement in the countryside dates to 1811, when roughly 37 percent of the population had taken up residence outside the walls and urban extramural neighborhoods of Locorotondo (see Chapter 6). In the decades which followed, the occupation of the countryside continued, culminating in the patterns described in Chapter 2. This chapter will examine evidence about settlement pattern, economy, and social structure before the early nineteenth century, and establish a baseline from which the important changes of that century can be better understood.

KINDS OF EVIDENCE

Before beginning this historical discussion, it is important to consider the general nature of documentary evidence for the area. The research reported here is designed in an opposite fashion to many other studies of South Italian history. Often historians choose problems to investigate because they know about a rich data source. Here, instead, was an anthropological topic – how Locorotondo's settlement pattern came about, and the particular social organizational patterns and problems which accompanied that development – and the problem became making the best of what historical documents are available. The historical record for any locale is a patchy thing; outstanding evidence may cluster around certain dates, and there may be long spans of time upon which documents cast little or no light. This is true for Locorotondo. Aside from some fragmentary evidence, reviewed below, a dark space gapes between the sixteenth century and the early eighteenth. Notarial transactions begin in the archives in Bari in the 1680s, but they are savaged by worms and obscured by mildew until 1725. A functionary in the late nineteenth century made a pastime of using old Locorotondese church records as raw material for creating papier mâché animals, and probably destroyed a patrimony of information (Baccaro, 1968: 59). The minutes of eighteenth- and early nineteenth-century town council sessions survive only occasionally. On the other hand, the notarial transactions (ASB–AN, 1683–1729, 1729–1780, 1734–1784, 1761–1796, 1777–1808, 1780–1838, and 1819–1867) which do survive contain rich qualitative data, and the property tax rosters (cadasters) of 1749 (ASB–CO, 1749) and 1816 (ASB–CP, 1816, ACL–CP, 1823–1930), and the census of 1811 (ACL–SP, 1810–1811) provide marvellous quantitative cross-sectional pictures of conditions. In many ways, documentation for the eighteenth and early nineteenth centuries is richer than for the later nineteenth, particularly given the existence of the cadasters. However, police and judicial records afford vivid glimpses of nineteenth-century life, as do the contents of prefectural files on Locorotondo which were kept in Bari. In sum, different periods provide different kinds of evidence and this account of Locorotondo's economic and social history must end up as patchy as that evidence.

BEFORE THE EIGHTEENTH CENTURY

Foundation of a territory

An amateur archaeologist has made surface finds just below the current historical center in the Contrada Grofoleo which suggest that a population lived there as early as the upper paleolithic, and continued to exist at least intermittently during the neolithic, the bronze age, the time of Greek colonization, and the Medieval period (De Michele, 1986; see also Baccaro, 1968: 57–58). Locorotondo probably appears in the historical record for the first time in 1086 as part of a feudal grant to form the Abbey of Saint Stephen, headquartered near what is now the city of Fasano on the coastal plain. At that time it would have been no more than a cluster of peasant and shepherd dwellings located on the ridge occupied by the present town. No building survives in Locorotondo which can be dated with any certainty before the fifteenth century. An Aragonese tax register dating to the mid-fifteenth century lists Locorotondo as having only 65 hearths, or households (Guarella, 1983: 76). According to best current methods of estimating the mean number of individuals in a taxable hearth during the epoch, this amounted to around 260 people (Villani, 1972: 1637).

On the thirtieth day of September in 1566 the town of Locorotondo bought its hinterlands from the Royal Court and its first set of
official borders became established (Sampietro, 1922: 254–263;
Chirulli, 1982). At that date, the town, numbering 308 hearths (in
1561, up 47.4 percent from the mid-fifteenth century) and therefore
between 1,230 and 1,380 souls, lay in the midst of a vast common
territory which stretched along the plateau from the territory of the
city of Monopoli to the northwest and down to the vicinity of Ostuni
to the southeast (Giustiniani, 1802: 282). Contemporary locals knew
this as the *selva*, or "forest" as opposed to the coastal plain, known
then, as it is now, as the *marina*. The inhabitants of Fasano,
Locorotondo, Cisternino, Martina Franca, and Castellana, as well as
of the city of Monopoli, enjoyed rights to pasture animals, draw
water from catchment basins, cut wood, and spend the night in this
territory.

Around the middle of the sixteenth century, citizens of these towns
began to abusively enclose land for private use as woods, pastures,
and fields. The Commissars of the Royal Court imposed sentences,
but fines went uncollected, giving the impression that this was wild
territory in which such impositions were difficult to enforce, and that
the Royal Court wished to rid itself of the bother. In 1566, it sent an
agent to the area with the explicit task of enforcing the previous
sentences and forcing usurpers of common land to destroy the walls
they had built, but also with the clandestine task of negotiating the
sale of promiscuous rights with the heads of the towns involved.

The officials divided the territory proportionally among the towns
according to the number of hearths in each, and with each subdivision went the legal jurisdiction (*baglivo*) over the territory and right
to rents paid for the privilege of pasturing animals. A surveyor
marked crosses on trees and piled up *specchie*, mounds of rocks, to
mark out borders. The territory of Locorotondo, according to a
mid-eighteenth century map which notes the old borders (ALM,
1810), and the document drafted at the time (Chirulli, 1982:
217–241), was defined as triangular, except where it bordered the
Difesa of Ostuni, which was not part of the territory being sold.[1]

The *trullo* form of construction and some indication of habitation
in the countryside are already apparent in the boundary establishing
document.[2] At least one sixteenth-century *trullo* survives in Marziolla
in the northern part of Locorotondo's territory, and the builder
commemorated its construction by scratching the date 1599 on the
lintel stone (Plate 4.1). This is the oldest securely dated *trullo* in the

entire *murgia* area, but it is not easy to determine whether it was a habitation or a field hut. It consists of a single circular space about five meters in diameter at floor level, from which the corbeled dome arises directly. People in the neighboring hamlet tell tales of treasures – golden statues of goats – guarded by large serpents found inside.[3]

The notary's description of the actual process of walking over the landscape and establishing boundaries in 1566 testifies that land in the zone had been enclosed. The document mentions many *clausurii* (enclosures) and vineyards belonging to owners from Locorotondo and Martina Franca (Chirulli, 1982: 217–241). In the countryside there are also cisterns, catchment basins, and threshing floors. The road network is also visible, at least where it crosses the boundary line, and about 40 percent of roads which cross the line in 1756 (date of the mid-eighteenth-century map) were noted in 1566. Importantly, the document mentions two *jazzèlere* – Trito and San Marco (under the name Santa Maria di Sisignano).

Land involved in this set of transactions was to remain open except under the following circumstances defined in the agreement between all the towns concerned (Chirulli, 1982: 242–244). "Item: that it would be legal in said territory to plant vineyards and make gardens and to enclose them, but not impermanently planted fields, under the penalty of fifty ounces." The document also stipulated that on *masserie* one tenth of the land be defined as *mezzano*, which in this era meant pasture set aside especially for plow oxen, and which seems to have been closed for at least part of the year. Other enclosures which the town's citizens had made were to be opened again by dismantling the stone walls.

The stipulation having to do with vineyards and gardens has significance because it said that land could be "captured" from the commons by private parties through investment in intensive cropping. The mechanism by which it could be acquired is, however, not defined, nor have the stipulations by which common land was used in Locorotondo after 1566 survived the centuries. Cofano, who writes of Martina Franca (where such statutes do not survive either) notes, however, that towns regulated not only the rights to use of common land, but also had the right to cede land to private parties with the obligation that the latter improve it and make it more productive (1977: 58). Sometimes the concession, particularly when it was of land for cereals, was not definable as true private property in the sense that it had to remain open between the harvest and sowing.[4] Whatever the mechanisms of land acquisition, all common land in Locorotondo had passed into private hands by the middle of the eighteenth century, and a universal commons, in the strict sense of the term, no longer existed.

The seventeenth century

Only counts of taxable hearths in various years survive before the eighteenth century, although now only secondary sources can be consulted because the originals perished in a fire in the State Archives in Naples (Giustiniani, 1802: 282). By 1595 the number of hearths in Locorotondo had risen to 429 showing an increase of 39.3 percent above the mid-sixteenth-century figure reported above. This was a peak because the count fell again to 400 in 1648 and to 342 in 1669. By 1749, year of the cadaster, the number of hearths had risen once again to 622 and the population registered numbered 2,182. Then a hearth averaged 3.5 individuals.

Locorotondo's mid-seventeenth-century population decline had parallels elsewhere in Apulia, and was a symptom of general crisis which included economic decline, increasing taxes, plague (1656), popular insurrection, bandits, and bad harvests, all of which culminated around mid-century (Masella, 1979: 36). The national expression of these troubled times was the famous insurrection of Masaniello in Naples in 1647 (Villari, 1985). Although warfare between European powers and the Ottoman Empire had calmed since the sixteenth century, during the seventeenth century pirates still plagued the Adriatic coastal cities and their hinterlands with raids. This made sea trade and travel dangerous and costly.

Despite this, during the sixteenth- and seventeenth-centuries there was some development of commerce in the Apulian Adriatic through the coastal grain ports of Trani, Barletta, Manfredonia, and the olive-oil ports of Monopoli (nearest to Locorotondo), and Bitonto. In each of these towns local bourgeois merchant families arose, and traders from elsewhere, Venice in particular, established themselves. The Terra di Bari, in which Locorotondo lay, saw some expansion of grape and olive-oil production because of this, and was probably the most developed zone in Apulia (Masella, 1979: 35). As early as 1551 a geographer comments about the coastal zone around Monopoli, "that, in truth it is a thing which is very difficult to believe for those who have not seen the forests of olives . . . all of this region, or rather the Terra di Bari, contains" (Alberti, 1551: 198).

THE ECONOMIC BASIS OF EIGHTEENTH-CENTURY SOCIETY

Population and settlement

Abrupt growth in Locorotondo's population during the eighteenth century parallels other parts of Apulia, where between 1710 and 1790 the population doubled, although not uniformly. Expansion was more rapid in the Terra di Bari. According to Massafra (1979a: 79), by the end of the eighteenth century a little less than half of all centers with more than 10,000 people in the entire kingdom were concentrated in Apulia, and of these, 56 percent were in the Terra di Bari.

The first half of the eighteenth century was economically bright in the Bari area; the second less so. Commerce and intensive tree crop agriculture expanded further for several reasons. In 1707, as a result of the War of Spanish Succession, the kingdom became an Austrian Viceroyalty. The almost thirty-year period of Hapsburg domination (until 1734), with its emphasis on Adriatic commerce and effective control of pirates, gave new life to commercial activities in the Barese port towns and this, in turn, stimulated intensification of olive cultivation along the coastal plain (Rosa, 1979: 65; Massafra, 1979a: 79). This expanding monocrop specialization created, at least in the zones of Monopoli and Fasano, a market for wine produced just inland on the Murgia dei Trulli. The first Bourbon King of Naples, Charles I, took the throne in 1735 after the fall of the Austrians, and, until mid-century, Apulia and especially Terra di Bari continued to enjoy a degree of prosperity and development within the confines of the feudal order. The second half of the eighteenth century was not so advantageous, and dire crises, culminating in the revolution and French invasions of 1799, characterized its last decades.

Charles I mandated the compilation of the *catasto onciario* – ("ounce cadaster") in 1740–1741 to make the taxation system of the kingdom more efficient and equitable; a portion of church wealth now became taxable. Between 1741 and 1788 local commissions drew up the cadasters based on declarations of property by the citizens of each town (Dal Pane, 1936: 10), although some town administrations stalled because of threatened interests. The document was not based upon accurate land surveying, but each declaration was discussed by a commission of townsmen, and estimates were adjusted accordingly.[5]

The document is a household census as well as a register of property. For each household entry it lists the members by age, sex, and sometimes, for males of 16 years or more, occupation. There was some undercounting of very small children because they made no fiscal contribution, and their survival beyond the first years of their lives was problematical. There is no record of ages for the 49 priests recorded because they paid no head tax, which depended upon age. The sturdy yellow pages note whether each family owned its house or rented it, and if so, the name of the landlord and the amount of rent paid. There follows a listing of properties by location with the names of other individuals owning adjacent fields. Field sizes are given in *stoppelli* (one *stoppello* equals 1,074 square meters) and *tomoli* (eight *stoppelli* constitute one *tomolo*), and *quartieri*, a measure equivalent to a *stoppello* but used only for vineyards. The use of fields is not often clearly specified, and the compilers cared more about recording whether a field was common land or enclosed, than what was planted on it. They designated much land simply as *terra*. Taxable property such as buildings (besides the family dwelling, which was not taxed), animals (excluding courtyard animals and pigs), and workshops were recorded in detail. In addition, the debts and emphyteutical rents collectable were noted down with indications of the debtor's identity. Finally, the document records debts payable, including emphyteutical rents, and the names of creditors. Estimates of annual incomes and debts were ascribed to all the above categories in ducats and a tax "drawn" from these figures in *oncie*, or "ounces," a currency of accounting. In short, each entry portrays the economy of a hearth using figures reflecting estimated yearly averages of some kinds of income and expenses. Unfortunately, no estimates of wages or professional earnings survive.

The document has liabilities. Since the land areas it records were estimates declared by the proprietor, the possibilities for false declaration or unconscious inaccuracy were myriad. A local committee reviewed declarations, but patronage and kinship relationships between heads of household and the committee members surely presented opportunities for distortion. Analysts of this data must rely on the law of large numbers, and adhere to comparisons which stress relative proportions of property instead of absolute quantities. This makes comparison with other towns, or with later data sources for Locorotondo, difficult, at least in absolute terms. Despite potential distortions, the document provides a wealth of material from which to reconstruct mid-eighteenth-century demography, social structure, and economy in Locorotondo.

It is also synchronic data. The *catasto onciario* can reveal little about social change, and its analysis must be contextualized using other sources, both published and documentary. Notarial acts contain descriptive material which helps flesh out the cadaster's skeletal nature, and the lucky survival, noted above, of the mid-eighteenth-century map in an early nineteenth-century copy has helped form a spatial sense of this small Apulian town and its territory. Similarly a late eighteenth-century survey of the properties of the Duke of Martina Franca (also the Baron of Locorotondo), which includes several maps done in bright water colors, has remedied the lack of information in the cadaster about the feudal lord's properties in the territory of Locorotondo which were exempt from taxation (ACMF, 1797).

The age and sex pyramid at Figure 4.1 presents an approximate image of the population structure of Locorotondo in 1749 as recorded in the *catasto onciario*.[6] The median age for both men and women was 26 years, making this a young population. The marked triangular form of the graph (allowing for inaccurately recorded child cohorts) is typical, as one would expect, of a pre-industrial population experiencing high fertility and high mortality. Population density in Locorotondo was around 44.2 people per square kilometer, considering the modern figure of 47.5 square kilometers as a measure of surface area. The official boundaries were different in the eighteenth century, but judging from the cadaster itself and from notarial transactions, residents of Locorotondo worked, and, in some cases lived, in a territory which was approximately equal to the current one.

Before the 1811 Napoleonic census (see Chapter 5) there are only scraps of evidence from which to infer the nature of the settlement pattern. According to the instructions decreed for its compilation, the *catasto onciario* should have listed the domiciles of the heads of household being assessed, but neither in the individual declarations of property preserved in Naples, nor in the two copies of the document, are locations for the hearths to be found. Evidently the town was small and socially compact enough that the officials who drew up the

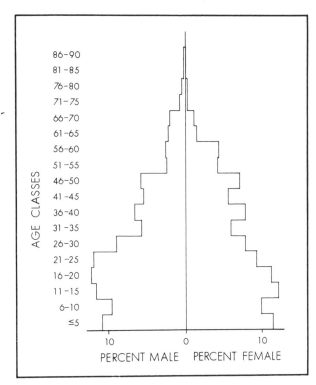

Fig. 4.1. Population pyramid for Locorotondo, 1749. (Source: ASB-CO, 1749)

cadaster knew the whereabouts of each household. This in itself suggests that most people did live within, or at least near the walls, instead of being dispersed around the territory, and other evidence suggests this as well. However, there is evidence which points to some residence in the countryside. Unfortunately it is not evidence which allows quantitative statements. Some of those who resided in the countryside were undoubtedly *massari da campo*, or estate overseers employed by landowners. For the early and mid-eighteenth century, little evidence of land renting survives in the notarial transactions and therefore the figure of the sharecropper or tenant farmer residing on the *masseria* is difficult to discern (but see below).

However, the territory of Locorotondo as revealed in the cadaster presents an odd characteristic. Unlike other territories in the Southern Italian countryside, in which the town was closely ringed by a zone of intensive cultivation of tree crops, vineyards, and gardens, Locorotondo had concentrations of vineyards in areas toward the periphery of its zone. In particular, there were concentrations of vineyards in the northern part of the territory in the vicinity of roads which eventually lead off the plateau toward the coastal-plain city of Fasano. The area of San Marco, which was mentioned in the 1566 purchase of territory, was particularly rich in vines. Vineyards in Locorotondo, and elsewhere in Apulia at this time, often belonged to small proprietors instead of larger landowners. Throughout the end of the seventeenth and the totality of the eighteenth century, in the notarial transactions having to do with sale, mortgage, inheritance, and marriage settlement, there are references to the combination of vineyards, *trulli*, grape crushing floors (*palmenti*), and outdoor hearths (*fornelli*) for concentrating must into syrup to fortify the alcohol content of the wine. These were clearly in the hands of peasant small proprietors. Concentration of vineyards far from the walls would have provided an incentive to live nearby because of the distance which had to be traversed to arrive on the job, and it is likely at this time that at least San Marco, which had its own church, was a separate *jazzeile* populated by people who identified with Locorotondo.

A notarial act, drawn up in 1725, reveals something of the nature of San Marco and life in it (ASB–AN, 1683–1729: Sept. 21, 1725). The act consists of a division of a man's property between two unmarried daughters. One of them inherits some land, including a *quartiero* of vineyard "with the new *trullo* where the bed is . . . and half the *trullo* with the hearth, half the fruits of the fig trees which are above the *trulli*, half of the olive tree in front of the *trulli*, a fourth of the well which is in the common *chiazzile* and in front of the *trulli*."[7] The word used for *trullo*, *casella*, in this instance signifies a single space covered by a *trullo* roof, a cluster of which, indicated by the plural *caselle* forms a dwelling. She also inherits half use of a *bascio* (ground floor, one room, dwelling) in town. Her sister inherits another portion of land including vineyards, "as well as the big *trullo* where the loom is, and the same loom, and half the *trullo* of the hearth," and a share in the use of the well, the *chiazzile*, the above mentioned trees, and the *bascio* in town. Clearly the will divides a domestic situation; there is a bedroom, a hearth, and a loom. Furthermore, the share in the cistern is a one-fourth share which suggests that other relatives not mentioned also live around the *jazzeile*.

In this act there is an indication of a dwelling in town as well as in

San Marco. The notary labels the dwelling as a *bascio*, in modern Italian, a *basso*, or a humble one room, ground-level dwelling. Such a dwelling would have been more restricted and uncomfortable than the *trullo* being divided in the will and was probably merely a place to rest, change clothes, and otherwise sojourn while in town on Sundays when people went to Mass. Another 1725 notarial transaction, a marriage settlement in which the bride receives a *bascio lamiato* (pitched-roofed one-story house) in town, in which it says that the bride and her husband to be, "may use said house for necessities of sickness, or for needs when they come to hear the Mass on feast days, and *not otherwise*," attests to this practice (ASB–AN, 1683–1729: August 12, 1725, author's italics). The injunction "and not otherwise" points to a value placed on residing only in the countryside which the father in question is trying to enforce in the agreement being drawn up over the marriage of his daughter. It has long been a practice among wealthier Locorotondese peasants to maintain a room in town for just these purposes, and for taking care of business which requires a night's stay.

Other *jazzèlere* existed at least in incipient form. For example, in an act of public testimony regarding the Masseria Serrapizzuto in the zone to the south of the town center, one reads that three men "expert at cultivating the land . . . were called (to testify) from the countryside where they live" (ASB–AN, 1734–1784: November 10, 1768). One of these men is Oronzo son of Francesco Nardelli who lived near the *masseria*. From a marginal note in the *catasto onciario* at Nardelli's entry one sees that he, in fact, bought several fields in this area soon after the initial drafting of the document. Just south of the *masseria* in question there is a hamlet now known in dialect as "Ronsidde" and in Italian on the topographic map as "Ronziello," a contraction of "Ronse" (short for Oronzo) and "Nardidde," dialect for "Nardelli." The eighteenth-century map plainly indicates the *caselle di Oronzio Nardelli* with three schematic *trulli*.

Life in the *jazzèlere* of Locorotondo's countryside in the present, and in the memories of living people, contains situations which lead to conflict over the use of common space. Yet another transaction from the year 1725 hints at such conflict, in this case, arising from the control of pigs. In a will which divides the components of a *jazzeile*, the dying father, who has called the notary to his bedside, refers to a will made previously with a priest and reiterates, because he worries that quarrels will arise among his heirs, that "if said heirs wished to raise porcine animals, that each must keep them confined to his own portion." (ASB–AN, 1683–1729: January 6, 1725). This will under-lines the fact that people were living in the *jazzeile* on a permanent basis because they would not raise pigs in the countryside and then retire to the town at night leaving the animals at the mercy of thieves. It also implies that cohabitation of a common space between dwell-ings was an expectable source of conflict, in this case over cleanliness and invasion of the kitchen gardens.

However, from other notarial transactions it is also clear that the majority lived in town within the walls. Marriage settlement con-tracts list in detail what a bride brought to the marriage, and more rarely what the groom's parents contributed. It was possible to inspect all twenty marriage contracts recorded by Locorotondese notaries during the decade before 1749 (ASB–AN, 1729–1780; 1734–1784) and identify the households which had been formed by consulting the cadaster. In these contracts parents supplied the brides of peasant grooms with dwellings in town which were clearly more than places to sojourn from the countryside, and in cases where this was not possible they supplied portions of houses, or sometimes a year or two of rent, so that the new couple could get on its feet. In essence, inheritance of houses was matrilateral and Locorotondo's walls probably contained uxorilocally tending neighborhoods such as those described for the present day by Davis in his study of Pisticci in Basilicata (1973).[8] According to Delille (1988) this pattern was widespread in Apulia. Currently, and for as long as any rural informant could remember, it is the groom's family's responsibility to help provide housing. Informants marveled at the idea of women inheriting a house as long as there were male children in the family. Therefore, a likely correlate of the change to settlement of the countryside by the Locorotondese peasantry is a change in the pattern of inheritance of houses.[9]

Land and land use

As one would expect of a small rural town, wealth in Locorotondo was based almost entirely upon the possession of land, although several of the town gentlemen amassed large amounts of income by lending money against the property of their debtors. There were no craft industries beyond those necessary to supply local needs. Land in Locorotondo was unequally distributed, although 82.36 percent of all hearths had at least a small field or vineyard. For all land, and for

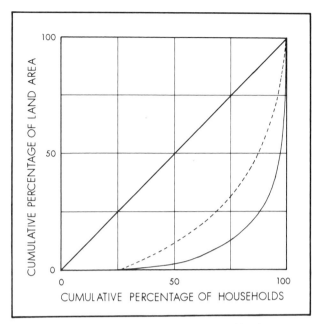

Fig. 4.2. Lorenz curve showing distribution of land in Locorotondo at mid-
    eighteenth century, landless households included. Vineyards only =
    dashed line; all land = solid line. (Source: ASB-CO, 1749)

all hearths, including landless ones, the Gini coefficient equals 0.81
(see the corresponding Lorenz Curve at Figure 4.2). This figure is
reasonably typical for the era.[10]

The *catasto onciario*, which is most silent about land use, only
clearly distinguishes vineyards. Occasionally the term *seminativo*
(sowable field) occurs, but not with enough frequency or consistency
to allow quantification. Designations of fields more often have to do
with whether they are open or closed. Terms such as *chiusura* and
serrata indicate land which is enclosed with walls and the words
demaniale (commons), and *mezzano* indicate land which is at least
partially open. However, the document simply calls much land *terra*,
with no indication of use, although we can assume most of this was
planted to cereals or légumes. Vineyards are the only category for
which use is certain (see Table 4.1).

Since viticulture in Locorotondo is key to the development of the
particular patterns of peasant culture found there later, it deserves
emphasis because the eighteenth-century data provide a baseline for
what was to come during the nineteenth. Vineyards were measured in

Table 4.1. *Land categories designated in the* catasto onciario *with frequency and income statistics. Land amounts are in* stoppelli *(1 stoppello = 1,074 square meters); land values are in ducats.*

Land class designated in cadastral entries	Total amount of land in class	Percent of total amount	Total income from class	Percent of total income	Income from one stoppello	N owners of land category	Percent of all 635 hearths
Vines	2299.45	5.18	738.50	17.61	0.32	470	74.02
Demaniale	8067.64	18.16	441.80	10.54	0.05	165	25.98
Mezzano	4185.03	9.42	460.60	10.98	0.11	156	24.57
Enclosed	3613.50	8.13	400.81	9.56	0.11	101	15.91
Other	26262.34	59.11	2151.29	51.31	0.08	467	73.54
All land	44427.96	100.00	4193.00	100.00	0.09	523	82.36

a special unit, the *quartiero*, which was equivalent to a *stoppello*, the unit of measure used for other kinds of land.[11] Vineyards constituted 5.2 percent of all land registered in 1749 in the cadaster. This proportion would expand to 16.6 percent of land by the next full cadaster in 1816. This expansion accompanies both demographic expansion and diffusion of population into the countryside.

The mean income from a *quartiero* was almost a third of a ducat, or 32 *grana*. Declarations of value for vineyards were automatically fixed at 3 *carlini* (1 ducat equaled 100 *grana* or 10 *carlini*) per *quartiero* with little regard for variation between locations. However, even if a third of a ducat per *quartiero* was an approximate figure for vineyard income, it was more than three times the level of income which could be produced from any other kind of field noted in the cadaster. Therefore, even though vineyards accounted for only 5.2 percent of fields they produced fully 17.6 percent of income from land. This high yield must have provided incentives to plant vineyards.

Vineyards were the backbone of small property in Locorotondo. Almost three-quarters of the households recorded in the 1749 cadaster cultivated them. These were more uniformly distributed than any other kind of land, with a Gini coefficient of 0.56. This more uniform distribution of vineyards (and the high income from them) somewhat lessened the general inequality of distribution of wealth. The 244 agricultural worker (*bracciale*) households in the cadaster cultivated an average of 1.9 *quartieri* each. The 158 *massaro* (integrated farmer) households each tended vineyards averaging about 4.5

quartieri. There was a good reason for peasant proprietorship of vineyards. For the peasant planting and cultivating vineyards required less capital outlay than cereal cultivation which ideally required animal traction, which in turn implied the necessity for pastures or land for growing fodder crops. Viticulture could be carried out solely with investments of family labor and simple hand tools such as hoes and pruning hooks. Of course these investments of human capital were massive, especially in the initial creation of vineyards.

Cultivation of grapes for wine making was a market oriented activity for the *massari* in the population and probably for many agricultural worker headed households. According to Calella, who wrote of Locorotondese viticulture before mass use of chemical fertilizers and rototillers, and before many vineyards had been planted in richer and deeper soil in the dolines and other depressions of the local landscape, a hectare of vineyards produced an average of about 60 quintals of grapes and therefore a *quartiero* produced an average of 6.4 quintals (1941: 90). From the 1982 sample survey a family used about 7.2 quintals of grapes to produce the wines, both simple and fortified, consumed with meals during the year. With its nearly two *quartieri* the average *bracciale* household of the eighteenth century is likely to have outproduced its consumption needs, especially as, according to the recollection of informants, current consumption of wine by rural households is less frugal than in the past. Some remember a time when only the males of the house drank wine. Eighteenth-century *massaro* production far outstripped table needs.

Vineyards were distributed in most areas of the town territory except in the eastern side where the Duke of Martina had large estates, and in the northern side where there were smaller estates belonging to the Duke and to the Bailey of Santo Stefano in Fasano. Again, there was no notable concentration of vineyards just around the walls of the town as there was in other locations, and as is typically the case even now in many Southern Italian town territories (cf. Blok, 1974: Plate I). High concentrations of vineyards cluster roughly along an axis running from the northwest zone of the territory, through the town, and finishing to the southeast near borders with Martina Franca and the Difesa of Ficazzano belonging to the city of Ostuni (See Figure 4.3). These concentrations border roads which lead off the plateau toward the northwest to the coastal

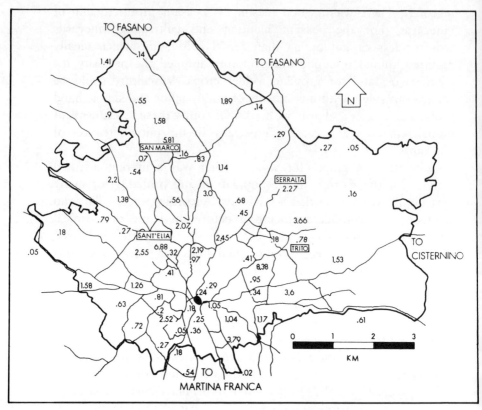

Fig. 4.3. Vineyard concentrations and road network, mid-eighteenth century,
superimposed on the modern commune border. Figures show
proportion of total land surface in 1749 planted in vineyards at specific
locations. (Source: ASB-CO, 1749; ALM, 1810)

plain and the town of Fasano (double the size of Locorotondo in the
eighteenth century) and the city of Monopoli (almost three times the
size of Locorotondo), or which lead toward Martina Franca with a
population of about 9,200 at mid-eighteenth century (Boso, 1969:
17–18; Assante, 1964: Appendix III).

There is little evidence from this period of wine exportation
through Monopoli, the nearest port which would have served Locorotondo, and markets for wine were probably strictly local. The
coastal towns would have provided such markets because their
burgeoning monocrop economies specialized in olives and oil. The

hotter spring and summer months on the coastal plain would have created a demand for the stronger fortified wine produced in Locorotondo, and the presence of outdoor hearths for reducing must to syrup as part of the vineyard, *casella*, crushing floor combination testifies to this.[12]

Although the territory of Martina Franca shared some of the Valle d'Itria with Locorotondo, Boso, in his analysis of its economy from the *catasto onciario* completed there in 1755, concludes that the city specialized in livestock raising and leather working, the former absorbing 30 percent of the employed work force (1969: 33–37). If this is so – and Boso's analysis of the cadaster is not a complete one – Martina would have also provided a market for wine. There were 436 artisans, many of them leather workers of one kind or another, who, not being food producers would have consumed local wine. Martina would not truly specialize in wine production until the end of the next century. Locorotondo, therefore, found itself perched between several potential markets for wine which would expand as population increased throughout the rest of the century. Proximity to markets explains both the location of vineyards and of population between the walled town center and the edge of the plateau to the north and northeast, and between Locorotondo and Martina.

Vineyards were probably walled with stone to keep animals out and to prevent soil erosion on terraced hillsides. Untransformed fields in the area contain much rock, and the process of creating vineyards produced a surplus of stone which had to be disposed of in piles called *specchie* or used either in constructing walls or *trulli*. The 1756 map shows some walled vineyards. The right to enclose vineyards and gardens had, it must be recalled, been won in 1566 with the establishment of the territory.

Little description of vine planting techniques survives, but one emphyteusis contract from 1756 specifies that vines were to be planted "according to the measure of Martina," five *palme* apart (ASB–AN, 1729–1780: 25 August, 1756). Wall builders and traditional masons now remember the *palma* as equal to 25 centimeters. Therefore vines were planted about one-and-a-quarter meters from one another. Another lease from the end of the century contains some specific stipulations about cultivation (ACMF, 1796). Each year eight days (the season is not specified) had to be spent "burying" offshoots to provide root stock. The vineyard was to be "cleaned" of weeds, and pruned so that useless branches were removed. The contract states that legumes such as favas and peas, with the exception of chick peas, could be planted between the vines (presumably on ridges), but not other crops. The contract is vehement about these last points, which leads to the conclusion that planting crops between vines had to be carefully limited by the landlord because there must have been temptation for peasants to plant cereal crops there as well. The stipulation is a harsh one which gives the landlord, who is the baron in this case, the right to uproot, at the tenant's expense, any illegal planting. There existed recognition that cereal crops and chick peas competed with vines while other legumes did not. Clearly, vineyards provided staple food as well as a cash crop.

Because of the specific right to enclose vineyards granted in 1566, the sixteenth century can be seen as the era in which peasant–proprietor viticulture had an origin. A typical contractual mechanism which provided incentive for the investment of human capital in tree-crop agriculture in Southern Italy was the emphyteusis contract, which was a form of perpetual lease under which peasants took land from a landowner with the stipulation that within a specified number of years it be improved. For vineyards this was emphyteusis *ad meliorandum et pastanandum* (to improve and plant vineyards). Some of these contracts were written with a clause allowing for their redemption with a cash payment which gave full title to the tenant. However, there is little evidence of this form of contract in Locorotondo at mid-eighteenth century. Only 0.44 percent of the vineyards of Locorotondo registered in the cadaster were held by proprietors through emphyteusis (in almost every case the Duke of Martina was the landlord), and among the notarial transactions, emphyteusis contracts having to do with vineyards are rare until the end of the century and the beginning decades of the next. Rosa notes that concession of land under emphyteusis was common in the Kingdom of Naples during the first two decades of the eighteenth century, and that in neighboring Martina leases were drawn up by religious institutions with priests, but also with secular small proprietors, which let 340 *tomoli* (292.13 hectares) in emphyteusis. Tenants had redeemed many of these contracts by 1720 thereby taking possession of the land free and clear (Rosa, 1974: 82). Early eighteenth-century notarial transactions for Locorotondo are severely damaged, and many of the books cannot even be opened; the 1725 volume is the first which may be examined easily. Therefore it is difficult to know whether a similar trend toward concession of land under emphyteusis took place within the town's boundaries.[13]

Twenty-one percent of Locorotondo's vineyards were laden with tithes of the tenth or the fifteenth part of production payable to one of three ecclesiastical organizations – the Bishop's Refectory of Monopoli, the Abbey of Sant'Angelo in Grecis (affiliated with the Bailey of Santo Stefano in Fasano), and the local chapter of the church. These tithes may represent old perpetual emphyteutical concessions of land by church organizations, although the epoch of such concessions remains obscure. Villari (1977: 73) notes such a phenomenon for the commune of Brienza near Salerno. Poli (1981: 330) writes of perpetual emphyteusis concessions by ecclesiastical organizations in the vicinity of Molfetta, at the northern end of the Terra di Bari, during the end of the sixteenth century and the beginning of the seventeenth. He argues that they represented attempts by church landlords to reclaim soil fertility on exhausted lands, and to improve marginal areas so that they rendered some income.

Land bearing the designations *demaniale* (commons), and *mezzano*, or *menzano*, (literally "middle" land) appear to have been mostly in pasture. Twenty-seven-and-a-half percent of taxable land falls into these categories. These forms of common land had fallen totally into private hands by mid-eighteenth century. They were bought and sold, and passed to heirs in the notarial transactions, without restriction. A universal commons no longer existed at this point, and there were no commons associated with the local estates of the feudal lord. This privatization of commons was, according to Cormio, typical of all the Murgia dei Trulli (1974: 31).

Mezzano, according to a common definition in Apulia, was pasture land held on a *masseria* for animals of traction, especially plow oxen, to graze in during periods of work. The term *mezzano*, meaning "middle," probably derived from the notion that for convenience this sort of land was located in the midst of other fields being plowed. During the eighteenth century this kind of common land was no longer explicitly associated with estates, nor was it well associated with the possession of plow oxen. The *bracciale* households of Locorotondo possessed an average of 1.5 *stoppelli* of *mezzano* land each, but almost none of them owned plow oxen. In some cases it was sown, but whether with fodder crops or with cereals or legumes for human consumption is unclear. Sometimes in notarial transactions the designation *mezzano seminatorio* appears. Angelo Massafra, historian at the University of Bari, who kindly examined the cadaster in response to a query, suggests that this category of land represented pasture which was reserved for the use of the proprietor during the winter months (from Saint Michael's in September to the middle of May), but which then became subject to public use during the summer months (personal communication). This would have allowed winter pasturing or sowing of a fodder crop to be harvested in May, but of course would have precluded a cereal crop or fava beans, which are both harvested later. The other category of common land, *terra demaniale*, had the least value of any kind of land according to the assessments in the cadaster, and probably was lesser quality pasture land mostly.

The cadaster indicates possession of cattle, plow oxen, horses, donkeys, and sheep and goats, but never courtyard animals such as pigs, chickens, or rabbits. That country people kept pigs and chickens is clear from clues in the notarial transactions. *Massari* and priests were the livestock raisers of Locorotondo. In particular the town's 49 priests specialized in raising sheep and goats in partnership relationships with *massari*. They also rented flocks to shepherds in return for an annual payment. These strategies of course relieved priests, who did no manual labor, of the burden of husbanding the animals themselves. Peasant workers in the cadaster were notably without larger animals – among 244 households there were but ten cows, two horses, and fourteen donkeys. Plow oxen were totally absent among them, and this goes far toward explaining the peasant worker specialization in viticulture. This lack of animals, even of a few sheep or goats, suggests that the supply of truly open common land was inadequate for the poorest peasant households.

Some fields are clearly defined as enclosed with the words *chiusura* and *serrata* which derive from Italian and Latin verbs meaning "to close," and "to bar," respectively. I have found no direct indications in the documents which allow *serrata* land to be distinguished clearly from *chiusura* land and the two terms may have been used interchangeably. However, a clue may exist in the two kinds of walls commonly found in the zone. The first is low but thick, and serves to keep grazing animals out of fields. It is easily vaulted by a man, a dog, or indeed, a wolf or a fox. There is usually no real gate; the opening is closed by some sturdy branches propped across it. The second kind of enclosure found in the area associates with larger estates and consists of smaller fields, often containing fruit trees or grapevines, surrounded with high walls obviously designed to keep people or marauding animals out. A true gate which could be barred, i.e. *serrata*, is possible in these enclosures.

The average income deriving from these enclosed field types was eleven *grana* to the *stoppello*, making them more productive of income than average. Occasionally, both in the cadaster and in notarial transactions, enclosed fields are indicated as used for cereal cultivation, but it is also quite likely that they were often planted with tree crops. The vast olive groves of the coastal plain have never penetrated to any great extent to the plateau, and there is evidence that olive cultivation was not attempted with much success before the 1830s; the altitude of the plateau too readily exposes olive trees to dangerous frosts (ACL–ABF, 1856a). Tree crops included almonds, walnuts, figs, cherries, pears, and apples. The notarial acts refer only to small numbers of trees, giving the impression that in no location in the territory of Locorotondo were there orchards of much consequence.

There was an association between the possession of enclosed, non-vineyard, fields and the possession of greater amounts of capital and power in the social structure.[14] Enclosing a field must have represented a considerable investment, and afterwards a constant expense, because the dry stone walls of Locorotondo require maintenance, especially if they are terrace walls with the pressure of soil behind them. High concentrations of enclosed fields among those who did not do manual labor must have kept the town's two *paretari*, wall builders, regularly employed. The *massari* and *bracciali* probably built and maintained their own walls, as they do now.

The greatest part of the agricultural surface area was undifferentiated and probably not walled, since the cadaster and notarial transactions go to great lengths to designate enclosed land. In the calculations reported herein designations which appear infrequently and inconsistently, such as *seminativo* (sown field), *chiascia*, (high field), and *palude* (low field situated in a fertile enclosed valley or doline) were lumped with the simple designation *terra* (land). This residual category comprised 59.11 percent of land registered and rendered an average taxable income of 9 *grana* per *stoppello*. Probably fields designated simply as *terre* were cereal and legume fields, but there were also small gardens, woods, and *macchie* (brush) in this category.

The cadaster also lists entire *masserie* (estates) as units of property ascribed to hearths. The significance of the term *masseria* varies from small enterprises comprising as few as twenty *tomoli* to large estates with hundreds of *tomoli*. The land designated as *masseria* totals a minimum of 1,444.9 *tomoli* (surface area was not always recorded). Eighty-eight percent of this fell in the hands of the wealthy – priests, professionals, landowners living from estate income, and church organizations. *Massari* and an occasional shepherd owned the remaining portion. Clearly the word *masseria* had a meaning similar to the one current for the twentieth century, and designated the large and medium estates belonging to elite families, and only rarely the enterprises owned by *massari*.

In sum, elements of Locorotondo's present-day landscape were present during the eighteenth century in incipient form. The view from the town walls revealed *trullo* homesteads and *jazzèlere*, but the latter were smaller and much more infrequent than now. The impression of a crowded countryside was not yet apparent. *Jazzèlere* were no more frequent than the 23 *masseria* headquarters which can be located in the mid-eighteenth century map. Pastures and cereal fields surrounded *masseria* headquarters. Fewer vineyards would have met the eye than now do, and all were cultivated according to the traditional system. They were planted on hillsides and on higher land; the fertile bottom soil of dolines and other depressions in the karst landscape was reserved for cereal production. Vineyards and other walled enclosures were isolated in a landscape which was mostly unwalled and contained much more pasture land with grazing flocks of sheep and goats, and small groups of horses, donkeys, and oxen, than would have been spotted even in the early twentieth century. The tightly wall-constrained quality of the landscape now visible on the Murgia dei Trulli, and remarked upon by Tommaso Fiore, was absent. The "population of ants" had yet to do all of its work.

The traveler encountered rare patches of intensely cultivated vineyards, often at a distance from the town center, and associated with the patches were small clusters of *trulli*, some of them inhabited permanently by peasants. A thick network of roads, most of which were little more than pack-animal trails, serviced the rural hinterlands and connected Locorotondo with other towns. Since a minority of peasants dwelt in the countryside, at dawn and dusk there was much coming and going along the roads and trails which radiated from the towered walls of town – a town with social structure already in transition from the constraints of the old order.

Chapter 5

SOCIETY AND TERMINAL FEUDALISM

With the succinct decree – "Feudalism, with all its attributes, stands abolished" – the feudal order legally ended in South Italy in 1806, but of course it had taken the occupation of the Kingdom of Naples by Napoleonic forces to bring about this change (Villani, 1968: 100). However, feudalism was hardly a monolith at the time of its legal abolition. In differing areas of the kingdom the degree of feudal control varied, as did the degree to which power and wealth had already come into the hands of middle-class men. Also, as Aymard points out, the feudalism of the Kingdom of Naples, and of Italy in general, was qualitatively different from the more commonly known "standard" model of feudalism and the manorial system developed by historians from the English and French cases (1982).

The great feudal issues of the eighteenth century concerned the inalienability of baronial land and the feudal commons. The primary benefits of feudalism to the southern nobility were legal jurisdiction over their territories and the power which accompanied it, and exemption from property and other taxes (Villani, 1968: 56). Abortive political attempts at reforming feudalism before the Revolution of 1799 and the French decade (1805–1815) must be understood in the context of changing class relations in the Kingdom of Naples during the second half of the eighteenth century, especially the strengthening of individuals interested in enriching themselves through various entrepreneurial activities involving the acquisition of land. The latter were, writes Villani (1968: 62), "tenants, usurers, livestock raisers, administrators of feudal holdings, governors of feudal territorial jurisdictions, mayors and officials of the towns and cities, and medium and small merchants," and they were not conscious of constituting a new elite class.

The first clear views of Locorotondese social stratification afforded by the *catasto onciario*, and other eighteenth-century sources, show a microcosm of what Villani describes for the kingdom. In fact, the processes of which he writes were more pronounced in the Terra di Bari, particularly in the coastal cities where the development of Adriatic Sea trade fueled the engines of social change. By mid-eighteenth century local feudal power was much in crisis, and in Locorotondo and Martina Franca, the seat of the Caracciolo dukes, there existed an elite class which in part challenged the feudal system, and in part lived symbiotically with it. Villani's characterization of it as lacking consciousness of class probably fits, although, of course, inferences about such matters are difficult from the surviving documents.

FEUDAL LORDS AND REGIONAL MAGNATES

In 1749, year of the cadaster, Locorotondo was subject to feudal relationships with several kinds of lords – its baron and several church organizations. It lay within the baronial legal jurisdiction of Francesco II Caracciolo, also the powerful Duke of neighboring Martina Franca (Cofano, 1977: 125). It is unclear whether, at that time, the Locorotondesi really paid tributes to the baron, although he did claim a twentieth part (*vigesima*) of grain, barley, favas, and wine production; a tax on mills, bread ovens, meat, and notarial acts; and the tenth part of small animal production (ASN-CO, 1749: Atti Preliminari, Vol. 8697, foglio 16). Whether the Locorotondesi paid these tributes is unclear because the local bourgeoisie hotly contested the lord's rights to privileges and tributes in legal battles throughout the second half of the eighteenth century (Baccaro, 1968: 90; also ASB-AD, 1810).[1]

The "Illustrious Baron," as documents refer to him, exerted several kinds of power over the Locorotondesi. First, he owned a considerable amount of land within the municipality, some of which he had let in emphyteusis by 1749, but most of which consisted of wooded estates rented to *massari* who paid an annual rent under a six-year contract. These lands, which contained no commons and were enclosed (they are called "parks"), amounted to almost 420 *tomoli* (361 hectares, assuming the accuracy of late eighteenth-century surveying), or about 8 percent of the 1749 total. These land holdings must have been sources of power with respect to granting leases to *massaro* tenants.[2] Other rural property consisted of many smaller fields conceded under emphyteusis contracts, some of them long enough before 1749 to have been converted into vineyards, and another part of them "just now given to many citizens in emphyteutical concession to be planted to vineyards" (ASN-CO, 1749: *ibid.*). Francesco II also owned three underground snow-storage facilities in the countryside. The upper classes of Martina and Locorotondo probably enjoyed fruit flavoured *sorbetti* even during the eighteenth century.

The baron also held urban properties which included a bread oven, a tavern, a butcher shop, several artisans' shops, the crumbling castle with its ground-level shops or dwellings, and several multi-storied dwellings. His property declaration for the *catasto onciario* (although he was exempt, he made a cursory declaration which fails to record property sizes or values) also lists people and institutions, the local church chapter and the Chapel of the Blessed Sacrament, owing him debts. A record in the ducal archives shows that without the lost tithes on produce, or on courtyard animals, the baron's income from properties in Locorotondo in 1757 alone amounted to 1,431 ducats, 55 *carlini*, 6 *grana* (ACMF, 1757: Busta CM 53–52), a tidy sum considering that the declared taxable wealth of the richest houses in Locorotondo averaged 86.75 ducats a year. Therefore baronial power and riches had a base in landlord–tenant relationships both in urban and rural property.

Baronial power also had a strong basis in legal jurisdiction. A governor, who was supposed to be educated in law, or in a smaller town like Locorotondo, a *luogotenente* – lieutenant – presided over the local court (*corte locale*). The lord appointed this officer (Baccaro, 1968: 91). Local magistrates had the right to try civil and criminal cases when they did not concern privileged matters (such as highway robbery, or poisonings), or noblemen (Dibenedetto, 1976: 127–128; Galanti, 1969: 174–178). In the worst cases, the baronial courts could condemn convicts to the galleys, to have limbs severed, or to death, but such drastic measures were subject to review by a higher provincial level court (*Udienza Provinciale*). The magistrates of the latter court, however, could often be intimidated by a powerful nobleman such as the Duke of Martina Franca. Until 1737 the feudal lord imprisoned his enemies in a "black hole" under the castle in Locorotondo.

In 1728 the Duke appointed a key figure in Locorotondese society, Vitantonio Montanaro, as governor of Martina Franca. The latter must have had considerable influence to obtain the appointment, and then must have reaped power and income from holding it. Theoretically he earned 72 ducats annually for his trouble, but as Galanti notes, the governor's salary often went unpaid, and as the manuscript quoted below asserts, the appointment was often purchased from the local nobleman (1969: 176). Its purchase must, however, have brought dividends in the form of either income or political power and influence, which outweighed the initial investment. This eighteenth-century manuscript, quoted by Cofano (1977: 134), describes baronial justice under Francesco II as follows:

> Because of the abuses introduced in the ducal court, justice had been reduced to an illicit commerce; grave crimes which required an effort [to prosecute], and which didn't produce a profit, were not punished . . . and if some higher crime occurred for which it was necessary to gather information and prosecute, the case was soon dropped in the court in Lecce. If some civil suit was being brought, the most arrogant party always won; the suits of the poor were either ignored or judged in favor of the person with the ability to pay such that the jurisdiction was a real business, as it was a business for the Duke who habitually sold letters of appointment (to office) for 250 ducats.

The extent of legal jurisdiction of the Bailey di Santo Stefano, which was the feudal authority for neighboring Fasano, and which exacted tithes from Locorotondesi working fields in the northern reaches of the territory, is uncertain, but some individuals, particularly those living in the countryside in that side of the territory outside Locorotondo's official boundaries, may have fallen under it. Fasano was a fief of the Bailey and its leader appointed a governor of a local court, just as the Baron of Locorotondo did.

Other regional magnates controlled land in Locorotondo. At the time of the cadaster the grain bank (*monte frumentario*) derived from the will of Signora Pelligrini-Castelli, widow of an eminent Martinese gentleman and a lady associated with the Ducal court (see below). Until the latter part of the century when it passed under municipal control, the ducal house in Martina administered this resource, rare at that time in the Terra di Bari. Also several wealthy churchmen, one a citizen of Taranto and the other of Francavilla, owned large estates within the communal boundaries and figure often in notarial transactions.

SOCIAL STRATIFICATION WITHIN LOCOROTONDO[3]

Gentlemen and professionals

Although some *massaro* households equaled or even surpassed, the professional and gentlemanly households in wealth, the latter emerge as a clearly distinguishable local controlling class exhibiting strong differences from the landowning peasantry. The cadaster and the notarial acts refer to both sorts of household head with the title "magnificent" (*magnifico*), and the former source describes the seven gentlemen living from estate income or interest on mortgages as living "civilly," or "nobly" (*vive civilmente; vive nobilmente*). Several priests must also be included in this category. The documents designate no *massaro*, no matter how wealthy, in such a manner. (Occupational statuses and landed wealth are shown in Table 5.1.)

Two cases in particular stand out from among the leisured households. These are the Morelli brothers, both priests; and Vitantonio and his uncles Don Venanzio and Don Martino Montanaro (here the title "Don" designates membership of the clergy rather than the highest class). The street name, Via Morelli, and the ornament encrusted *palazzo* they left behind them, recall the eighteenth-century importance of the Morelli family which represented long established wealth and elite status. The 1566 document which defined the territory of Locorotondo shows that a Marino Morelli held the title of mayor (Baccaro, 1968: 114). The Morelli brothers, both of whom owned large extensions of land and many animals, rented (in 1762) for 2,350 ducats a year the rights to collect the tithes and to sublet properties within the territories of the Abbey of Sant'Angelo in Grecis (ASB-AN, 1734–1784, contract drawn up by Not. G. Ventrella of Naples inserted in 1767 volume), which extended through the plateau zones of Fasano, Monopoli, Ostuni, Cisternino, Martina Franca, Ceglie, and Locorotondo. Their ties to the powerful ecclesiastical organizations headquartered in neighboring Fasano, as well as their personal patrimonies, would have been significant sources of power, and it is notable that one of them, Don Angelo Morelli, was a leader in the legal struggle against the Duke's attempts to enforce his feudal privileges and tributes in the 1750s. Baccaro asserts that it was Don Angelo's death in 1785 which prompted the Duke to reopen the controversy over feudal privileges because he believed that no one in Locorotondo remained who would stand up against him (1968: 90). Morelli wealth seems to have been consolidated in a single line of relatives as there are no other Locorotondese household heads in the cadaster bearing that surname (a Rocco Morelli was mayor in 1788, however), and in 1816, the year of the reformed cadaster, the family was no longer present (Baccaro, 1968: 114; ASB-CP, 1816).

Table 5.1. *Occupations recorded for hearth (household) heads within the* catasto onciario *(1749) with indications of land ownership. Amounts of land are in* stoppelli *(1 stoppello = 1,074 square meters).*

Occupation of hearth (household) heads recorded in the *catasto onciario*	N heads of hearth	Percent of all hearth heads	Amount of land owned in hearth	Percent of all land owned	Mean amount land/ hearth	Standard deviation
Widows	49	7.99	1242.99	2.89	25.37	39.44
Bracciali	241	39.31	9549.38	22.23	39.49	451.45
Massari	158	25.77	12024.69	27.99	76.11	104.38
Shepherds	8	1.31	460.83	1.07	57.60	95.58
Gardeners	1	0.16	11.50	0.03	11.50	0
Gualani	1	0.16	36.00	0.08	36.00	0
Trullo builders	1	0.16	2.00	0.00	2.00	0
Rural wall builders	2	0.33	12.16	0.03	6.08	4.84
Stone breakers	5	0.82	93.00	0.22	18.60	14.91
Zavattini (?)	1	0.16	0	0	0	0
Servants	1	0.16	0	0	0	0
Pack animal drivers	22	3.59	254.99	0.59	11.59	19.74
Cut stone masons	11	1.79	102.00	0.24	9.27	7.57
Tanners	1	0.16	0	0	0	0
Shoemakers	19	3.10	180.50	0.42	9.50	11.67
Butchers	1	0.16	3.00	0.01	3.00	0
Carpenters	5	0.82	69.00	0.16	13.80	22.98
Smiths	6	0.98	25.00	0.06	4.17	5.42
Tailors	5	0.82	0	0	0	0
Pharmacists	1	0.16	0	0	0	0
Grocers (cheese/oil)	3	0.49	69.50	0.16	23.17	25.04
Lay nuns	6	0.98	61.83	0.14	10.31	12.07
Medical doctors	4	0.65	608.50	1.42	152.13	158.27
Notaries	2	0.33	335.50	0.78	167.75	158.75
Lawyers	1	0.16	0	0	0	0
Priests	49	7.99	12074.00	28.10	246.41	371.80
Students	1	0.16	0	0	0	0
Living from estates	7	1.14	2501.00	5.82	357.36	505.99
Duke	1	0.16	3249.10	7.56	3249.00	0
Totals	613	100.00	42966.47			

Vitantonio Montanaro headed another kind of elite household (ASB-CO, 1749: foglio 463). This consisted of Vitantonio, his second wife, and his two priestly uncles, both of whom were well off. Baccaro (1968: 9–11) briefly chronicles Montanaro's life. He was born in 1694, and died at the age of 85, leaving his third wife widowed, but never produced a direct heir to his fortune. After finishing preliminary studies, Montanaro completed a degree in law at the University of Naples. Probably the fortunes of the Montanaro had recently blossomed as there were several potentially related Montanaro households recorded in the *onciario* (the key to this is in first-naming patterns) which were headed by *massari*, and not particularly rich (ASB-CO, 1749, foglio 80 and 255). Vitantonio's elder sister Anna was married to a *massaro* (ASB-CO, 1749, foglio 367) and his future third wife Maria Maddalena Pinto, just four years old in the year of the cadaster, was the daughter of a rich *massaro* (ASB-CO, 1749, foglio 220). In the cadaster Vitantonio has a unique double designation, "doctor of law," and "living nobly," and the compilers therefore ascribed to him both the highest leisured rank and that of a professional. His taxable annual income in 1749 all came from interest on mortgages (although it is possible that he owned property which was taxed in another town, or that part of his patrimony had been ascribed to one of his priestly uncles who, because of their clerical status, were largely exempted from taxation). At some point after the original cadastral entry, and before 1765, according to a note in the margin of the record, he purchased an estate which rendered the considerable sum of 360 ducats a year. He later inherited his uncles' properties. Baccaro also notes his position as a prodigious money lender, and writes from documentary evidence that Montanaro's debtors not only came from Locorotondo, but were scattered about the region (1968: 11). Montanaro's legacies to the town, since he had no direct heirs, consisted of the money to build a larger Church of Saint George (the currently existing building), and of a charitable fund (the *Monte Montanaro*), which bore his name. The town used this fund in the late nineteenth century to finance the construction of the Montanaro Hospital.

His connections to external power as governor of Martina Franca would have lent him considerable local leverage as a patron. He can be described as a man with a rising career and this probably accounts for his unique double ascription as both a professional and a man who "lives nobly." *Massaro* relatives suggest recent entrance into urban elite middle-class status.

Many priests in Locorotondo were wealthy by town standards, although it is also clear that not all priests were men of substance. Priests held a little more than 28 percent of the land registered in the cadaster and averaged 246.41 *stoppelli* per head, as a social category a holding second only to the average holding of those who lived only from their estates (357.36 *stoppelli* per household). There were tax advantages to priestly property ownership, and according to Cofano (1977: 203) the tonsure could be purchased abusively from several unscrupulous archbishops in nearby cities. A portion of priestly wealth consisted of a kind of dowry given the priest by relatives as a source of income as he undertook his orders. This was to be enjoyed as long as he lived, and then reverted to the family line (ASB-AN, 1729–1780: April 20, 1745). Profits garnered from this land could, of course, be reinvested, and before the decree for the formation of the *catasto onciario* priestly property was tax exempt. After, even though priests became liable for some taxes, taxation could be escaped. Therefore a part of the capital of a wealthy family could be sheltered from taxation for many years and then be returned to the line. Some priests came from the ranks of the elite families which practiced primogeniture, and their entry into the priesthood allowed the family to avoid providing a permanent inheritance for them, and their vows of celebacy helped avoid squabbles over inheritances which might have arisen had they formed families.

Such clerics without vocations easily gave themselves over to worldly activities, and often kept mistresses. The sensual interests of at least one churchman were portrayed in a public act, notarized in 1702, in which a Locorotondese worker declared that he would not return to a church-owned estate in the territory of Martina Franca where he was sharecropping some fava beans. During the night, while he, his wife, and her sister were sojourning there to work their plot, he had heard his sister-in-law being "played with" by a certain ecclesiastic. She had reclined in the evening with her skirt on, but in the morning wore only her top. The man's wife gave her sister a good beating at dawn, and presumably wounded honor and legal obligations prompted him to declare his decision not to return (ASB-AN, 1683–1729: foglio 71).

Just below the leisured elite who had no professions were the educated professionals. Education beyond basic literacy skills was not locally available and meant attending boarding schools in cities such as Bari, and then attendance at the University of Naples, which, along with the ancient medical school at Salerno, constituted the only degree-granting institution in the Kingdom of Naples during this epoch (Galanti, 1969: 258–266). Considering the expenses of supporting a son in the capital, professional education represented a considerable financial sacrifice even for wealthy parents. These heads of household were not always particularly wealthy in land and sometimes stood below the richest *massari*, although no information about their professional incomes survives. Such income must have compensated in part for what persons of this rank may have lacked in land and animals, but of course meant that they worked for a living – a prestige-reducing characteristic in a society which idealized the leisured style of the nobility and declared so in official documents by labeling those who lived only from estate income as "living nobly."

Both the landed elite and the professional families of Locorotondo had a wider and differing set of contacts outside the town than the peasant or artisan groupings below them in the hierarchy. Undoubtedly expectations that marriages be contracted with individuals of the same, or higher, social level forced families which were well-ensconced among those who "lived nobly," or from the professions, to look outside Locorotondo for marriage partners because of the limited possibilities existing in town. Marriages between elite families of differing towns also created politically and economically useful networks and alliances. In cadastral entries or notarial acts there are often indications that one of the parties to an elite match came from another Apulian town, among which Martina Franca, Grottaglie, Castellana and Francavilla. In addition the out-of-town partner often brought lands in his or her home territory.

Ethnographic and oral historical work in Locorotondo confirms the persistence of the pattern into the twentieth century, and members of the recently declined landed elite clearly indicated that their social circles extended far beyond local boundaries, and that, especially as youths, they attended social functions among their peers in neighboring towns and made contacts during their years away at school. This was true of the eighteenth century as well, particularly with respect to the social circles of neighboring Martina Franca – a short gallop away on horseback.

Entry into such social circles constituted an important indicator of elite status. Other kinds of locals, particularly wealthy *massari*, surely had contacts outside the town, but these would have been commercial, mostly in the context of livestock fairs held in Locorotondo and surrounding towns on important saints' days. *Massaro* families which invested resources in the education of children for the priesthood or a profession simultaneously invested in social legitimacy, which would eventually permit participation in elite networks, and provide mobility for their heirs and useful ties for themselves. Judging from the marriage of Vitantonio Montanaro's sister to a *massaro*, and especially his own third marriage to the daughter of a *massaro*, marriage into higher ranks may also have provided a means for connection to broader social networks. Montanaro's young widow remarried into a prominent landed family in Martina Franca after his death, and his sister's children inherited wealth from him, enriching their *massaro* father's line (Baccaro, 1968, 10).

"Massari" and "bracciali"

The gulf between the town elite and the peasant elite could be bridged, but most *massaro* families were not adopting such strategies. In fact, there are several distinctions to be made among the households of this peasantry. There were some particularly wealthy *massaro* households. One of them (ASB-CO, 1749: foglio 115) was a joint family composed of three brothers with their wives and children, and an unmarried sister, living together and farming a large extension of land in common. This is the sole record of a multiple household strategy among brothers in the population. Another rich *massaro* household head (ASB-CO, 1749: foglio 220) was an entrepreneur of 33 years, who, among other properties, possessed two large estates, one indicated as recently purchased, the other owned jointly with an uncle. Notably, he would become the third father-in-law of the elderly Vitantonio Montanaro. The third extreme case among the *massari* was a rich peasant who declared that his 24-year-old son was an agricultural laborer, and that his younger two sons (13 and 15 years old) were students (*scolari*). Here we see indications of a social mobility strategy toward a profession or the priesthood for his children.

A second grouping of *massari* consisted of middle category peasants who derived their income from mixed agricultural enterprises composed of pastures, grain fields, and vineyards, with no indication of other strategies toward exceptional wealth or mobility. These represent most of the 158 *massaro* households in the general population. Larger *massari* derived their incomes from their own lands and were likely to have had to hire labor on occasion. Smaller *massari* probably utilized family labor exclusively, and may have had to supplement family lands with rented property (of which there is no precise indication in the documents), and the wages of children. It is common to find boys in *massaro* households at all levels defined as *bracciali*.

Other heads of household the cadaster defines as *massari* were completely or nearly landless. Their ages rule out retirement as an explanation and this means that they were *massari da campo*, or salaried overseers of large estates. Such employees would have been responsible for husbanding animals, and such expertise would have distinguished a salaried *massaro* from other agricultural laborers. Mature *bracciale* households almost never possessed animals, and salaried *massari* would have learned their jobs as *gualani*, or salaried shepherds who resided on the estates and worked under the supervision of the *massaro da campo*. Only one head of household in the total population was a *gualano*, which is expectable because they were usually unmarried youths who boarded on large estates.

Clearly, neither were all *massari* the same nor was the category equivalent to a rigidly definable social class. This was also true of the category *bracciale*. *Bracciale* (the southern dialectal form of the word *bracciante*, derived from the word *braccio* meaning "arm") ostensibly meant rural day-laborer. However, important to the compilers of the cadaster in assigning this classification was not lack of land so much as lack of animals. They applied the label *massaro* to heads of households possessing sheep, goats, cows, or oxen, who possessed amounts of land greater than, or equal to, but sometimes *less than*, day-laborer households that were better off.

However, the lines between *bracciali* and *massari* were not as clear as they appear in the cadaster, which is a synchronic document. In the general population the heads of *bracciale* households were on the average 37.2 years old (standard deviation 14.9). In contrast, the *massaro* heads of household in the population were on average 44.7 years old (standard deviation 14.1). The mean age of artisan heads in the general population was 36.1 (standard deviation 12.1), but the lack of any individual who had survived his sixty-first birthday accounts for the low mean age in this category. These figures suggest that many heads of household labeled *bracciali* were beginning the first phase of a career which would take them into the *massaro* category upon the acquisition of more land and animals. This is supported by the frequent classification of sons of *massari* as *bracciali*, and by the many *bracciale* households in the population which consisted either of young single male heads living with unmarried siblings and often their mothers, or of newly formed couples.

A young man began his career as an independent adult supplementing his income from a small property, often a vineyard, given to him upon marriage, or coming with his wife's marriage settlement, and by working for others. If fortunate, he would accumulate savings, acquire more land and eventually some animals, particularly oxen for traction, and would achieve a status which the compilers of the *catasto onciario* would have labeled *massaro*. Not all *bracciale* householders attained this mobility, however. If, in the general population, 27 percent of them were more than 45 years old, there was a strong likelihood of remaining in that status until death. It is likely that those whose fathers had attained the status of *massaro* form the nucleus of those who eventually changed status from day laborer to *massaro* peasant. Unfortunately, because these terms do not remain in use in later documents, particularly those of the Napoleonic era, it is impossible to verify this.

Workers and *massari* related to land through other kinds of tenure besides ownership and employment, but the cadaster contains only hints because fields which were let under leases other than emphyteusis were ascribed to the landlord for taxation and not usually recorded as rented. There is no way of judging the extensiveness of land renting, unless it was a matter of emphyteusis. Not until the end of the century do many rental contracts appear and these are mostly for entire estates. There were also various kinds of oral agreements which went unrecorded by the notaries. The early nineteenth-century cadaster housed in the town archives contains entries which record emphyteusis relationships noted as having been contracted orally many years previously (ACL-CP, 1823–1930). Several notarial documents (ASB-AN, 1683–1729: 1702, foglio 71; ASB-AN, 1734–1784: April 4, 1735) record indirect evidence of sharecropping small extensions of land on estates in Martina Franca to grow fava beans, a local food staple. This is a practice which continued into the recent past and was never formalized by a notary (see Chapter 2).

Many *bracciali* were poor. An illuminating portrayal survives in a declaration of property by the widow of a rural worker (ASB-AN, 1734–1784: August 18, 1736). She had three children who were minors and wished to inventory her deceased husband's property so that it would not be dispersed before her children reached adulthood and could inherit it. The possessions he left included a red skirt, a canvas bed sheet, a frayed green wool blanket, a red sash, a pine table, two used chairs, a small garden hoe, an old medium sized hoe, a *one-fourth share* in a wall builder's hammer, a pine chest, a wooden ladder, five clay jugs, four plates, and a large clay pot. In addition, there were a few small fields, a vineyard, a *trullo*, and a share in the threshing floor, grape crushing floor, cistern, and corral of a *jazzeile* in which the *trullo* was located. The widow declared that to feed her three children she mortgaged most of the land and the *trullo*. The death of her husband, perhaps sudden and premature as there was no will, placed her at the edge of survival. The hammer, one-fourth of the use of which was to be inherited by two male children, tells the tale of poverty in this case.

On the whole, artisans were poorer than *bracciali*. Most were landless, and few had workshops which were separate from their living spaces. They appear to have suffered conditions which led to shorter lives than other townsmen. Douglass, basing his conclusions upon early nineteenth-century church records, also notes a difference in life expectancy between artisans and other townsmen in Agnone, the Molisano town he studied (1984: 70). A local doctor, who began his practice before the Second World War, and the significant improvements in medical treatment which have come about in the post-war era, noted that artisans and their families were particularly subject to respiratory diseases because they spent their lives confined to the cramped and dank street level and subterranean work spaces of the town.[4] Stone workers, who worked outside, suffered respiratory problems from breathing limestone dust. If eighteenth-century earnings for artisan work were as poor as those of the late nineteenth and early twentieth centuries, men following these occupations, and their families, had poorer diets than those who could either afford to eat better or who had enough land to grow a few vegetables (cf. Lisi, n.d.). Marriage contracts from the decade preceding the *catasto onciario* further suggest the poverty of artisans. In contrast to the *massari* and *bracciali* who often received houses from their bride's parents at marriage, artisan grooms did not often begin their *ménages* in a house they owned. Also brides of artisans brought dowries containing two of each item of linens (*panni due*) to the marriage, when worker brides brought three or four, and brides who married men already established as *massari* brought four or five. However, the superior wealth of the peasants may not have guaranteed them a higher place than artisans in the local stratificational system, if more recent values can be projected backwards in time.

HOUSEHOLD STRUCTURES AND MARRIAGE

The evidence from the *catasto onciario*, which is a household census as well as a tax record, points to a strong pattern of neolocal nuclear households. The mean recorded household size, excluding the ducal family, non-residents, and ecclesiastical organizations, was 3.5 (standard deviation 2.16). The compilers always defined the head of household as the eldest male unless none was present; therefore eldest brothers were often the heads of households containing sisters or a widowed mother. They recorded few multiple or extended families, and most records represent nuclear families somewhere along a continuum from a newly formed couple to a lone widow or widower. Along this continuum were couples with children, single parents caring for children by themselves, and unmarried brother and sister households formed by the death of parents in a nuclear family. Even considering Douglass' point – made about the Molisano town he studied – that ideals about extended and joint families may only be realized infrequently in pre-industrial settings in which short male life expectancy intervenes in cultural strategies meant to produce them, extended family and multiple family households were so rare in mid-eighteenth-century Locorotondo that the existence of such ideals, except idiosyncratically, can be precluded (Douglass, 1980: 348, see also Giacomini, 1981). Table 5.2 gives the relative proportions of these household types.

Widows and spinsters had special status in the eyes of the compilers of the *catasto onciario* and they were separated from other households in the document. They paid neither head taxes nor taxes on work, and only paid tax on property if the income surpassed six ducats a year after deductions for debts (Dal Pane, 1936: 20). This special treatment was an official recognition of the precariousness of the position of lone women. However, not all widows had able-bodied offspring to support them, and in the notarial acts one often encounters mortgages and sales of property by widows who declared that they needed money to feed their young children, pay other debts, or provide dowries for daughters (cf. Giacomini, 1981: 27–31).

It was the custom in betrothals to make out a contract, known as a *Capitula Matrimonialia*, with a notary. It is probable that some notarial records are missing for the mid-eighteenth century in Locorotondo because in the decade before the cadaster only twenty

Table 5.2. *Categories of households discernible from the* catasto onciario.

Household categories	N	Percent
Solitary male	82	13.10
Solitary male with mother	12	1.92
Unmarried solitary female	14	2.24
Unmarried female with mother	1	0.16
Solitary widow	13	2.08
Single male with lateral kinsmen	1	0.16
Coresiding unmarried sibs, male head	22	3.51
Coresiding unmarried sibs, male head + mother	30	4.79
Coresiding unmarried sibs, male head + aunt	1	0.16
Coresiding unmarried sibs, male head + non-relative	1	0.16
Childless couple, head 30 or less	46	7.35
Childless couple, head 31–60	39	6.23
Childless couple, head 61 or over	16	2.56
Simple nuclear family	276	44.09
Solitary father with children	16	2.56
Remarried father, wife, and step children	9	1.44
Widow with children	18	2.88
Upward extended family, male head's mother	8	1.28
Upward extended family, male head's mother-in-law	1	0.16
Downward extended family, head's sibs' children	1	0.16
Lateral extended family, head's unmarried siblings	6	0.96
Multiple family, head and son both married	3	0.48
Multiple family, two or more brothers married	1	0.16
Unmarried woman + aunt	1	0.16
Unmarried female + sister	8	1.28
Total	626	100.00

such contracts come to light among the notarial records, and in the cadaster there are forty-nine married couples with no children in which the husband is less than thirty years old, not to mention the young nuclear families which have produced children. There is little reason to believe, however, that the contracts which exist inaccurately reflect general custom with respect to dowry practices.

In the matrimonial contract the parents or guardians of the bride specified what *dote* was to be given upon marriage. This consisted of her trousseau (*panni*), land, and often a house in town or a portion thereof.[5] An elder brother or an uncle sometimes contributed to the *dote* as well. An elder representative of the groom usually took part in the transaction, and sometimes contracts also specify his *dote*. Contracts often noted *doti* as constituting a share of the inheritance an individual would eventually split with siblings and therefore, strictly following Davis' suggested terminological distinctions (1977: 184) must be considered "settlements" in this system of partible inheritance.

From the twenty marriage contracts Locorotondese notaries drafted in the decade before the compilation of the cadaster, it is possible to trace 17 unions (which, given a widowhood, involve 16 men and 17 women) in the latter document, and identify the ages of the fiancés at the time their marriage contracts were settled. Since the traceable group of families neither constitutes a large nor a random sample, projection of statistics from this group to the population is fraught with peril which cannot be mitigated even with tests of significance. However, for the group under consideration the mean age at marriage agreement for males was 26.13 (standard deviation equals 7) years, and for females 21.65 years (standard deviation equals 4). This disparity of four-and-a-half years is consistent with the four-year average disparity between husbands and wives recorded in the cadaster. However, precise age at marriage is difficult to derive from these figures because there is little way of knowing when, after the contract was drafted, the couple actually married.

The patterns of eighteenth-century family life are not easily discernible from the legalistic records which survive and which cluster around moments in family cycles – marriages and deaths – when property passed from one generation to another. One can assume that since formal education of any kind was unlikely for all but very few elite and wealthy *massaro* children, work for most people began at a tender age, perhaps at an even earlier age than it did for modern elderly informants, who had a year or two of schooling at least. In the eyes of the legal system a male was a tax-paying adult at the age of fourteen and was accessed a head tax.

The *catasto onciario* never ascribes female children an occupation but they probably worked within their households weaving (looms show up as important items of property in contracts), minding smaller siblings, working in the fields, and sewing and embroidering their dowries.[6] Some women may have exercised the craft of seamstress, but the cadaster leaves no indication of this. It is an Apulian tradition that women go to the fields with their husbands, fathers, and brothers, and there is little reason to believe this was not true during the eighteenth century also. The account of priestly amorous activity, cited above, shows a work party consisting of a man, his wife, and her sister who resided temporarily on a *masseria* to sharecrop some favas.

THE CHURCH AND THE GRAIN BANK

Several town-wide institutions merit attention in considering the Locorotondese social system during the waning century of the old order. Indebtedness was common. Most recorded debts were simply mortgages of property contracted with private individuals, sometimes relatives, other times with local magnates, or wealthy local priests. However, the local church chapter was the primary lending and mortgage institution during these times (ASB-CO, 1749: foglio 568). The chapter possessed a little more than 150 *tomoli* of lands located in 33 differing locations throughout the town's territory, which rendered, according to the cadastral entry, 248 ducats annually, although the means by which they were cultivated are not specified; they were probably rented out, but no contracts survive to verify this. In addition, the chapter owned 17 buildings which brought in almost 79 ducats a year in rents. Immovable properties accrued to such organizations through foreclosure on mortgages, and through gifts of income producing estates left to the church to pay for masses for the soul of the deceased.

Another 453 ducats per annum accrued to this institution from the 60 debts owed by individuals or their heirs. Further, as noted earlier, a little over 52 ducats came to the institution from 86 emphyteutical rents. In short, the chapter grossed 832 ducats annually in incomes of various kinds. It claimed expenses amounting to 473 ducats annually for masses (of which 2,360 ordinary, and 71 sung), and other functions. Despite these expenses it was a considerable financial power in the town and functioned as a bank from which cash could be borrowed against property at an annual payment rate of 5 or 6 percent. Most loans were for 2 or 3 ducats, but in one case the chapter had loaned an individual from the city of Monopoli the sum of 2,500 ducats and reaped, at 4 percent per annum (perhaps a discount considering the large sum involved) 100 ducats interest. The pecuniary nature of Locorotondo's church chapter was by no means unusual for the area (cf. Rosa, 1974: 66).

Those in need of seed in Locorotondo were fortunate that the town boasted one of only 5 grain banks in the entirety of the Terra di Bari during the latter part of the eighteenth century (Masi, 1962: 370). Of these, only those of Locorotondo and Canneto survived the crises of the last decades of the century and continued to function satisfactorily at the beginning of the nineteenth (Masi, 1962: 374). Locorotondo's *monte frumentario*, had been founded by the wife of a Martinese notable, Madama Pelligrini-Castelli, who in her will, drawn up on May 4, 1699 (ACMF, 1699), declared that the supply of about 1,300 *tomoli* of grain she possessed in the territory of Locorotondo be set up as a grain bank for the benefit and needs of the peasants of that town. The Duchess of Martina Franca, Madama Pelligrini-Castelli's heir and mistress (the woman had been the Duchess' wet nurse), was to officially constitute the *monte*. The acts of foundation of the Monte Frumentario Madama Pelligrini date to January 22, 1711, and inexplicably by that time the supply of grain on hand had decreased to 760 *tomoli* (ACMF, 1711). This made it of medium size among the grain banks in existence at mid-eighteenth century; that of Minervino Murge began with 1,700 *tomoli* and that of Cassano with 200 (Masi, 1962: 371).

The operating rules of the bank were established at its foundation. Grain could not be denied to those who regularly sowed, but could be to those who did not. From the first fruits of the institution's operations a granary to house its capital was to be built, and rent paid on the warehouses currently being used for storage. Clothing and shoes were to be provided for the poor from the income. If the price for grain outside of Locorotondo was higher in some years than locally, it was legitimate to sell what remained every year and realize a profit, but the original capital had to be reestablished (*rifatto*) each year. Interest was not to exceed the amount of one *stoppello* for every *tomolo* of grain given out. Grain could be lent only for sowing or consumption. Those who took grain fraudulently to speculate on the market had to pay back not only the principal and interest, but also any profit made. The *monte* was to remain secular and not be church run (ACMF, 1711). At mid-century it was administered by a board under the control of the Duke, but by the end of the century it had passed into municipal hands (Baccaro, 1968: 37–38). The availability of loans of grain during those times must have helped maintain the small proprietor–peasant population of Locorotondo in the face of adversities when similar small proprietor populations elsewhere suffered great losses. In fact, during the last decades of the eighteenth century and the first decades of the nineteenth this grain bank was one of the factors which facilitated the further development of small property and dispersal of more small holders into the countryside – the subject of the next chapter.

Chapter 6

RURAL SETTLEMENT IN THE NINETEENTH CENTURY

This chapter will examine the economy and population of Locorotondo as it appears from nineteenth-century documents. It will concentrate upon the documentary evidence for movement of peasants into the countryside, describe the extraordinary effort of the town's upper classes to curtail this movement in 1827, and portray, insofar as the evidence allows, aspects of nineteenth-century peasant life in rural Locorotondo.

THE NINETEENTH-CENTURY ECONOMY AND POPULATION OF LOCOROTONDO

The Catasto Provvisorio and the 1811 Census

The *catasto provvisorio* (provisional cadaster) contains most of what can be learned about the economy of Locorotondo during the early decades of the nineteenth century. The Murattian government issued the official decree for its formation on April 4, 1809, and the cadaster constituted one of the major economic reforms of the Napoleonic period. It was called "provisional" because this descriptive cadaster was to be replaced by a permanent "geometric" one which would actually map fields. But it remained provisional for almost a century. The new cadaster was compiled in a more orderly manner than the old *catasto onciario* and much reflected the new French order and its enlightenment roots (Dibenedetto, 1976: 106–110).[1]

The *provvisorio* differed in some important ways from the *onciario*. First, it did not constitute a list of households because the taxable unit was now the individual owner. Since the *onciario* provides no ways to ascertain which properties in it belong to which members of recorded households, the two cadasters are difficult to compare. The *provvisorio* provides little evidence, beyond the application of titles such as "Don" or "Signore," of occupations or social statuses for the owners listed, and unfortunately does not list their domiciles. The boundaries of the commune were not precisely the same for the two cadasters. In the nineteenth-century document rural zones (*contrade*) became officially established and remain essentially the same now, although exact definitions of their boundaries do not survive and may not have been accurately formulated at the time. Taxation laws under the French did not exempt the property owner's dwelling, so for the first time one gains some sense of urban space. The nobility became taxpayers with the end of feudalism and their properties appear in the provisional cadaster. However, the nineteenth-century document, even though better organized and probably more quantitatively accurate, is not so rich in information about society as the *onciario*, and therefore not susceptible to the kinds of analysis possible with the latter. Its primary value lies in what it records about land use and distribution.

Fortunately, another closely contemporary document exists which amplifies an understanding of Locorotondo in the second decade of the nineteenth century: the census of 1811 (ACL-SP, 1810–1811).[2] The Ministry of the Interior issued instructions to compile this census, or *Statistica* as it is called on the document's first page, on September 12, 1810. It records the population of Locorotondo household by household, giving names, sexes, and ages (but unlike the *onciario*, not relationships) of the members.[3] Occupations are listed inconsistently for the individuals recorded, along with an indication of their marital status, and their health, the latter roughly indicated as "optimum," "good," "mediocre," or "ailing." Head-of-household occupations were more often recorded than those of other family members. Of the variables recorded, names, ages, and sexes are the most consistent; other variables went unrecorded for many entries and must be used carefully.[4]

In addition to the cadaster and the census, several other kinds of nineteenth-century records have proven very useful. These include notarial acts (which are more carefully indexed in this era), various forms of correspondence between the town administration and the provincial bureaucracy, and police and court records.

Population

In 1811 the population listed in the census of Locorotondo numbered 4,523 residents, of which 49.9 percent were male and 50.1 percent

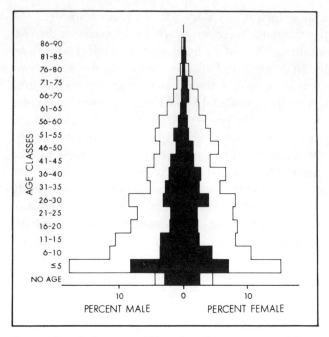

Fig. 6.1. Population pyramid based on the 1811 census. The rural portion of the
population in black. (Source: ACL-SP, 1810–1811)

were female. This represents a doubling of population since the
mid-eighteenth century. The population resided in 1,117 households
with an average of 4.05 individuals each. Figure 6.1 shows the age
and sex distribution of the population which, like the mid-eighteenth-
century counterpart, continues to be distinctly triangular and represents a high birth rate with a relatively high death rate. Birth rates
may have been slightly higher than in the mid-eighteenth century if
the narrower base of the 1749 pyramid (compare Figure 4.1)
represents anything more than the underrecording of young children.

   The census provides, for the first time in Locorotondo's recorded
history, a precise look at town and country settlement. After recording all the households residing in the town at street addresses, the
compiler turned to recording the country dwellers. This seems to have
been a somewhat difficult task because the details of domicile are left
out, and ages and other details, such as occupation and health, are
more frequently ignored. The census compiler adopted no way to
refer to rural household locations – there is no specification of
contrada or (except for a few cases) rural section. He did take pains,

however, to record patronymics for the rural heads of family, and their wives, and organized his compilation by first name as in the eighteenth-century cadaster.

Of Locorotondo's total population, 62.6 percent of individuals (2,837) resided in 61.3 percent of the households in the town, and the remainder resided rurally. The compiler of the census defined country residence as more than mere domicile outside the crumbling walls. In fact, 16.3 percent of households (included in the town figure above) were domiciled in the *borghi*, or extramural, but urban, neighborhoods of San Rocco, Santa Maria dei Greci, Santo Spirito, and Bonifacio.[5] The census indicates whether town properties were rented or owned by the family occupying them. In the town 58.8 percent of habitations were the property of occupants, and the remaining 41.2 percent were rented. Although the compiler recorded the names of landlords, he did not record the rents.

People recorded in the census as residing in the country were mostly *trullo* dwellers. Schematic *trulli* are found in turn of the century maps. Since information about rental of housing in the countryside was not given in the census, one can assume that most *trullo* dwellers owned their own rural houses. However, a proportion of rural dwellers were *massari* who had taken on *masserie* from elite owners in rental and sharecropping contracts and who, therefore, probably lived in estate housing provided by landlords. From a document dating to 1816 which carefully lists information about all *massari* who lived in the countryside, one knows that 55 *massari* cultivated land for owners other than themselves, and one can assume that the vast majority of these were heads of household because a *massaro* needed a family labor force to comfortably take on a *masseria* (ACL-ABF, 1816). Therefore the proportion of tenant *massaro* to small proprietor households can be estimated at approximately 12 percent of the 433 rural households listed in 1811 for Locorotondo. The document also supplies information about the length of time *massaro* households had held their *masserie* at the time of compilation, and only a handful had been renting or sharecropping for more than 6 years (the length of an average rental contract). This suggests considerable turnover in *masseria* rentals and considerable instability among *massari* both in terms of livelihood and residence.

The census reports occupation for only 1,503 residents – about 60 percent of individuals above the age of 14 (see Table 6.1). Therefore the absolute numbers reported here cannot be considered a representative sample, and must be understood, instead, as minima.

Table 6.1. *Occupations recorded in the census of 1811 (ACL-SP, 1810–1811).*

Occupation	Number in Town	Number in Country	Total
Males			
cultivators	193	263	456
shoemakers	45	2	47
rural wall builders	43	12	55
massari	33	22	55
landowners/gentlemen	11		11
pack animal driver	23	1	24
priests/monks/deacons	27		27
students	9		9
quarry workers	6		6
gardeners	3	2	5
barbers	2		2
shopkeepers	4		4
lawyers	3		3
*manipoli**	5		5
grocer	2		2
corduroy maker	2		2
medical doctor	4		4
notaries	4		4
surveyor/engineer	1		1
scribes	5		5
butchers	3		3
trullo builders	1		1
school masters	1		1
usher	1		1
hearth builder	1		1
*mazzieri**	1		1
*centimolari**	1		1
millers	2		2
shepherds	3	1	4
stone cutters	1		1
carpenters	8		8
blacksmiths	8		8
stone masons	11		11
undertakers	1		1
tailors	19		19
pruners		1	1
Total males	487	304	791
Females			
cultivators	8	4	12
spinners	259	215	474

Table 6.1 *(cont.)*

Occupation	Number in Town	Number in Country	Total
Females (cont.)			
weavers	44	10	54
landowners/gentlewomen	3		3
beaters of cotton or linen	17		17
wool carders	17		17
corduroy makers	1		1
*farcellare**	7	2	9
midwives	1		1
millers	2		2
knitters	14		14
servants	4		4
seamstresses	7	1	8
soap makers	1		1
bakers	1		1
Total females	386	232	618

* Designation either uncertain or unknown.

Occupations in the countryside are generically recorded and give the impression of blanket assignment of categories based upon residence. Most rural males are *coltivatori*, or farmers, and their wives or widows are listed as *filannare*, or spinners. This document does not make the distinction between *bracciale* and *massaro* noted in the *catasto onciario*, and it may be that many men recorded without occupations were propertyless manual laborers. Other rural male occupations occurring with some frequency are *massaro* and *paretaro* (wall builder). The latter occupation expanded extraordinarily, from two, in 1749, to at least 55 men residing both in the town and in the country in 1811. This suggests increasing enclosure of rural fields, probably as vineyards, and a corresponding demand for wall builders.

The town housed over 150 men listed as *coltivatori* indicating that Locorotondo was far from developing the urban and rural division of agricultural labor which would characterize it later. Despite population increases, the number of priests in Locorotondo had been cut in half since mid-eighteenth century, and this probably reflects the lessening fortunes of the church in a somewhat more liberal kingdom. The numbers of shoemakers and tailors had considerably increased by 1811. There were at least 47 artisans involved in making footwear (2.7 times the 1749 figure), and 19 tailors – almost five times as many as in the *catasto onciario*. Expansion of these trades beyond the level of simple population expansion may reflect a certain prosperity and therefore greater demand for clothing, or indeed it may reflect the establishment of the artisan hierarchy which existed until the mid-twentieth century.

The *catasto onciario* did not indicate female occupations, so only in 1811 can a sense of what women did be gained. Women, in both town and country, were overwhelmingly involved with the production of textiles and clothing. Occupations such as spinner, weaver, seamstress, knitter, linen and cotton beater, wool carder, and corduroy weaver occurred. With the exception of corduroy production, these were *strictly* female activities. A few women also made soap, worked in flour mills, and baked professionally.

The distribution of wealth

Wealth in Locorotondo can be measured from the *catasto provvisorio* in two forms: area of, and income from, various kinds of land, and numbers of, and taxable income from, buildings, including houses and property devoted to economic activities such as mills and pharmacies. Since the cadaster does not double as a household roll it only reveals property owning individuals and institutions. However, various population figures survive from the French decade and a comparative sense of the ratio of property owners to population is recoverable. Demarco (1970) provides tables derived from the provisional cadasters of 53 towns and cities which allow comparison on several points between locales in the Province of Bari. From these tables it results that Locorotondo had a population of 4,716 in 1806, and in the cadaster, according to summary tables, there resulted 1,589 entries for property owning units, most of which were individuals, and which now included the baronial family in Martina Franca.[6] (Church organisations and a few other corporate bodies also had entries.) From this one can calculate a ratio of property owning units to population of 0.34. The mean for the province was 0.316 (standard deviation 0.131), and the median was 0.29. This places Locorotondo at the eighty-first percentile, well above the central tendencies of the leftward skewed provincial distribution, indicating that property in Locorotondo was fragmented into small units with

Table 6.2. *Comparative ratios indicating land and income distribution from
selected towns from the Terra di Bari, 1806. (Modified from cadastral figures
reported in Demarco, 1970.)*

Unit	Population	Entries/person	Land/entry	Taxable income/entry
Locorotondo	4,716	0.34	2.49	16.88
Cisternino	4,116	0.34	2.61	13.93
Alberobello	3,395	0.24	2.23	11.72
Monopoli	13,362	0.16	11.93	100.91
Fasano	8,226	0.19	8.35	66.52
Mean, 53 towns Terra di Bari	6,333	0.32	5.47	39.05

wide distribution among households. The latter is confirmed by
Locorotondo's ratios of land area per entry (2.49 *tomoli*) and income
per entry (16.88 ducats), which fall respectively at the thirty-second
and fifth percentiles of the provincial distributions to which they
belong. Neighboring Cisternino's ratios are close to Locorotondo's,
and Alberobello's are lower but follow the same pattern. Other
neighboring places such as Monopoli and Fasano show lower ratios
of entries per person (0.16 and 0.19 respectively), but much higher
figures indicating income and land area per entry. This indicates
greater concentration of wealth and the presence of much larger
properties which pull the means upward (see Table 6.2). Therefore
Locorotondo, and its hill neighbors, differed distinctly from immediate coastal neighbors.

Figures which are internal to Locorotondo reflecting distribution of
wealth are of course calculable from the *catasto provvisorio*, but they
are only tenuously comparable to earlier ones deriving from the
catasto onciario for reasons mentioned above. The best which can be
done is to compare only landowning units from each source (remem-
bering that the earlier units are households and the latter ones are
individuals, with the hope that the process of conversion of raw
scores to percentages mitigates this difference).[7] In doing so it is
apparent that the distribution of land quantities is essentially the
same in both cadasters. In 1749 the Gini coefficient for households
owning land was 0.774 and in the early nineteenth century it was
0.772. There does not seem to have been a concentration of property

from the eighteenth to the early nineteenth century. Similarly landed *income* continued to have about the same distribution it had in 1749. Considering only landed entries in each case, G for income from land in both 1749 and 1806 was 0.67.

The lack of change contradicts general expectations for concentration of wealth following from the considerable upheavals of the end of the eighteenth century, and the profiteering and foreclosure on land leases typical of that time in the Terra of Bari noted by various authors (cf. Masi, 1968: 90). This supports the idea that during the eighteenth century in Locorotondo, land, even commons, was already securely held by small and medium proprietors. This interpretation is further supported by a document in which an agent of the Feudal Commission recounted his investigation of the nature of common lands in and around Locorotondo in 1809 (ASB-AD, 1809) in which the common fields of Locorotondo are defined as *demani appadronati* – commons possessed by single owners – and were declared to be the outright property of those to whom they were ascribed. Usurpation of commons within the municipal territory, since there was no universal commons, was not, unlike the cases of many nearby municipalities, a factor in contributing to the rise of a new gentlemanly class, at least in the early nineteenth century. Certain family names – De Bernardis, and Aprile-Ximenis, among them – which suddenly appear in the provisional cadaster attached to wealthiest households, would grow in prestige soon after the French decade through the acquisition of ducal lands. Apparently they obtained these lands through purchase, and not through usurpation of commons, as some local historians, who project the historical experiences of other towns in the region on Locorotondo, believe.

The lack of a change in the distribution of land between the two cadasters may also reflect the persistence in Locorotondo of a grain bank which allowed peasant small proprietors to weather the end-of-century storm. In many other towns the local bourgeoisie drained away the patrimonies of, and destroyed, grain banks and charitable institutions, especially those run by religious confraternities, which had already been assailed during the 1790s by various extraordinary taxes imposed by the crown to meet the growing threat of French invasion. Although there were some irregularities in the management of the charitable fund, the Monte Montanaro (it was investigated by higher authorities), the Madama Pelligrini grain bank continued to function and to lend out grain both for planting and for tiding hungry

Table 6.3. *Land in* stoppelli *by use and by land quality category assigned by the compilers of the* catasto provvisorio. *(Source: Calculated from the* Stato di Sezione *portion of ASB-CP, 1816.)*

Land use categories (aggregated from finer categories in the cadaster)	Land quality classes			Total all land	Percent each land use
	First class	Second class	Third class		
Woods, brushy land	3690.00	4593.00	112.00	8395.00	22.51
% woods, brush in each class	43.95	54.71	1.33	100.00	—
Pasture	1.00	0	0	1.00	0.00
% pasture in each class	100.00	0	0	100.00	—
cereal fields	6577.00	7976.50	6955.50	21509.00	57.68
% cereal fields in each class	30.58	37.08	32.34	100.00	—
Small garden	342.00	328.50	152.00	822.50	2.21
% garden in each class	41.58	39.94	18.48	100.00	—
Vineyards	3045.00	2199.50	936.10	6180.60	16.58
% vineyards in each class	49.27	35.59	15.15	100.00	—
Farmyard (*jazzeile*)	326.50	31.00	23.00	380.50	1.02
% Farmyard in each class	85.81	8.15	6.04	100.00	—
Total in each quality class	13981.50	15128.50	8178.60	37288.60	100.00
% land in each quality class	37.50	40.57	21.93	100.00	

peasants over the winter (Monte Montanaro: ASB-ICO, 1809; Madama Pelligrini grain bank: ASB-CB, 1798–1807).

There is a major difference between the two cadasters with respect to reported land use. Categories reported in the *catasto onciario* which concerned enclosure or common use no longer interested the compilers of the *provvisorio*, who concentrated on categorizing land quality and cultigens. All land was classified as belonging to either first, second, or third, category with respect to its quality. Table 6.3 breaks down the land recorded in Locorotondo by use and category. As one would expect of a predominantly subsistence agricultural system, nearly 58 percent of all land consisted of fields sown with grain or legumes such as fava beans. Of this only about thirty percent was select land belonging to the first category. Twenty-two-and-a-half percent of the land surface was uncleared and categorized as "brushy" (*macchioso*), "herbaceous" (*erboso*), or woods (*bosco*). It is interesting that, except for a trivial amount, uncleared land was not at all classified as third quality land, and that 44 percent, a large part of which is "herbaceous," was first class land. Criteria for classification do not survive, but one can surmise that grazing land, and land which supplied fuel, had high value. Also there may still have been areas of deeper soil which were as yet uncleared.

The third largest land use category consisted of vineyards. Of this, a bit over 49 percent was first class land. Vineyards constituted 16.6 percent of all recorded land and, significantly, this represents a more than three-hundred percent increase over the proportion of land used for growing grapes recorded in the cadaster of 1749. The proportion of land devoted to viticulture in Locorotondo at the provisional cadaster was at the high end of the range for the Terra of Bari. Demarco gives figures for nineteen municipalities in the province with surface areas over 10,000 hectares (thus excluding Locorotondo), and for these territories vineyards comprised only 6.36 percent of the land surface with a mean per town of 7.66 (Demarco, 1970: 224 and Table 24). Neighboring Alberobello showed no proportion of its surface in vineyards, and Cisternino, always most similar to Locorotondo, showed 12.1 percent according to figures reported by Salvemini (1982: 833). From Demarco's figures, clearly only Bari, at 18.82 percent, surpassed Locorotondo's development of viticulture. (There was another zone of viticultural expansion stretching northward along the coast between Bari and Trani.) As in the eighteenth century, vineyards were more uniformly distributed among the population than other forms of land, as indicated by a crop-specific Gini coefficient of 0.596 (as above, considering only property owners).

Larger properties within the commune's borders which could be labeled *masserie* vary from a size of 4 or 5 to a maximum of 322 *tomoli*. In 1816 there were 55 farms cultivated by *massari* for various elite landlords (ACL-ABF, 1816). Only 17 of these *masserie* also employed an adolescent boy charged with taking care of livestock. Only 30 properties were indicated in the *catasto provvisorio* as having a house for the owner on the premises. The largest property was the Parco del Vaglio, which belonged to the Duke of Martina Franca, as did another estate of 61 *tomoli*. Both were predominantly covered in oaks. The oaks provided a bountiful crop of acorns which could be utilized as animal fodder. According to a surveyor's report dating to 1817 (ACMF, 1817) the soil of Parco del Vaglio was sown with grain. This large estate provided income to the Duke from rental to a Locorotondese *massaro* for about 700 ducats a year under an eight-year contract (ACMF, 1796: contract dating to January 21,

1794). It was probably surveyed at the time in preparation for division and sale because, in the opening phases (1823) of the cadaster kept in the municipal archives of Locorotondo, the estate no longer belonged to the ducal family, which had divested itself of properties in Locorotondo, and had been split into several pieces owned by the major agrarian families of the town. The estate was valued in 1817 at 16,490 ducats.

Another large wooded area, Parco Talinajo, belonged to a religious institution in Fasano and consisted of almost 200 *tomoli*. It would remain intact until 1879 when the owner sold it off to 8 buyers, some of whom further divided their portions into small parcels (ACL-CP, 1823–1930). A Martinese gentleman, whose surname survives in its name, owned the Masseria Marinosci which totaled 178 *tomoli*. A large part of this estate remains intact even now, but in 1874 a portion was divided and let to 29 emphyteutic tenants. A gentleman from the distant town of Trani owned 114 *tomoli* on the western side of the communal territory. The other twenty-five estates measured under 100 *tomoli*, and 50 percent of the entire distribution of "large estate" land, measured under 27 *tomoli*. In all, 35.42 percent of the land surface taxed in Locorotondo was occupied by estate land. The rest was in small parcels. The land recorded for most of these estates consisted of cereal fields and uncultivated fields left in scrub or in woods, and used as pasture or as a source of wood.

Twenty-seven of the 30 *masserie* with owner's housing included what the document refers to as a *casa d'abitazione*, "inhabitable" house, and 3 had a *casino* or a *casinotto*. The key to the meaning of the first term is the identity of the kind of person for whom a dwelling was or was not "inhabitable." By this date most of the *casette* listed in the document were inhabited on a year round basis by peasants. The *casa d'abitazione* referred, instead, to the pitch-roofed "great house" of the *masseria* which was meant for the periodic habitation of the landowner, and which was therefore "habitable" by the upper classes. Most *masseria* headquarters listed in the cadaster can still be identified in the modern Locorotondese landscape, although many of them have ceased to be estate headquarters. Only a handful of these buildings seem to have been built since the early nineteenth century, and some of these were built after larger estates such as Marinosci and Parco del Vaglio became divided. A *casino* or *casinotto* was probably a more modest landowner's dwelling. In the early nineteenth century the custom was for elites to spend the autumn months in the country, as the following vignette from a manuscript reporting on the weather in 1836 and 1837 notes:

Autumn in our town brings to mind festivals dedicated to the inventor of the vine, and it is the custom of citizens, who betake themselves to live in the country, to celebrate with some feasts. Therefore, they wish as much as possible that the months of September and of October, period of residence in their villas, proceed serenely, as much for the blooming of pleasures, as for the good success of the wine. (ASB-PI, 1822–1844)

Nineteen larger estates were surveyed as part of the adjustments to the cadaster which took place in 1815 (ASB-LRCP, 1815–1817). The surveyor drew sketch maps which show only a rough outline, but in the case of a number of *masserie*, these maps already show the results of a process of nibbling away of land, and division. Five of them are divided into two or more separate parts. These and others have outlines which feature odd "dog legs" and indentations which may represent cession of fields in emphyteusis or sale. The Masseria San Pantaleo, for instance, was divided into two sections between which stood the *trulli* of a peasant nicknamed "Pasqualicchio."

Five-hundred individuals owned a piece of urban property, according to the cadaster. Of the total of 1,208 urban properties, 1,033 can be considered some form of dwelling. The rest range from stairways and portals to various kinds of shops and institutions. The largest category of dwellings consists of one room spaces, either at ground level (*sottano*), of which 536, or a story up (*soprano*), of which 218. The third largest category is the *soprano con suppigno*, a single upper-story space capped off by the loft under the pitched roof of the house. Larger dwellings were comparatively few. There were only 44 ground-level houses with more than one room, and 47 similar upper-level houses. Upper-story houses with more than one room and a loft seem to have comprised the dwellings of more elite inhabitants and account for 59 entries. There was even a ten-room example which must have been grand for the times.

The town center of Locorotondo boasted 11 churches, most of them very small. Eight flour mills milled grain. The Duke owned and rented the town's only inn and tavern to an innkeeper. He also owned some rental housing and one of three ovens, as well as the ruined castle and the town walls with towers. There were 6 shops (*speziarie*) which sold staple groceries, probably mostly spices, oil, cheese, and perhaps wine. Of these, 3 included work space, which suggests local food processing. Scattered along the narrow, labyrinthine alleys of the town are 19 artisan workshops. Obviously, then, as in the days of the *onciario,* few artisans owned workshops separate from their dwellings.

EXPLICIT DOCUMENTS AND THE SETTLEMENT PATTERN

The census taken in 1811 allows the observation that about 37 percent of the population lived in the countryside. Another document, a set of testimonies dating from 1812 which were taken to establish a case for an indemnity to be paid to some peasants because they had been robbed of most of their household possessions by bandits, demonstrates that this pattern of residence was unusual in the Terra of Bari during the French decade (ASB-PA, 1812). The town magistrate asked each witness whether the victims lived with their families "in all seasons of the year" in their rural *trulli* in the *contrada* of Serralta. The care taken in establishing this for the benefit of the provincial Intendant suggests that the general expectation in the Apulia of those times was that peasants did not live permanently in the countryside, but only temporarily for particular purposes, and not with their families.

Further, there is indirect demographic evidence which suggests that the degree of rural settlement measured in 1811 was the result of recent trends. In Figure 6.1, the rural segment of the population pyramid was set off and shaded. Figure 6.2 is another pyramid which represents the rural population alone by percentage of individuals falling within male and female age cohorts. It is drawn to the same scale as Figure 6.1 and distinct differences from the overall age/sex distribution are visible. To further illustrate this, Figure 6.3 graphs positive and negative deviations from a hypothetical rural population pyramid exactly proportional by age cohort to the overall pyramid – in essence a miniature of the latter. Positive and negative deviations in given age classes indicate more or less people in the countryside than would be expected if the population were uniformly distributed by age across both town and country segments. The graph shows that the country population exceeds expectations for young children, for men in their thirties, and for women in the latter half of their twenties and in their early thirties. (Individuals, from an inspection of the document likely to be mostly small children, for whom no age was recorded, are also overrepresented in the countryside.) Older children, adolescents, and adults over 45 are underrepresented in the

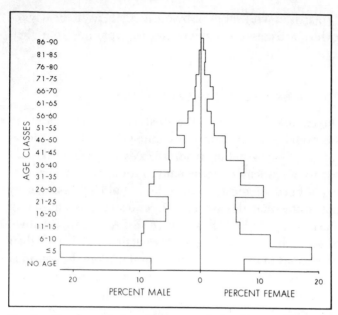

Fig. 6.2. Rural population of Locorotondo in 1810–11. (Source: ACL-SP, 1810–1811)

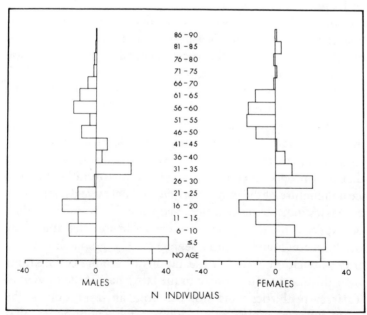

Fig. 6.3. Positive and negative deviations between the actual rural population pyramid and a hypothetical rural pyramid exactly proportional by age cohort to Locorotondo's overall pyramid. (Source: ACL-SP, 1810–1811)

rural zones. One explanation for these deviations would be some factor or factors operating in the countryside to cause higher mortality in the adolescent and early adult cohorts, and among old people. This seems unlikely, especially given the tendencies for greater longevity among peasants than for townsmen noted in the *catasto onciario* and described in the last chapter. Instead these profiles suggest that adult and young child bulges in the rural pyramid represent a trend toward establishment of young families far from the bells of Locorotondo, probably in the decade or so before the census. In addition, the mean age for rural heads of household (45.56 years) was 3.34 years less than the mean age for town heads of household (48.9 years). The fact that thirty to thirty-five-year-old males and twenty-six to thirty-year-old females are overrepresented in the rural zones follows estimates of marriage ages and age differences between spouses made in Chapter 5. The underrepresentation of older adults in the countryside probably indicates the recentness of trends toward rural settlement. This lends support to the idea of then recent trends toward establishment of younger couples in the countryside.[8]

On Sunday February 11, 1827 Mayor Antonio Aprile delivered the following words to the *decurionato*, the town council, of Locorotondo:

Gentlemen, the representation of the town rests in your bosom and therefore it is in your maximum interest that the people represented by you be orderly, obedient, and furnished with the best morality and religion. You are not unaware, however, that the majority of these citizens live permanently in the countryside in the guise of brutes, and further you see that men and women die there indiscriminately without medical assistance and deprived of the sacraments. Such a system is completely reprehensible because they are running with great strides toward animality and toward general corruption without knowing the Christian duties and the principles of that holy religion which must constitute the guide to good living far from the rule of law and from the surveillance of the Magistrates. And not participating in church and its sacraments they enter upon immorality and they become worse every day. The collection of royal taxes, the execution of conscription, civil service, and all which concerns the purpose of the public good, become bound up and difficult. I would therefore be of the view that such an abuse come to be repressed with great haste, and I would think therefore that all of them should come back into the inhabited part of the town with the exception of the estate overseers, shepherds, and others who might be regarded as necessary for the cultivation of the lands or for the care of the flocks. So doing we would move toward rectifying fairly corrupt public custom, religious principles would be cultivated for the good of the spirit, and we would avoid those disturbances and inconveniences which derive from living licentiously, and from immorality. The inhabitants of Cisternino, of Fasano, and of other more populated cities of the province go to work in their respective fields but they re-enter the town in the evening. Our population alone leads a capricious life in order to escape the vigilance of the authorities and that cannot be permitted as it damages the public good. (ASB-ACA, 1827)

The minutes go on to report that having heard the Mayor's discourse, the thirteen *decurioni* found it "just" and "regular" and "applauded it with a unanimous vote." This extraordinary speech was the first official move in a flurry of memorials to the provincial Intendant, and the archibishop of the Diocese in Ostuni, which had as their object forcible displacement of the rural peasant population back to town. Other letters to the Intendant, sharing many phrases with each other and with the mayor's speech, came from the town's leading churchman and from the Justice of the Peace. Both added that women gave birth in the countryside without midwives, and the Justice of the Peace declared that a killing which had taken place on the 10th of February "would not have been consummated if public custom had not been aborted because of the degeneration of those principles which impose good upbringing, which is neglected in the country as much as it is cultivated in town."[9] The churchman hoped the Intendant would issue the appropriate orders to the Minister of the Police immediately.

Upon receiving these letters and the council meeting minutes, the provincial Intendant wrote the archbishop of Ostuni stating that what he heard from Locorotondo astonished him, but the measure requested seemed to him "rather strong to avoid the cited inconveniences, as the matter concerns families which for a great length of time have found themselves established in their miserable huts, not having shelter in the town center, and without means of subsistence other than that resulting from diligent residence on their own farms," which subsistence, he believed "must be quite limited." "How," he wrote, "can one pretend that all these people withdraw within the town?" However, he did find it "intolerable and quite irregular" that they live "almost by beastly customs" – and asked the archbishop whether a way might not be found for these families to hear Mass in a central place. The archbishop, who had also heard from Locorotondo, answered that indeed a church, with an adjoining residence for a priest, ought to be built in a central location in the territory of Locorotondo.

The Intendant wrote back to Mayor Aprile with this solution, but the latter answered that the town was the central location of the territory, and that, in the Contrada San Marco, in the countryside, there already existed a church in which peasants heard Mass every day. He lamented that the solution proposed by the archbishop and the Intendant "does not attain the purpose of bringing these citizens who live in the guise of beasts and without constraints under the surveillance of the authorities," and further that since the provincial authorities would not order the withdrawal of these people within the walls of the town, the best thing was to leave things as they now stood.

In this exchange remains the first clear indications in the documentary record that a majority of the population of the town had come to reside in the countryside. Further it provides an indication that this was not the case in surrounding towns. Fasano and Cisternino, the peasants of which returned within the walls after working the fields, are specifically mentioned. The provincial Intendant considered residence in the countryside "astonishing" and the local churchman, Paolo Baccaro, thought it a "system to be rectified." One also gains the sense that the Intendant, or his advisors, already knew about this settlement pattern, because he noted that peasants had lived in their "miserable huts" for a long time and that they cultivated small properties. The unusual nature of the country residence pattern is underlined in these documents through certain language usages. The mayor asked that the peasants be forced to live in the "inhabited" part of the town, and all parties refer to rural residence as having "beastly" qualities. To these elite political figures it went against human nature to live permanently away from town.

From the same year dates a document Locorotondese amateur historians call the "Convertini Manuscript" (Guarella, 1985). This was an attempt by Don Angelo Convertini, medical doctor, to describe the geography and some of the history of Locorotondo. His motives for doing this are uncertain, and his words are often garbled by poor syntax. He relates fantastic legends about Locorotondo's origins and history, but also includes descriptions of Locorotondo as it existed during his time. Unfortunately, the original manuscript was lost in 1932 when its possessor died, but local intellectuals have circulated faithful copies, and recently one of them published the text and a commentary in book form. For present purposes, the following is the most salient passage:

In this city of Locorotondo the majority live in the country, on the *masserie*, for the cultivation of same, and most of them are grouped in huts [*abituri*], [groups

of which] number 46 . . . [there follows a list] of which Li Corrieri, Trito, and San
Marco are the most populated and in all seasons carry on their business. How
also in San Marco even before the sale of the Territory of the Royal Customs
House in Monopoli to the six towns, there was a parish which went under the
title of Santa Maria of Cignano. For these clusters, which are dispersed all over
the countryside according to the usages of the first natives, and which in many
places, for the number of huts, are today reduced to hamlets and hay lofts, our
Archbishop, Monsignor Consiglio has decreed among other things upon his Holy
Visit that there be a parish priest in the countryside to administer the Holy
Sacraments in all the hamlets; and he has selected the priest Don Leonardantonio
Palmisano, confessor of one and the other sex, to begin on the 10th of January
1827. (Guarella, 1985: 192)

Here, Don Angelo Convertini lists the *jazzèlere* existing in the early
nineteenth century, some with the names of people who are visible as
massari, or in other roles, in eighteenth-century documents – Erasmo
Serra (Serra), Oronzo ("Ronse") Nardelli (Ronziello), and Madame
Pelligrini-Castelli ("Mamma" Pelligrini). He names the three most
populated hamlets: San Marco, Trito, and Li Corrieri. Only a few
current rural population centers are missing from this list. Convertini,
like other members of his class encountered in the peasant removal
documents, who fail to mention peasant small holdings, seems mainly
concerned that peasants dwell in the countryside to work on the
medium and larger estates. His indication of the "first natives" is
obscure and refers to a fanciful and mythological notion of the
founding of the town after the Trojan Wars, but he hypothesizes that
the hamlets of the countryside were once larger. This is unlikely, at
least in the century before. The plot thickens about the availability of
religion in the countryside because Convertini notes that a priest was
to take service there a month before Mayor Aprile delivered his
impassioned speech before the town council. The administration's
concern did, indeed, revolve more around control of the dispersed
householders and their families than around saving their souls (see
Chapter 7).

The next documentary reference to population in the countryside
comes from the year 1855, and is a letter from the Intendant of Bari
Province to the President of the General Council of Hospices, in
which the former states that in Locorotondo "there are three villages
known as San Marco, Pastini, and Trito about three miles distance
from that center of habitation, which taken together number 1,500
souls." These lack churches, says the Intendant, except for a small
one in San Marco (ASB-OP, 1855). Probably Pastini can be considered equivalent to Li Corrieri mentioned above, and did not

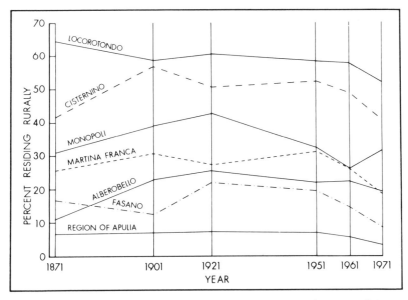

Fig. 6.4. Percent of total population residing rurally in selected municipalities
    and in the Region of Apulia, over time. (Source: Drawn from national
    census data in Liuzzi, 1981; 99, 150.)

represent a newly ascendant hamlet. The word "*pastino*" means
"newly planted vineyard."

Eleven years later the Municipal council deliberated about changing market day from Monday to Sunday to avoid competition with
Martina Franca's market, which was to be established on Tuesdays.
No longer concerned about removing the peasants from the countryside, the mayor noted that all the inhabitants of the town's rural zone,
"in the proportion of almost two-thirds of the population," come
into town for provisions on Sundays anyway (ASB-AIC, 1866).

From 1866 it is but a short step to 1871, year of the first census
which records the percentage of population dispersed in the countryside. Thereafter, the national bureaucracy produced figures tracing
the profile of dispersed population, which I have graphed alongside
figures from adjacent communes at Figure 6.4 (Liuzzi, 1981).
Throughout the period for which data is available, and for all the
Murgia dei Trulli towns, Locorotondo had the highest percentage of
population distributed in the countryside. Cisternino to the east
approached it, but differed, like other towns (except Fasano), because
the proportion resident in rural zones climbed from 1871, at which

point in Locorotondo the already high rural proportion began a slow decline. In 1827, one must recall, Locorotondo's mayor cited Cisternino as exhibiting the "natural" pattern of peasant residence in town.

Other *Murgia* towns had dispersed population levels notable for Apulia, but they never reached those typical for Locorotondo and Cisternino. A little further afield the coastal city of Monopoli climbed from 31 to 40.8 percent from 1871 to 1921 and then fell from 22.8 to 21.7 percent between 1936 and 1971. Other Murgia towns such as Noci, Castellana Grotte, and Putignano climbed abruptly from levels below 10 percent in 1871 to highs between 20 and 30 percent in 1936, and leveled off in the teens in 1971. These abrupt later nineteenth-century increases in rural population represent a well-documented expansion of viticulture and rural residence in response to sudden international demand, created by the lethal spread of the vine disease phylloxera in France, and the crisis in cereal agriculture (see Maranelli, 1946, and Presutti, 1909).

The neighboring coastal city of Fasano is, along with Locorotondo, the only zone which showed a drop in dispersed population between 1871 and 1901. Its history of settlement most directly parallels that of Locorotondo because the Fasanese *contrade* having dispersed settlement are high on the plateau directly adjacent to the territory of focus, and there was a trend toward Fasanese settlement of the plateau edge in the early nineteenth century which was related to the similar trend in Locorotondo. The lowland parts of Fasano, on the other hand, were almost totally planted in olive groves, and most of the peasant population of the coastal strip resided in town and commuted to the fields as indicated by the mayor in his speech before the town council in 1827.

PEASANT LIFE IN RURAL LOCOROTONDO[10]

Evidence from the *catasto provvisorio* portrays the very early nineteenth-century Locorotondese countryside as unevenly populated. *Trulli* and vineyards, and from this one can infer population, were particularly concentrated in areas bordering the upper reaches of the territory of Fasano, along the edge of the plateau, in the *contrade* known as Pantaleo, Lamie di Olimpia, and a bit to the south at Serralta. The latter two *contrade* contained no less than 279 recorded vineyards and along with San Marco (with its 158 vineyards) constituted the areas of major viticultural development in the commune. In San Marco there were 69 *trulli*. This was, and has continued to be, the most significant *trullo* village in Locorotondo's territory and, as was clear from the eighteenth-century data, it is the *contrada* most likely to have had a significant population under the old order. San Marco and the three *contrade* noted above, along with several smaller ones, lay along roads which, after a short journey, directly joined the two major arteries which led to the territory of Fasano. They also bordered florid developments of viticulture and peasant country settlement over the border in Laureto, a plateau zone of Fasano.[11]

Movement of population to the countryside of Locorotondo was therefore part of a larger trend which included movement of Fasanese peasants into grape growing and rural residence in the uplands of the commune and over the border into Locorotondese territory. Many Fasanesi owned land within Locorotondo's boundaries in the border *contrade* and, vice versa, Locorotondesi cultivated vineyards in neighboring *contrade* in Fasano. The years during which the Napoleonic cadaster was being compiled was also the period during which the modern borders of the communes were sorted out. Many Locorotondesi and Fasanesi owned land in vaguely defined border areas which various old regime documents called *territori promiscui* – promiscuous zones. When Locorotondo's borders were established, many people who had previously identified with Fasano found themselves to be citizens of Locorotondo. Most of the population of owners in Serralta, for instance, were listed in the cadaster as *"in Fasano,"* even though Serralta eventually fell well within Locorotondo's borders. Statistics reported above which show early highs in rural population in Fasano, and a later minor decrease which parallels the pattern in Locorotondo, support this hypothesis. The facts further suggest that plateau dwellers were meeting market demand for wine on the olive monocropped coastal strip.

In Locorotondo's hinterlands most of the larger concentrations of *trulli* lay at least two kilometers from the walled center. There were few *trulli* in the immediate vicinity of the town because peasants who cultivated lands near the walls and resided in town had little distance to travel and had no need of rural residences. In the direction of Alberobello, on the western side of the commune, stood several small hamlets which were probably comprised in the area labeled "Li Corrieri" in several documents. Another major *trullo* village was Trito, in 1806 a cluster of 20 *trulli*, which was about three kilometers from the walls and located near the point at which the road forked toward Cisternino in one direction and toward the main Fasano road in the other. Trito, Mavugliola, and Pappariello bordered the large baronial estates in the eastern end of the communal territory, and, besides containing small proprietors, these hamlets supplied labor for the larger *masserie* acquired from the baron by town *galantuomini* in the 1820s.

Certain documents help build a sense of life in rural Locorotondo in the early days of the nineteenth century. Among these are various kinds of contracts, especially marriage contracts, or *capitoli matrimoniali*. During the decade before the 1811 census Locorotondese notaries drafted at least 217 marriage contracts. These can be compared to the much smaller number (20) which survive for the decade before the *catasto onciario*.[12] Often these early nineteenth-century contracts contain only vague clauses which specify, for instance, that the bride or groom is to be given a portion of the eventual parental inheritance. Other contracts specify the transfer of a sum of money after several years' time "to buy *beni stabili*" (immovables) with annual 5 percent interest payments in the meantime. They are, in essence, debts to children contracted by parents. The high frequency of this kind of settlement probably reflected the hard times of the decade in question. The necessity to marry children off arrived before families could provide them with the expected settlements. Many contracts specify the transfer of little in the way of a settlement – one, in fact, states that the bride's widowed mother "isn't giving anything because she doesn't have anything" (ASB-AN, 1780–1838: January 25, 1800). Here the bride might have turned to the Monte Montanaro charity for a minimum dowry. The number of contracts which specify detailed inventories of goods to be settled upon the marrying couple is much smaller than the total.

Marriage contracts provide evidence about residence at marriage. The reader will recall that eighteenth-century contracts indicated a pattern of bridal inheritance of town housing. This continued to be a trend at the beginning of the nineteenth century because the contracts show that females inherited town property upon marriage 2.5 times more frequently than males. This was often encumbered, however, with stipulations that widowed mothers continue to have rights of habitation, and many times the settlement consisted of a share of the whole, and represented a division between sisters. Further, such inheritances did not necessarily mean residence in town. Comparison between marriage contracts and the 1811 census shows a few cases in which couples who had inherited town housing ended up in the countryside.

New in the nineteenth-century contracts was the frequent settlement of rural housing upon grooms. There are 31 instances in which the male was provided with an already existing *trullo*, or the construction of a new one was promised. Parents gave *trullo* buildings to only 14 brides. This, of course, suggests a rule by which urban housing preferably devolved to women and rural housing to men. The latter is the current rule and has been as long as rural folk in Locorotondo can remember. Now, and probably during the era under consideration, many of the exceptions are explicable by cases in which all the heirs are of one sex, or in which there is only one heir.

Twenty-three contracts stipulate residence which is other than neolocal, and in nineteen of these the pattern mentioned is patrilocality. The bulk of the patrilocal cases concerned peasant grooms who were to live with their fathers either temporarily (sometimes until the upcoming harvest is over – August fifteenth) or permanently, but with the stipulation that should separation occur, a house, often clearly a *trullo*, would be settled upon them. During the remembered past it has been the rule that the youngest son inherit the parental household and that he divide the *trullo* to set up a household for himself and his bride, and to be close to aging parents. Nineteenth-century cases of patrilocal residence may represent this custom, but there is no indication of birth order in the contracts.

In sum, movement of peasants to the countryside brought with it changes from female settlement with, and inheritance of, housing (and neighborhoods containing related women) to male settlement and inheritance of *trulli* and the formation of *jazzèlere* consisting, at least initially, of households related through males. Female inheritance of housing, if there was any to pass on, probably persisted among artisans and town-dwelling rural workers for several decades, but appears to have disappeared as a rule during the nineteenth century, because it is not remembered by elderly townspeople. Interviews with older artisans lead one to the conclusion that they rarely owned housing and were forced to rent living space. In the early nineteenth century there had been strong increases in renting, as a comparison between the 1749 cadaster and the 1811 census demonstrates (see below). Even now, there is considerable artisan envy and resentment expressed toward the rural dwelling peasantry about their achievement of house ownership.

Sometimes fathers promised the construction of a new *trullo* for country dwelling sons, and in a few cases there were precise specifications. For instance, Santo Convertini promised his son Antonio a new *casella* measuring twelve *piedi* (feet) with a kitchen measuring 7 by 8 feet (ASB-AN, 1777–1808: October 13, 1808). Vito Michele Conti promised his son Quintiliano a *trullo* measuring internally 16 palms (roughly 4 meters) with an alcove and a kitchen, but with the specific stipulation that he and his son would build it together (ASB-AN, 1780–1838: January 8, 1804). Lorenzo Felice's father gave his son a *trullo* "adjacent and contiguous" to his own in Trito (ASB-AN, 1777–1808: November 2, 1806). Gennaro Neglia committed himself to building his son a *trullo* next to his in the Contrada of Cerrosa within the space of four years after the marriage, and to provide housing for the couple until it was finished. Giovanni Grassi's father Vincenzo pledged to divide a *casella* – the other half went to another son – and to build a chimney on Giovanni's half, presumably so that it could be converted into a separate household with a separate hearth (ASB-AN, 1780–1838: August 29, 1806). *Trulli* of this vintage often contained kitchens reminiscent of tipis. These consisted of no more than a domed space with a chimney cut into the apex of the cupola to allow the exit of the smoke from the hearth, which was a raised pedestal on the floor. The conversion of a room or an alcove in half an existing *trullo* would have presented little problem to the *trullaro*. The provision of several sons with *trulli* adjacent to their father's dwelling would have quickly created small hamlets inhabited by patrilineally related kinsmen and their spouses.

The closest view of rural Locorotondo in the early nineteenth century comes from the aforementioned document concerning the payment of an indemnity to two peasants, brothers-in-law, who lived in the hamlet of Serralta (ASB-PA, 1812). The local magistrate interrogated many witnesses and they each gave their occupations and domiciles and described what they were doing in the zone on the day of the robbery, or the day after when the victim went looking for his stolen property. Both peasants who commuted from Locorotondo and Fasano, and some who resided the year round, cultivated the area between Serralta and Lamie di Olimpia, which lies on the border with Fasano.[13] Along with the 1811 census, this confirms for Locorotondo, at least, that the pattern of residence of the entire peasant population in the countryside, which later developed, had not yet been established, and that the French decade was part of a transitional period. One Locorotondese witness was a rural wall builder, and one Fasanese declared himself to be a tailor who resided rurally in the Fasano side of Lamie di Olimpia. Certain artisans, then, both resided in the countryside and in town, and cultivated land. A witness who declared himself a salaried *massaro*, and another who was a farm laborer, lived inside walled Locorotondo. To repeat, the investigator took considerable pains to establish that the victims of the brigand attack resided throughout the year in their *trulli* in Serralta. In the morning and evening hours there must have been considerable foot traffic on the roads as people walked between their houses, either in rural *contrade* or in the towns, and their fields. In this zone of Locorotondo, and in others characterized by high concentrations of vines, which require considerable intensive labor, there must have been many people at work in the fields at once.

The case of the Serralta brothers-in-law provides some precise information about the kinds of valuables peasant small proprietors kept in *trulli*, because the thieves took everything except the benches and stools the inhabitants sat on by the hearth, the marriage beds, the communal plates they ate from, and their cooking utensils. They had chosen Pietro Rosato as a victim because at a fair, in front of the ducal palace in Martina Franca, they had overheard him say that he had money in his house which he was saving to pay a debt, and because they thought he had a firearm which they relished. They robbed his brother-in-law, Antonio Lo Russo, who lived in the *jazzeile* of Serralta in an adjacent *trullo*, as an afterthought. According to the cadaster, Rosato was a small proprietor who owned two small vineyards amounting to 9 *quartieri*, and 2 cereal fields which together measured 4.5 *tomoli*. (Lo Russo cannot be individualized.)

The stolen items in both cases included clothing, linens, and foodstuffs. The robbers took what were probably Rosato's best clothes, which consisted of a new pair of shoes with silver buckles, a wool cloak, a blue velvet vest, a blue corduroy jacket, and a cotton sash. The brigands cleaned out the family's supply of seven-and-a-half *tomoli* of grain, and a *tomolo* and a half of oats, along with three cheeses. They also emptied Rosato's wife's dowry chest which had contained sheets, handkerchiefs, napkins, clothing, and jewelry, among which: silver shoe buckles, silver pins and buttons, two pairs of gold earrings, a gold pin, and a six stranded gold chain. The brigands stole a similar inventory of items from Lo Russo and his wife. In addition they appropriated Rosato's mare to carry the booty.

From this comes the sense that such small proprietors cut fine peasant figures on saints' feast days and at the associated livestock fairs. Men wore blue velvets and corduroys (there are other bits of evidence which show this to be more than Rosato's preference, and that blue homespun was preferred by peasants throughout the century), and women were well decked out with ornaments of precious metal which also most certainly served as wealth in reserve for emergencies. Everyday clothing was made of homespun wool and cotton. Rosato had traveled to, and met with, witnesses at fairs in both Fasano and Martina Franca – his range of commercial interests was not limited to the local countryside alone, and in this era he may have considered himself more Fasanese than Locorotondese (see below).

In Lamie di Olimpia and Serralta there were complex relationships with the land, and individual households engaged in agriculture through more than one mode of land tenure at a time. Rosato cultivated the soil in his vineyards and his cereal fields to raise a subsistence crop and make some wine for sale. He may have held some, or all, of his vineyard land in an emphyteusis contract and therefore have owed an annual rent upon it (the cadaster records emphyteusis as simple ownership). His brother, Angelo Cosimo, was mentioned as a tenant in such a contract which, in 1801, ceded 470 *tomoli* of land in Serralta to 14 Fasanese peasants under the condition that it be transformed into vineyards. Much of the land on the hill was held in this way, and the victims were part of the Fasanese settlement of the area.

The document shows that a year before the incident, which took place in November, Rosato had bought a wheat field from another small proprietor, Giuseppe Carparella, who resided in the Fasanese half of Lamie di Olimpia. The latter had allowed Rosato a year to pay for the land and was owed 70 ducats. In addition, Carparella's testimony indicates that to supplement the production of his own lands, Rosato also held a field *a società* (in a sharecropping arrangement) in a *padeule*, or deep soiled karst depression, on the *masseria* Lamie di Olimpia, which at that time belonged to a Fasanese landlord. The deep well-watered soil had produced high-quality grains of wheat which witnesses recognized as a trail left behind by the brigands as they escaped. This suggests considerable variation in quality of wheat produced in fields with differing soil depths. Unfortunately, Pietro Rosato did not recover his possessions, despite this clue.

Others who were witnesses on the day of the theft, or on the day after when Pietro Rosato and his brother-in-law went in search of the mare and their property, worked in their own fields, plowed behind a pair of oxen as a hired *massaro* in a field belonging to the elite Locorotondese Lelli family, or worked in fields sharecropped with another Locoroton-dese landowner. The document yields an image of the countryside in this zone as a patchwork of small peasant properties, either owned outright or held under emphyteusis, and small, but in the case of Lamie di Olimpia, rich-soiled, *masserie*, either worked directly with hired labor or given out to local peasants to sharecrop. Rosato was a small-scale entrepreneur like his neighbors.

There is also a sense of moral community in the countryside in the form of mutual knowledge and concern which is visible in these documents. Local witnesses respected the victim because they vouch for his and his brother-in-law's honesty, and testify that both were prosperous enough to have owned all the things which were taken. Even Carparella, to whom Rosato owed the considerable sum of 70 ducats, and to whom the debt was overdue, showed a genuine concern and respect for his fellow country dweller in his statement. Obviously falling victim to the sort of attack suffered by Rosato and Lo Russo was a potential problem with which all who dwelt in isolation from the safer haven of the towns of Fasano or Locorotondo could sympathize and identify.

From two contracts among the acts of the baronial court dating to 1803 and 1806 one also knows that Locorotondese peasants contrac-ted in April to do harvest labor considerable distances from their homes. Unfortunately, one does not know if the individuals involved in these contracts were rural dwelling peasants, or if they were landless workers from town. Oral history and folk memory, however, suggest that both situations were the case. The work was in Massafra and Palagiano, both in the Terra of Otranto to the northwest of Taranto. These territories had much lower population densities than those on the Murgia dei Trulli and were mostly planted in cereals or devoted to pastoralism; there must have been significant labor needs at the harvest. The later contract is more detailed; the earlier one contains more formulaic and vague language about food and lodging (e.g. "all as usual").

The more detailed contract specifies that Don Michele Lelli, acting as agent of the feudal lord of Palagiano, contracted 15 Locorotondese men to harvest grain and fodder crops in that territory when he called them (ASB-CB, 1798–1807: April 3, 1806). Their daily wage was to be 35 *grana*, fava bean mush with olive oil in the morning and evening, and rations of lettuce, onions, garlic, and other greens. Both after the harvest of fodder crops, and of grain, two sheep were to be provided, and each man was to receive a *rotolo* of cheese and be provided with wine on the day off, presumably Sunday. Lastly, the boss could not designate one of them as cook, but instead had to provide for the preparation of the daily fava bean ration himself. To assure their coming at the time specified, when the notary drew the contract up Lelli paid each man earnest money amounting to 12 *carlini*. The other contract was for similar work in the territory of Massafra, and paid less at 21 *grana* a day with earnest money of 10 *carlini* for each man (ASB-CB, 1798: April 24, 1803). The 1806 contract was favorable to the workers with its stipulation about feasts of mutton and a relatively high wage rate, and, as Assante points out, wages for those who wielded the sickle well at the harvest tended to be the best because of the necessity to attract good workers to the less populated areas of Apulia (1974: 205).

Later nineteenth-century peasantry

The only available window from which to glimpse the peasantry, between the middle nineteenth century to early twentieth century, distorts. That window, already utilized in these pages, is of course, criminal records. The reader should not remain with the impression that the countryside of Locorotondo was particularly rife with criminal activities or especially prone to conflict. In fact, leafing through the records of criminal cases and trials in the Bari Archives, one gains the distinct, although impressionistic, sense that there was considerably more criminality elsewhere in the Province of Bari, particularly in the more poverty stricken municipalities at its upper end. These records do, however, allow the investigator to reconstruct certain aspects of daily life, most particularly those things which led to conflict.

The aftermath of Unification was turbulent for the peasantry of Apulia, and many men, mustered out of the Bourbon army, and finding a day laborer's living difficult to earn, or threatened with

conscription into the new Italian army, took to the woods. Locorotondo, although occasionally touched by famous bandit gangs,
produced no bandits of consequence from among its peasant population. This suggests an occupied peasantry concerned with farming
small properties, and able to reabsorb those returning from the
military. The only Locorotondese arrested and tried as a bandit was a
very minor character whose name was Martino Tarì.[14] Tarì, aged
nineteen and labeled as a peasant by the authorities, ran briefly with a
small gang of minor bandits, led by an Alberobellese named Giorgio
Palmisano. This gang roamed the area between Alberobello and
Locorotondo, and often struck isolated *trulli* and *masserie* within
Locorotondese territory. These bandits were tried in 1864; Palmisano
received the death penalty, and Tarì, who had carried out thefts
during only two nights in November of 1863, was sentenced to
twenty years at hard labor. In his confession, Tarì claimed to have
been coerced by Palmisano and his gang to join. Unlike Palmisano,
and many other bandits, he had not served in the Bourbon army; he
was just unemployed. His confession conveys a certain embarrass-
ment at having been involved in robbing his neighbors, and in one
case, he claims to have begged Palmisano not to take the victims'
linens and gold jewelry because they were poor.

If rural Locorotondo, with its small holder peasant culture, was not
a producer of bandits during this era, it presented good pickings for
bandits from outside, such as Giorgio Palmisano, or the more
renowned Pizzichicchio (in whose band Palmisano served for a
period), or even the infamous Sergeant Romano, who in July 1862,
invaded Alberobello to furnish himself with arms from the arsenal of
the National Guard (Molfese, 1964: 171). The isolated *trulli* of the
area, inhabited by small proprietor peasants who had stores of food
and sometimes firearms and gun powder, were attractive to bandits.
However, the confessions of both Tarì and Palmisano, the latter of
whom was so clearly guilty of crimes he knew would lead to his
execution that he had little to lose in concealing minor details,
indicate that by no means were all the small proprietors and *massari*
of the area unsympathetic to their activities – they were local men,
well known in the area. On several occasions, particularly early in his
career, Palmisano hid out in Locorotondese *masserie* working for pay
for the *massaro* and once even rented a piece of land to work. Such
sympathies seem to have been motivated, however, by connections of
kinship and friendship rather than by a vicarious expression of class

conflict – "social banditry," in Hobsbawm's sense (Hobsbawm, 1959: 13–29). Palmisano was just a poor wretch who was forced by circumstance, poverty, unemployment, and conscription, to do what he did. The current peasant folk memory disapproves of thieving, but, in the case of rural men who were desperate, understands the motives. Something of the kind produced a certain sympathy for Giorgio Palmisano.

In fact, in nearly all instances in the accusations brought against Giorgio Palmisano and his henchmen, he victimized members of the local peasant world – *massari*, small holders, and carters. For instance, he threw a carter down a deep chasm to his death because the latter "had the face of a liberal," and wore parts of a Bourbon army uniform, but, with one exception, he left the local gentry alone. The exception was Don Leonardo Pinto, head of the Locorotondese National Guard, who had fired upon him and wounded him during an escape. Tarì testified that Corporal Giorgio (as Palmisano liked to call himself, recalling the much more notorious Sergeant Romano) once suggested that the band burn down Pinto's *masseria*, but that he had talked his leader out of it because the *massaro* was a sharecropper and this would ruin him. Later Palmisano descended upon the *masseria* and killed the animals in their stalls. Hatred directed against Don Leonardo seems to have been entirely of a personal nature rather than based in any firm consciousness of class. The sort of open-class warfare that erupted in places such as Gioia del Colle, and other latifundist areas, was less obvious around Locorotondo. The local liberal *galantuomini* were not great landowners for the most part, and no questions about usurpation of commons festered in Locorotondo to arouse peasant anger as they did in many other Apulian towns, including neighboring Alberobello.

Even after the end of the brigandage period, Locorotondese peasants continued to be convenient targets for thieves. In 1878 3 Locorotondesi and 2 men from Carbonara, a town now engulfed in the suburbs of Bari, were convicted of "criminal association with the object of committing crimes against property and persons" in the territory of Locorotondo. The plot to form a gang and meet where there were many "well-off peasants," was hatched while several of the thieves spent time in jail. The two Carbonaresi arrived on the *Murgia* and went to the house of the father of one of the Locorotondese ex-convicts, and, rather stupidly, began to ask about "well-off peasants and the customs of the area," such as "whether the peasants living in the countryside would go to the big festival being held in Locorotondo on Sunday evening." The father warned a neighbor that he should be on guard because he might be robbed and the neighbor informed the *carabinieri*. They rounded up and arrested the gang before it could commit a crime. The report finishes: "This arrest was learned of with the greatest pleasure by the good citizens of this town, who nourish the hope that the continual thefts which happen here and in neighboring towns, will finally cease" (ASB-CD, 1878).

It is not hard, therefore, to understand the diffidence sometimes shown even now by country dwellers toward people they do not know. One does not simply go up to a house and knock on the door, especially at night; one approaches slowly, calling out, or better, one nears the door accompanied by someone whose voice will be recognized by those inside. (Giorgio Palmisano used this tactic frequently in robberies, although he recruited such help at gunpoint.) Strangers who come to the door have long been either officials bearing unpleasant tidings (Palmisano also used to gain entrance by dressing in a stolen National Guard uniform), or people, such as salesmen, confidence men, and bandits, who seek to take advantage. The former sort of visitor explains the response a stranger gets when a householder answers the door – "What's happened?"

The first half of the nineteenth century, then, saw the permanent establishment of Locorotondo's peasantry in the countryside. From 1811 when two-thirds of the population lived in town, the situation reversed by mid-century when two-thirds of the population lived outside the walls, far from the church bells, independent of daily contact with townsmen, but endangered to a certain extent by brigands and thieves. The next chapter takes up the problem of explaining these changes in settlement pattern.

Chapter 7

HOW PEASANTS POPULATED THE COUNTRYSIDE

The evidence shows, then, that by the beginning decades of the nineteenth century a peasant population was well established in Locorotondo's countryside, and migration would continue, so that by mid-century fully two-thirds of the municipality's population dwelled rurally. The peasant removal documents of 1827 show that this was both a highly unusual pattern for the area and that elite townsmen felt alarm about it. It remains in this chapter to explore the "hows and whys" of population transfer into the countryside. The populating of the rural hinterlands of Locorotondo will be portrayed as a peasant adaptive strategy, and, in part, the consequence (unintended, given their alarm in 1827) of adaptive strategies adopted individually by elite landowners.

EMPHYTEUSIS BETWEEN THE OLD AND NEW ORDERS

A key element in understanding peasant and elite adaptive strategies in Locorotondo at the end of the eighteenth century, and throughout the nineteenth and early twentieth centuries, is the institution of emphyteusis, which in Locorotondo, and later in surrounding towns, directly affected the development and expansion of viticulture and of rural settlement. This kind of contract facilitated the development of peasant small proprietorship through the guarantee of secure land tenure in exchange for intensive labor. As noted at the outset, economic thinkers and reformers belonging to the Neapolitan enlightenment, Antonio Genovesi principal among them, proposed emphyteusis as a means to improve and develop the rural economy. Emphyteusis contracts provided certain advantages and disadvantages to the parties involved in them, and these bear exploration in attempting to understand how this land tenure system dovetailed with the development of rural settlement and the expansion of viticulture. However, there is no perfect span of records from which to gain a complete sense of the history of emphyteusis in the area. Also not all such agreements were legitimized by notaries. Marginal notes on the town's copy of the provisional cadaster refer to many properties which had been held in emphyteusis "for a long time" but which were never legalized as such (ACL-CP, 1823–1930). For instance, a contract dating to 1838 consists of a written renewal of a verbal contract which dated to 1810 (ASB-AN, 1819–1867: November 19, 1838). Often landlord and tenant drew up contracts after land had been divided, and even several years after it had been occupied – the written contract seems to have been an afterthought. Indeed, occasional emphyteusis contracts relevant to land being divided in Locorotondese territory may exist among the greatly larger number of protocols left by notaries who practiced in the larger cities of Monopoli, Martina Franca, and especially Fasano. Since the discovery and consultation of such documents is extraordinarily labor intensive, limited time and resources prevented the systematic examination of these non-Locorotondese records. Therefore the historical record is fragmentary and not easily subject to quantification.

To recapitulate a few significant points, there was probably a wave of emphyteutical leasing by church organizations during the late seventeenth and early eighteenth centuries. The 1749 cadaster listed 86 emphyteutical rents payable to the local church chapter, most of which were collectable from the heirs of those who contracted them. Unfortunately, in most cases the functionary who compiled the document did not specify the nature of the properties involved and some, perhaps many, of these properties were dwellings and other urban spaces. Less than 1 percent of the vineyards recorded in the mid-eighteenth-century cadaster were noted as emphyteutical holdings, and no records in the notarial transactions between 1725 and 1749 would account for 86 such leases. However, during the first 20 years of the eighteenth century, in neighboring Martina Franca, religious institutions ceded 340 *tomoli* (292.13 hectares) of land in emphyteusis to priests and secular small proprietors. By 1720 most of this land had become the outright property of those who had worked and improved it through enfranchisement (Rosa, 1974: 82). Concessions of this kind may account for the listings of the local church chapter in Locorotondo, and it is probable that enfranchised emphyteutical contracts account for many of the vineyards in Locorotondo, and probably for whatever rural settlement existed during those times.

Emphyteutical contracts became more frequent among the proto-cols of Locorotondese notaries in the last decades of the eighteenth century and the beginning of the nineteenth, but still no more than one or two a year were legitimized in writing. However, some of these contracts divided large amounts of land among many tenants. A particularly detailed contract dating to 1795 (ASB-AN, 1767–1796: March 15, 1795) divides 32.6 *tomoli* (28 hectares) of church-chapter land, some of it already enclosed, into 15 small portions ranging from 7 to 24 *quartieri* leased to peasants and artisans, and one large portion of 63.7 *quartieri*, leased to a priest. For each *quartiero* an annual rent of 6 *carlini* was to be paid to the church chapter on the 31st of August *in perpetuo, et mundo durante* (perpetually, and as long as the world lasts). This due date fell after the grain harvest, but before any income from grapes became available, and setting such a date reflected the economic reality that, until the tenants planted land to grapes, the principal income of the emphyteutical lessees came from other kinds of agricultural activities. The contract obligated the tenants to "improve the said portions from year to year with the planting of vines, and to keep them well manured and cultivated, such that within the space of fifteen years they must all be covered with vines and reduced to vineyards." If they failed to do this, the fields could be repossessed by the church chapter. Also if the lessee wished to sell his lease, the church chapter continued to be recognized as owner and to receive the rent, and permission had to be sought to make such a transfer. Three years' default on rent meant automatic return of the land and forfeiture to the chapter of the value of any improvements which had been made.

On the same day that the notary drew up this emphyteusis contract, the tenants on one of the portions being divided drew up an interesting agreement among themselves (ASB-AN, 1767–1796: March 15, 1795). They had, in fact, already taken possession of the land two years earlier and had begun to build on it. The contract says that together they had constructed a cistern which was to be held in common along with the *piazziletto* and threshing floor which fed it water. One of the tenants, Francesco Neglia, had advanced 57 ducats, 5 *carlini* of his own to pay a rural mason for the work, and for repairs on a *trullo* which fell in the portion of the tenant Cipriano Palmisano. The contract records 8 of the tenants as owing Francesco 5 ducats, 5 *grana* each, and Cipriano, to whom the *trullo* belonged, was noted as owing 12 ducats and 5 *grana*. This pair of contracts recorded the beginning of a *jazzeile*. Provision for the collection of rainwater to water animals and a place to thresh had already been made. One tenant, at least, already had a *trullo*.

The stipulations of this emphyteusis contract are typical in that few eighteenth-century contracts were specified as enfranchisable. Enfranchisement meant that the owner established a capitalized value based on the rent, which would satisfy him, and the lessee paid it to gain full possession of the property. Few records of enfranchisement survive. Only one such transaction survives from the eighteenth century and in it the church chapter demanded 30 times the annual rent (ASB-AN, 1729–1780: July 5, 1745). Another enfranchisement contract dates from 1800 which notes that a peasant paid 30 ducats to enfranchise 5 *quartieri* of vineyard (ASB-AN, 1797–1809: March 22, 1800). (See also below.) Sometimes there was a stipulation that upon sale of the contract the owner was to be paid a fifteenth of the price obtained.

Another detailed contract, which dates to 1801, records the concession of 179.3 *quartieri* (19.6 hectares) in Serralta to 20 tenants from Fasano at an average annual rent of 6 *carlini*, 6 *grana* per *quartiero*. The average concession was 8.9 *quartieri* (0.98 hectare) with a range between 2.9 and 13.4, so each tenant paid a mean of five ducats, nine *carlini* a year. The tenants were to transform the land into vineyards at the rate of one *quartiero* per year until completion, and if this was not accomplished the landlady had the right to compel them to do so under threat of expulsion from the contract.

The landlady, the Magnificent Barbara Barnabà, reaped 118 ducats, 6 *carlini*, 2 *grana* annually from her 20 tenants. The contract stated that she had come to the decision to divide her land in Serralta "for her own greater convenience and profit and to reduce it to an improved condition." As in all emphyteusis contracts the tenants were now to pay the land tax, and here there was also an annual feudal tithe owed to the Bailey of Santo Stefano in Fasano, which, unbeknownst to the tenants, would be cancelled five years later with the abolition of feudalism in 1806. This contract, unlike the one reported above, was enfranchisable in 3 cash payments, and is highly unusual among all the contracts examined in this project because it specifies a capitalized value (*capitale fondo*) for each portion. The annual rent was 5 percent of this value and did not accumulate toward enfranchisement. The contract was much like the loans against property of those times in which the principal was the capitalized value of the land, and the annual rent was 5 percent interest payable perpetually, or until the tenant found the where-withall to buy it out. No time limits were placed upon enfran-chisement and this contract, like all contracts of the time, also implicated the heirs and descendants of both parties to its terms. The total capitalized value of the land being divided amounted to the healthy sum of 2,372 ducats, 4 *carlini*. If the tenant wished to sell the contract to another party, the landlady had to be informed so that the personal qualities of the latter could be determined, and so that the old and new tenants would have to pay the transfer fees. Also the landlady was to be given the option to buy whatever improvements he had made.

This contract also contains clauses which point to the beginnings of the formation of a rural hamlet. There were stipulations about leaving corridors open to build access roads and paths to the fields of various individuals, to a commonly held grape pressing floor, to a *jazzeile*, and to a common cistern. Barbara Barnabà conceded rights to passage over these access roads to the tenants. As indicated in the last chapter, Serralta was an inhabited hamlet by at least 1812.

Because not all emphyteusis contracts survive, attempts at quan-tifying amounts of land let for improvement into vineyards founder on the rocks of sampling error and only minimum counts are possible. In the contracts recorded for the last decade of the eigh-teenth century and the first of the nineteenth, landlords conceded at least 178.35 *tomoli* (or 153.2 hectares) to 108 tenants, most of whom headed separate households. Two zones dominate in these conces-sions – Serralta and Pozzomasiello. The first zone was leased and then populated mostly by Fasanese tenants (of which 31), and the second by tenants from Locorotondo. The Morelli family, which took its major interests to Fasano in the early part of the nineteenth century, gradually conceded the second zone, which lies to the west of Locorotondo in the direction of Alberobello, to peasants. The 77 Locorotondese households which took land to improve during these years would have represented about 7 percent of all the households in Locorotondo in 1811. If, however, taking land in emphyteusis in this era also meant a move to the countryside by town-dwelling peasants, as the evidence suggests, this figure represents just over 11 per cent of the population still residing within the walls and *borghi* at the time of the Napoleonic census.

There are some patterns in the frequencies of emphyteusis contracts which Locorotondese notaries drew up during the early to mid-nineteenth century. During the first 3 decades of the century there was little emphyteusis recorded. Some years show no contracts, others one or two, although some of these involve considerable amounts of land and as many as 14 or 15 lessees. But the last 3 years of the 1830s saw considerable activity. Between 1837 and 1839 there were 19 emphyteusis contracts drafted in Locorotondo involving the passage of 99 *tomoli* (85.1 hectares) of land to 82 peasant households, about 6.3 percent of all households in the total population, and about 12.6 percent of the population likely to be remaining in town in that era.[1] Then until 1867, when the run of consultable contracts ends, there were only one or two contracts a year, although, once more, some of them ceded large amounts of land to many peasants.

Several factors explain the sudden concession of land in emphyteusis at the end of the 1830s. First, agricultural wages underwent a considerable increase during the second half of the decade, but fell again to early 1830s levels by the middle of the 1840s. This temporary increase in agricultural wages was a consequence of the grave cholera epidemic of 1836–1837, which, according to a local documentary account, did not cost lives in Locorotondo. However, in neighboring towns – Fasano, Monopoli, Ceglie, Francavilla, Martina Franca, Noci, Putignano, Cisternino – "Cholera swung his sickle and truncated the life of many victims" (ASB-PI, 1822–1844). High levels of sickness and death made able-bodied laborers scarce, and even if Locorotondo was not hit severely by the epidemic, there would have been a demand in neighboring towns for workers, and the local wage would have gone up. Weather conditions made the Locorotondese cereal harvests of 1836 and 1837, respectively, mediocre and poor (ASB-PI, 1822–1844).[2] In addition, during the second half of the 1830s there was a moderate, but temporary, increase in the price of wine which must have stimulated proprietors to consider planting vineyards (Assante, 1974: 211). Obviously, this labor-intensive alternative would have been difficult given high labor costs, and emphyteusis, which secured a steady income while motivating intensive labor, must have seemed a reasonable strategy.

Post-restoration contracts were a bit different from those clustering around the turn of the century. Generally speaking they were more accurate because, after the Napoleonic reforms, they were based upon the more precise cadaster which had three categories for land quality, and which resulted from actual surveying instead of mere declaration of surface area. There were often pacts specifying that olive trees (two to four per *quartiero*) were to be planted among the vines. This may have been a strategy meant to ensure that even after vineyards aged beyond peak productiveness a steady income could be produced from olives.[3] One contract even demanded that the olives be pressed at the landowner's mill (ASB-AN, 1812–67: 29 September, 1838). Rent came due in August during the first 10 years of the contract (before transformation was to be completed), and thereafter in mid-September after the grape harvest. There were specific stipulations that the land tax was to be paid by the lessee. Sometimes default on rent automatically gave the owner the right to appropriate whatever crops might be on the land in lieu of payment. In these contracts there was often the stipulation of a periodic renewal of the terms, often every 20 years, sometimes every 29 years. This was a hedge against the erosion of rents through inflation. The tenant could alienate the lease, but most mid-nineteenth-century contracts specified that a proportion, often a fifteenth, of the sale price was to go to the landlord. The contracts were usually permanent, but a few were specified as enfranchisable at the discretion of the landowner.

Peasant emphyteusis strategies included both planting vineyards and establishing residence in the countryside, and analysis of the French cadaster supports this statistically. On a *contrada* by *contrada* basis, the number of vineyards correlates highly with the number of *trulli*. In a stepwise multiple regression using the entire population of locations recorded in the cadaster (N = 106), with the number of *trulli* considered as the dependent variable, the first variable to enter the regression equation is the number of vineyards, and this independent variable alone accounts for 76.34 percent of the variance (r = 0.87). The addition of number of cereal fields to the equation accounts for another 11.55 percent of the variance (multiple r = 0.94). The problem of course remains that since the word used in the cadaster to specify a *trullo* is *casetta*, an italianization of both *casèdde* (rural dwelling) and *casidde* (*trullo* covered hut), the number of real dwellings is not precisely recoverable, although the 433 households indicated as located in the country in the census must have occupied most of the 495 *trullo* structures recorded in the cadaster.

By and large the lessees were defined in post-restoration contracts as peasants (*contadini*), although other rural occupations (pack animal drivers and rural wall builders, among them) were not lacking. Some contracts specified tenants' addresses. For instance, one lists 18 men as tenants, all but one of whom resided at town addresses (ASB-AN, 1819–67: 29 September, 1838). The exception lived in his rural *trulli* in a country hamlet. We may suppose that those with town addresses eventually moved to the countryside, because population figures strongly indicate the transfer of large numbers of people to the countryside between 1811 and the mid-nineteenth century.

Residence in the countryside was advantageous because the processes of transforming the natural land surface into vineyards was, until the recent introduction of earth-moving equipment, very labor intensive. There are few direct references to soil transformation in the documentary evidence, so it is necessary to project more recent practice back in time.[4] However, it is secure that transformation was necessary because the extremely thin soils which characterized the unmodified land surface of the Murgia dei Trulli, particularly on hilltops such as Serralta where many Locorotondese and Fasanesi took on emphyteusis leases, would not have supported vineyards. The process is worth describing in detail because of its labor intensiveness, and because it appears to be a unique system heretofore unknown in the general literature.

Vineyards were heavily modified artificial fields, traditionally located on hilltops and slopes. Doline bottom land was reserved for cereal production as late as the early twentieth century. (The modern trend of planting vines in richer valley bottoms began within living memory.) Small proprietor households transported earth and transformed fields during the summer months when other viticultural tasks were less pressing, and they created vineyards a row of plants at a time. This process began with removing whatever plant cover grew on the field. On uncultivated land this meant heavy labor because deep-rooted shrubs had to be cleared with mattocks. Peasants then stripped off the topsoil to expose the uppermost rock stratum and piled it nearby. The next step was fracturing and removing the bedrock, stratum by stratum, to a depth of between 50 and 100 centimeters depending on the irregularities which had to be overcome to create a level surface. Fields being terraced on hillsides, of course, presented more difficulties at this point because the down slope side had to be built up. The limestone strata were first pierced with an iron rod with a pointed tempered head and then chipped back from this initial opening with picks. (A similar procedure was adopted in excavations for house cisterns.) Small lenses of soil would be uncovered between the rock strata and these were swept up and combined with the stockpile of topsoil already set aside. The resulting pieces of stone were sorted into several categories by size and could be used for building and wall construction, or to backfill soil quarries. The peasant replaced gravel-sized stones on the new bedrock surface to form a drainage layer 20 to 30 centimeters thick.

Transformers of fields imported soil from deep deposits in sink holes and dolines. Teams of children, age nine and above, would carry baskets of earth from soil quarries up to vineyards and transport stones back down to refill the quarries. They deposited imported soil in a layer between 30 and 50 centimeters thick, and then the viticulturalist replaced the original topsoil forming a final layer 10 to 20 centimeters in depth. The fertile layer of topsoil provided rich nutrients to developing vines, the middle layer of less organic imported soil served to hold water and with time became more organic, and the gravel layer drained excess moisture (Ricchioni, 1958: 358). Also the imported soil was often of a type, called *u veole* in dialect, which was redder than the topsoil and less organic in content. The topsoil was deposited to hoe depth over the layer of imported *veole*, and *braccianti* hoeing vineyards would sink their blades into the soil only until they spotted the color change in soil strata. This protected the roots from hoe damage. If only small amounts of *veole* were available it was spread in only a thin layer to serve has a signal of proper hoe depth (Liuzzi, 1986: 12).

It is not entirely apparent from any of the sources, or from informants, how soil was acquired if it did not occur naturally on property belonging to the incipient vineyard's owner. One informant stated that in his youth (during the first three decades of the century) people never purchased soil, and that if one had a *tomolo* of land one could always find some soil to build up a vineyard. In the past, before massive transformation of most of the surface, such soil deposits may have been more widespread. At any rate, no one questioned remembers paying for such soil. Interestingly, one particularly detailed early nineteenth-century contract specifically stated that, in exchange for stones and manure, the peasants taking on land had rights to soil for transforming their fields from a *lama* (doline) which belonged to the owner (ASB-AN, 1812–1867: 1 May, 1837). Perhaps this was a precise specification of a more common custom. Naturally, the amount of soil imported depended upon the original soil depth in the field under transformation.

Of course the amount of labor, in man-days, necessary for the transformation of a given area of land into a new vineyard, varied according to several factors. Significant among these were the type of plant cover which had to be removed to begin the process, the hardness of the bedrock encountered, and the distance which had to be traversed to import soil to the site. Ricchioni collected quantitative data on transformation in 11 enterprises in the territories of Locorotondo, Martina Franca, and Alberobello in the 1950s. From these data he calculated an index equal to the number of man-days necessary to transform a hectare of land into a vineyard (1958: Tables 5 and 6). This ranged between 1,181 and 4,450 man-days and averaged 2,607, with a standard deviation of 51. (Some of the families interviewed had adopted explosives to fracture the bedrock and this accounts for the minimum he reports.) Estimates made by informants the author interviewed for this project, who remarked that there could be considerable variation, fall well within this range. The most thoughtful and careful informant on this matter, who itemized each activity as he answered interview questions, estimated 2,119 man-days of hand labor (without explosives or mechanized means) to transform a level cleared cereal field of one hectare into a vineyard. This figure, however, did not include enclosing it with stone walls. These estimates dramatize the impressive amount of labour which went into the creation of vineyards in the zone.

The peasant family with land to transform into vineyards, according to a schedule such as those specified in the emphyteusis contracts reported above, faced both the pressure of somehow securing an income to pay the annual rent while the transformation was underway and performing the transformation itself. Taking the middling estimated figure of 2,119 man-days per hectare reported just above, transforming a *quartiero* of land would cost a household about 233 man-days of back breaking labor a year. More would be involved if the land needed clearing, or if it was not level. Contracts specified that land had to be transformed into vineyards within 10 years (more rarely 15), and this meant that for larger parcels the labor had to be carried out at rates equal to and sometimes above one *quartiero* a year. All family members had to be absorbed into the process of creating vineyards and producing rent and subsistence, and residence in the countryside on or near the vineyard site facilitated this by saving transportation time to and from the towns. This would have been especially true for coastal Fasanesi, who took land in emphyteusis high in Locorotondese plateau territory. In addition, once vineyards were transformed, residence in their vicinity facilitated the intensive labor involved in cultivation and keeping up with wall repairs and eroding soil.

Emphyteusis, therefore, was a strong factor in the threefold increase in territory planted to vineyards in Locorotondo between the cadasters of the old and new orders. Undoubtably, peasants also purchased land for improvement into vineyards, and probably planted fields they already owned with vines. Given the fragmentary record, it is difficult to determine the proportionate contribution of each of these factors to the expansion, but emphyteusis stands out both in the documentary record and in folk memory as the most significant factor.

Further trends toward specialization over the first half of the nineteenth century emerge from a report about wine production, sent to the Provincial Intendant in 1856, in which the mayor gave the surface area covered by vines as 12,541 *moggie legali* – then the standard Neapolitan surface measure. Using the communal surface area surveyed in 1816, when the boundaries were established, and converting it to *moggie*, this equals 22 percent of the surface in vineyards (ACL-ABF, 1856a). In a later report, the mayor (ASB-AIC, 1871) wrote that vineyards totaled 966 hectares, or 25.8 percent, of the 3,752 listed as cultivated (however, the amount of uncultivated surface was not listed).

In 1856 the mayor sent the following report on wine production to the provincial Intendant:

In the countryside of Locorotondo there are vineyards in which the vines are all grown as low shrubs. In our parts two kinds of wine are prepared, that is, the fresh and the cooked. The first counts for a tenth portion of the must obtained from the vines and requires nothing but the stirring in of the dregs which rest in the wine until fermentation lifts them as a whole to the surface, after which clear wine is drawn off and put in bottles. The second is prepared by mixing the must with grape syrup in the proportion of eight *caraffe* of the latter in a *barile* of the former. Grape syrup for this purpose is made by reducing a quantity of must over the fire so that one fourth (of the original volume) remains. Wines which are thus prepared have much vigor, grace, raisin flavor, and sweetness, keep for many years without spoiling, and do not become cloudy even during sea voyages. Rather, they clarify and acquire quality, as experience demonstrates every day, such that Sicilians, Neapolitans, and Venetians buy them up and transport them by navigation in different regions of Europe. (ACL-ABF, 1856a)

After 1867 notarial contracts cease to be accessible for Locorotondo and one must depend upon published sources and oral history for information about emphyteusis and related strategies. During the later nineteenth century, especially beginning in the 1880s, because of international demand for wine created by phylloxera and industrial development in the north, and stimulated by the sudden drop in cereal prices, patterns already well established in Locorotondo, and to a somewhat lesser extent, neighboring Cisternino, spread to the other towns of the *murgia*. The spread of viticulture stimulated the construction of *trulli* and an increase in rural population in the general area.

According to Presutti, who conducted the Apulian section of the 1909 parliamentary investigation of the living conditions of peasants, the late nineteenth-century diffusion of viticulture in the towns of the Murgia dei Trulli, and with it rural population, was attributable to the spread of emphyteutic contracts of several kinds. Some were similar to those already reported for Locorotondo; others, more common in the large neighboring territory of Monopoli, took the form of delayed sales under which the peasant paid 6 to 7 percent interest on the price for a period of time varying between 12 and 20 years, and then paid the full price. In essence this was a contract which required enfranchisement. If this payment was impossible, the land reverted to the owner who paid the peasant for two-thirds of the value of improvements made on it (1909: 137). Another kind of emphyteutic contract reported in the literature on the area for the late nineteenth and early twentieth century required that a large entrance payment called a *morto* or *premio*, which amounted to a third to a half of the estimated value of the field, be paid in cash before the tenant could take possession (Ricchioni, 1959: 15). Some emphyteusis contracts were illegally defined as unenfranchisable. (Such clauses became illegal after 1861.) Sigismondo Calella, a Locorotondese gentleman, sometime socialist, later a fascist, and founder of the town's cooperative winery, deplored the kinds of delayed sale and emphyteutic contracts which developed after the First World War (1941: 111). They were less advantageous for the peasant, and he considered these forms of emphyteusis to be bastardizations of the more classic Locorotondese forms.

Although the later nineteenth-century contracts themselves are not accessible to the scholar and their details are therefore obscured, there is evidence from marginal notes in the running cadaster kept in the municipal archives of Locorotondo that estates continued to be divided by emphyteusis throughout the second half of the nineteenth century. For instance, the Grotta estate (now known as Vendura) was listed as totaling 45.5 *tomoli* under its original owner when the cadaster began in 1823 (ACL-CP, 1823–1930: entry for Dura, Don Angelo). In 1871 all but 1.5 *tomoli* passed into the hands of 31 emphyteutic tenants. Similarly the owner divided about 58 *stoppelli* belonging to the Marinosci estate through emphyteusis into two *stoppello* lots among 29 householders in 1873 (ACL-CP, 1823–1930: entry for Marinosci, Don Liborio). Calella notes that after Unification there was an explosion of emphyteusis in some bordering Martinese *contrade*, especially in the "peninsula" of Martina Franca which juts north between Alberobello and Locorotondo. Those who settled these zones long considered themselves Locorotondesi culturally, and some retired into the urban center (1941: 110).

Emphyteusis and transformation of property already under the control of small proprietors in the countryside of Locorotondo accounted for considerable expansion of surface area given to vineyards over the second half of the nineteenth century. The reader will recall that by 1871 about a quarter of Locorotondo's surface area consisted of vineyards. By 1905, according to data supplied to the Provincial Chamber of Commerce, vineyards in Locorotondo covered 2,125 hectares or 46.67 percent of the productive portion of the territory reported in the 1929 cadaster (De Felice, 1971: 469; ISTAT, 1933: *fascicolo* 71, p. 41). By 1929 vineyards accounted for slightly over half of agricultural and forest surface area. Similar expansions occurred elsewhere on the Murgia dei Trulli. Presutti reports, for instance, that in Martina Franca 8,000 proprietors and emphyteutical tenants cultivated 10,000 hectares planted to vineyards (1908: 138).

After the First World War, according to Calella and informants in Locorotondo, the institution of emphyteusis declined and direct sale of plots from divided large estates took its place (1941: 112). The sharp drop in the value of the lira during the First World War must have made long-term emphyteusis leases seem risky to landowners. Purchase became possible as returning emigrants brought home savings earned abroad, or local people borrowed money from relatives. According to Calella (1941: 112) members of the post-war gentry felt increased material exigencies and these inspired sale of estates. After looking for a buyer for his estate, and often failing because there would be few around with that much capital, a landowner in need of money would contract with a go-between, called in dialect an *'mbasciateure*, who would divide the estate in pieces of about a hectare and try to locate a collection of buyers among local peasants. For his trouble the go-between got a good price on a piece of land of his choice. (Essentially the same system had been used before in dividing land into parcels for emphyteutic leasing.) For example, after the First World War, a small group of related Locorotondese peasants settled temporarily in Century, West Virginia to work in coal mining, and returned during the early 1920s to buy portions of a large *masseria* which a gentleman who needed money to educate his children wanted to sell. Calella notes that in 1930 the proprietor divided the San Pantaleo estate (a total of 95 hectares) among 44 farm enterprises, and that in 1931 Casalini, amounting to about 46 hectares, passed into the hands of 32 peasant families (1941: 113). During the Great Depression the price of wine plummeted and many who had borrowed money to buy land lost what they thought they had gained, but by this time the patterns of Locorotondese intensive agriculture had been solidly established for more than a century.

In Locorotondo, by the last decades of the nineteenth century, peasants had totally settled in the countryside, and land which they took on under emphyteusis contracts, or bought, supplemented patrimonies which were eroding through inheritance fragmentation. Emigration formed part of the strategy to acquire enough wherewithal to buy land after the First World War. Unfortunately, year by year emigration statistics are unavailable for Locorotondo before 1900. Rates (see Figure 7.1) reported in official statistical sources for the period between 1900 and 1915 are substantially lower than those of the rest of the Bari area in the same years (Direzione generale della statistica e del lavoro, 1903–1918). This would indicate that, although emigration in Locorotondo, at least among country people, was a strategy for acquiring the capital to buy land, it was a strategy carried out by a lower than average proportion of the population than in the rest of the region, and this can probably be ascribed to successes at capturing land through the emphyteusis strategy in the previous century. Most emigrants returned from the Americas (Calella, 1941: 141). Unlike many other Southern Italian towns, Locorotondo has no significant diaspora which dates from that era (cf. Douglass, 1984).

Evidence suggests that over the second half of the nineteenth century local merchants sold Locorotondese wine on local markets

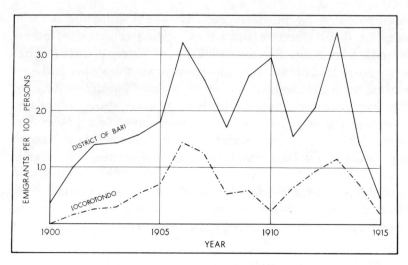

Fig. 7.1. Emigration from Locorotondo and from the District of Bari measured in
persons per hundred between 1900 and 1915. (Source: Drawn from
Direzione Generale della Statistica e del Lavoro, 1903–1918)

and shipped it to other Italian and foreign destinations from local
ports. Police records dating to 1880, which refer to a case of passing
counterfeit money, show that tavern owners in Monopoli, and other
coastal cities, acquired wine directly from peasant proprietors in
Locorotondo (ASB-CD, 1881). This sort of local commerce probably
goes back into the eighteenth century and helps account for the initial
expansion of vineyards along the Locorotondese and Fasanese plateau edges. Alongside direct sale of wine from the peasant household
to individual consumers and taverns, there developed in the countryside the figure of the peasant wine merchant who, alongside profits
from his own production, would buy and market wine produced by
his neighbors. Household produced wine was, however, of uneven
quality. Overseas shipment was well underway as early as 1856
(ACL-ABF, 1856a – see above), and of course expanded as demand
for wine in France grew, and later, after the tariff war, when
protectionism with the Austro-Hungarian empire was relaxed.

Beginning in 1919 major northern vermouth companies, among
them Martini and Rossi and Cinzano, established connections with
wineries in Locorotondo and Martina Franca, and bought most of the
grape production on the market for producing base wine for making
dry white vermouth in the north (Palasciano, 1986: 34). The new

Southeast Railroad, begun just after the turn of the century, which linked the Murgia dei Trulli with Bari and points north, facilitated this commerce. The qualities of local wine which made it ideal for use in vermouth production probably served to strengthen local viticulture and inspire the replanting of vineyards lost to phylloxera, and later to weather the economic crisis after 1929. The vermouth companies, and later, in 1933, the cooperative organized in Locorotondo, changed wine production for the market from an operation carried out by individual producers to one carried out with more quality control on an industrial basis. Of course, peasant households still made wine for their own use, but increasingly they became linked to national and world markets.

EMPHYTEUSIS AND VINEYARD PLANTING AS ADAPTIVE STRATEGIES

The wisdom of Antonio Genovesi's admonition to "divide, divide, but in small portions," would not have been lost on late eighteenth- and early nineteenth-century Locorotondese landowners. Probably the model for emphyteusis was established in the area as a result of earlier strategies undertaken by church organizations, and by 1769 when Genovesi wrote, local landowners must have known it as a possibility. During the old regime, Apulian feudal lords had used similar contracts to settle peasants on their holdings.[5] Recall that the Magnificent Barbara Barnabà specified in the contract described earlier that she was dividing her estate in Serralta "for her own greater convenience and profit and to reduce it to an improved condition." Landowners in Locorotondo sought to make gains from their medium-sized estates more secure. In doing so they took the step of relinquishing part of their control over the means of production, and to explain this we must pay particular attention to the kinds of advantages, both immediate and consciously calculated, and long-term and perhaps not so apparent, which benefited them because of this decision. This approach is informed by Bennett's useful discussion of adaptive processes with immediate and long-term returns, risks, and unforeseen consequences (1976: 282–28).

First it is necessary to recall the nature of the landscape. This is not, nor has it ever been, a naturally productive agricultural zone. Thin rock-strewn soils and exposed bedrock, coupled with the fissures which drained away moisture, conspired with steep slopes to guarantee that production of cereal crops, except in doline bottoms, could only be passable at best. Presutti reports that production of only 5 *quintals* of grain per hectare could be expected on most of the unimproved land in the Murgia dei Trulli area (1909: 155–6). This falls short of expectations in the large estate areas, even of Sicily, where 5 *quintals* per hectare would be considered especially low production, and one could expect double that amount on the average. In fertile Piedmont or Lombardy, 5 to 6 times Locorotondo's cereal production per hectare is common (Rochefort, 1961: 122–123). Therefore, profits from cereal production, once the costs of seed, labor, transport, and taxes were subtracted, provided little incentive for extensive agriculture especially on thin hillside soils.

The low productiveness of unimproved Locorotondese estate land was compounded by climactic fluctuation, especially of rainfall, and year to year risks were great. Of course, price fluctuation for grains and legumes also lent an element of risk to extensive agriculture. Concession of land under emphyteusis took most of these risks off the back of landowners and loaded them on peasant tenants who, in turn, were constrained by the legal threat of loss of land, and their invested labor, to meet a fixed annual payment despite the vicissitudes of the market or of the climate. Further, this secure rent payable to landowners came to them with a minimum of investment of time in agricultural management activities and freed them for leisure, politics, other entrepreneurial activities, or a profession. The symbolic gentlemanly value of landownership, often noted by others writing about the South Italian middle and upper classes (cf. Arlacchi, 1980: 163; Davis, 1973: 73), was preserved, but its risks and time costs were greatly reduced. All this was accomplished alongside unloading the tax burden for the land, and before 1806, tithes to church organizations, on the tenant. Therefore one would expect periods of high taxation to be periods in which emphyteusis proliferated. This fits the pattern of expansion during the last decade of the eighteenth century and the opening decades of the nineteenth when taxes rose.

Landlords probably foresaw several longer term secondary advantages. First, default on annual rent for three years meant the land reverted without compensation to the landowner with whatever improvements tenants had made. The economic and political crises of the late eighteenth century in Southern Italy saw many emphyteutical tenants elsewhere face loss of their lands because the annual rents could not be met (Masi, 1966: 40–42). Memory of this must have played a part in decisions to concede land during the earlier parts of the nineteenth century, because the concession of land in emphyteusis brought with it not only secure rents for a period of time, but also the distinct possibility of recouping greatly improved land without having made any investment. Such land could be cultivated with hired workers, sold, leased, or passed into another emphyteutical contract at a higher annual rent. Second, an emphyteutical contract forged a legal link between the landlord and tenant which must have been exploitable outside strictly economic terms. A lessee who was unable to come up with his rent would have been at the mercy of the landlord and the latter would have been able to extract favors and services in exchange for leniency. Third, as contracts drawn up during the first half of the nineteenth century show, sale of rights to the land by the tenant was legitimate, but only with the landowner's permission, and the latter expected to reap some of the price. Fourth, in individual cases profitable stipulations, such as the requirement that the tenants' olives be milled at the landowner's mill, could be included and enforced legally.

Landowners may not have consciously calculated other secondary advantages of their adaptive strategy, but these were apparent over the long run. In a society periodically subject to social and political upheavals, emphyteutical tenants and peasant landowners were less subject, as Genovesi put it, to "excitations and steam vents" – less likely to join in peasant rebellions, because, having captured relatively secure control of productive resources, their interests were privatistic. Unenthusiastic peasant reaction during the events of 1799, 1820, 1848, and the brigandage period reflected the essential rural conservativeness of the place. At the same time, the peasant who took land in emphyteusis faced immediate needs for cash to pay rent and taxes and was forced to continue participation in the local labor market until enough land was acquired for self-sufficiency, and to provide for his children at marriage. Therefore, the landowning class in general, in Locorotondo as well as in neighboring towns (where throughout much of the nineteenth century larger estates remained intact), was not entirely deprived of a labor force. Further, the continuing development of small proprietor viticulture in the Murgia dei Trulli area, as a commercial enterprise, contributed to the growth of its general economy during the nineteenth century. The 1883 *Annuario Storico-Statistico-Commerciale di Bari e Provincia* (a gazetteer and directory of businesses and institutions for the Province of Bari) notes that Locorotondese commerce in wine domestically and abroad "can be said to have given rise to the general and almost disproportionate prosperity of the town" (Mele, 1883: 230).

The adaptive strategy of emphyteusis carried with it some risks for the landowner as well. Rents fixed in the contract could be eroded by inflation, and therefore the secure income the owner bargained for in entering the relationship could be reduced greatly. (Conversely, during periods such as the middle of 1870s when the value of the lira grew, the peasant paid a higher rent than he had bargained for.) Middle nineteenth-century contracts began to stipulate a review and renewal after 20 to 29 years, probably as a hedge against this danger. A second risk was total loss of the land through its enfranchisement by the peasant tenant. Before laws changed to the contrary in 1861, this was sometimes prevented by clauses which ruled it out. Land-lords also took a risk with tenant competency to transform land into vineyards and to produce enough to satisfy the annual rent, or indeed with the competency of heirs or purchasers of the contract to do the same. The common stipulation that sale of the lease required the landlord's permission combatted the latter concern, and his rights to a portion of the price, or to an option on purchasing the improve-ments, may have operated to reduce the peasant's temptation to sell the contract at all, much less to incompetent tenants.

There were also several long-term risks of which landowners could only become conscious as time went on. The same stability of smallholder peasants which quelled the temptation to participate in peasant uprisings and produced a general peasant conservatism, could also mean that peasant labor, although never totally absent for reasons noted, could at the same time be scarce, and expensive for elite landowners. It is notable that labor in Locorotondo was, at least within the memory of informants, recruited on an individual basis and not at the early morning town-square labor market common in other Southern Italian locales, including neighboring Martina Franca, which had a town dwelling peasantry. In essence laborers did not have to sell themselves in Locorotondo, they had to be sought out by prospective employers. Similarly, movement of the peasantry outside the town, in conjunction with the expansion of viticulture through emphyteusis, complicated control by elite interests. Evidence of this concern first appears in the document from 1827, cited earlier, in which the town administration attempted to move the straying peasantry back within the crumbling walls. (Other attempts to control the peasantry will be examined in Chapter 9.)

What the peasant maximized through emphyteusis and rural settlement as an adaptive strategy was control over land when none had been owned before, or more was needed to provide dowries and settlements for children. Land, until recently the basis of almost all wealth in South Italy, not only had symbolic value for the higher classes and stood at the basis of their ascendancy, but meant a measure of security and independence for the Locorotondese peasantry, which invested enormous amounts of human capital in its capture. Once a peasant family acquired land, the incentive to get more, and cultivate well what had been captured, continued because of the necessity of providing the following generation with an adequate patrimony. Land, even in small amounts, meant a degree of independence for the peasant, particularly in this adaptive strategy which also included rural residence. At the least it meant a patch of ground upon which to grow food; in the long run it meant partial escape from the unemployment and underemployment typical of the uncertain agricultural-worker labor market, and from dreadful poverty, amply described for other locales in the south (cf., Dolci, 1959: 168–173; Blok, 1974: 47; or Snowden, 1986: chapt. 2).

The drive to develop and perpetuate a patrimony was a powerful one which must have been possible only with an attitude which did not figure labor costs in a strictly capitalistic fashion. Such an attitude is similar to that hypothesized by Chayanov (Chayanov, 1966: 4–6) for the peasant household, but that model is difficult to apply fully to Locorotondo because it was developed for a peasant agricultural system isolated from wages and production for profit measured in money. As noted in the description of soil transformation earlier, the investment of labor in the prospect of capturing land was enormous. The adaptive strategy was fed by, and in turn fed, a driving attitude toward hard work. Even now it is common to hear peasants' sons, who primarily work in the building trades, talk about how they are well aware that cultivating family vineyards and fields after work, and on weekends, is uneconomical if one considers family labor in terms of wages. But they feel driven to try to keep land producing to maintain the patrimony and produce "genuine" wine, olive oil, and flour for home consumption. The major calculated objectives of the peasant strategy in Locorotondo were therefore the acquisition of land, the ability to transfer that land to heirs, and for some kinds of emphyteusis, the eventual possibility of outright ownership through enfranchisement. Locorotondese peasants sought to satisfy both a yearly need for subsistence, and long-term sets of needs concerning the marriage of children and their entry into the rural peasant adaptive strategy.

Certain unforeseen advantages also accrued to peasant tenants. Unpredictable periods of inflation eroded long-term rent payments. Moving to Locorotondo's countryside from the town, and, as noted, to an extent from the neighboring town of Fasano, served to reduce stress produced by deadlines for transformation within emphyteusis contracts. Enormous amounts of labor were necessary for transformation, but the peasant grape grower lived near his fields and wasted little time in travel, and could therefore pour more labor into their cultivation. The formation of peasant hamlets, the *jazzèlere*, which contained shared facilities such as threshing and crushing floors, and cisterns, provided the kind of fixed capital that a large landowner had to provide individually for his enterprise at his estate headquarters. This move to the country, so nicely crystallized in the "church bell" proverb, had the consequence of creating a separate Locorotondese peasant culture which evolved a values system that rewarded hard work and "taking a step ahead" for coming generations. It also created a structure for prestige divorced from the heartless stratificational system typical of other South Italian towns (cf. Snowden, 1986: 47 ff.).

It should not be forgotten that in return for the rewards of the strategy, peasants paid high prices. The Italian literature on the area which I have cited (Presutti, 1909; Calella, 1941; Maranelli, 1946) tends to draw the contrast between the peasantry of the Murgia dei Trulli and the more proletarianized peasantry of other nearby zones quite sharply, and to ignore the difficulties the strategy held for its peasant protagonists, who are seen as nobly conquering land with the sweat of their brows. One price was increased exposure to theft of household objects, gold, stores of food, or animals. Rural isolation presented easy opportunities to thieves. Such dangers increased somewhat during periods of social upheaval or economic crisis, such as the periods of brigandage experienced during the French decade and later after national unification. *Trullo* doors traditionally had holes bored in them for a shotgun muzzle and large iron hooks and eyes which braced them securely shut from inside.

Another cost was that, unlike Chayanov's model peasant household, the Locorotondese peasant household could not operate on a purely subsistence basis because the landowner's side of the strategy demanded the production, not only of crops, but also of cash. Money was necessary for paying taxes and for paying emphyteutic rent. Emphyteutic contracts read that the annual rent was to be paid in cash, often in silver coin, as opposed presumably to payment in kind or lesser coinage. During the first years of transformation, before a salable crop was established, these exigencies must have guaranteed that tenant peasants and their family members worked long hours for others to earn wages in cash. Subsistence crops of fava beans and sometimes grain, planted almost seed by seed on the ridges between vines, helped feed families, and residence in the countryside probably facilitated this "agricultural involutional" practice (cf. Geertz, 1963), but despite peasant ideals about distance from town, participation in a cash economy kept them connected to the "bell towers" and the *piazza* of Locorotondo, and, ultimately, to international markets.

OTHER FACTORS IN PEASANT RESETTLEMENT

The population of Locorotondo doubled over the sixty years which separated the *catasto onciario* and the census taken in 1811 and did so again by the early twentieth century. This population expansion created a need for additional housing. In fact, some of the expanding population spilled outside the old crumbling walls of the town into the new neighborhood, or *borghi*, which probably arose during the late eighteenth century, and which, by the 1811 census, housed about 6 percent of the total population of households recorded. The largest of these extramural neighborhoods, the Borgo di Bonifacio comprised 38 households, and the smaller Borgo di San Rocco housed 23. A map published by Baccaro (1968: 3), based on one drawn during the first decades of the nineteenth century, shows these *borghi* clearly, and another smaller one, Borgo di Santo Spirito. That author (1968: 33) ascribes the church of San Rocco, which was outside the walls, to the latter part of the eighteenth century, and it is reasonable to suppose that a suburb grew around it.

Alongside promoting the formation of extramural town neighborhoods, population increase and shortages of housing within the walls must have played a part in driving landowning peasants into the countryside, into either newly constructed *trulli* or habitations remodeled from what had been field *trulli* meant as temporary shelters. By 1811 41.1 percent of households recorded in the town rented their cramped housing – recall that the vast majority of town

dwellers occupied bottom floor, one-room houses. This figure represents an expansion of five times the proportion forced to rent housing
recorded in the 1749 cadaster (8.3 percent). Times were hard during
this period. Such expansion of renting must have represented increasing financial inability to construct new housing at the point of
household formation, although expansion into new town housing
outside the walls indicates that this was not true of all new families.
New construction in the *borghi*, carried out by the middle and upper
classes, also provided rental housing and income because these classes
resided above the ground floor and their houses included ground-level
rental space for artisan shops or living quarters.

House rentals, unfortunately, went unrecorded with notaries and
the amounts of rents were not recorded in the census. However, the
catasto provvisorio and the documents which went into its preparation, provide a sense of the average values of various kinds of
buildings. The preparatory materials for the cadaster assumed that
annual taxable income for a building could be figured at 5 percent of
its market value – an estimate of what it would rent for. An
examination of even minimal town dwellings, usually with an alcove
and perhaps a small second room, in comparison with simple *trulli* in
the countryside, shows that the former were taxed on the average at
just over five times the value of income from the latter. An upper
one-room dwelling, was taxed at almost seven times the assumed
taxable value of a *trullo*.

There are few contracts which record the sale of *trulli*, but one
dating from 1796 legalized the sale of a double *trullo*, obviously
comprising a habitation and small proprietor enterprise with a
chicken coop, a pigsty, and certain rights in a *jazzeile*, such as a
portion in the common cistern, threshing floor, and grape squeezing
basin, for the sum of 40 ducats (ASB-AN, 1761–1796, *Emptio
Casellarum et aliorum membrorum*). Prices for town house sales
during the period 1798–1808 were recorded among the preparatory
papers for the *catasto provvisorio*, and although some ground-floor
dwellings sold for as little as 25 ducats (there is nothing in the record
about condition or size), most, especially those with access to a
cistern, sold for prices around 100 ducats, and sometimes more. In
1798 a *sottano* in the Borgo di San Rocco with a cistern and other
unspecified amenities even sold for 200 ducats (ASB-LRCP, 1815–
1817).

Peasants in the decades around the beginning of the nineteenth century faced several choices about housing. Given inheritance of a town dwelling, or an adequate cash marriage settlement, they could reside within the walls or in one of the growing *borghi* outside them without paying rent. Often, however, marriage settlements which included town housing stipulated that space had to be shared with sisters, or that aged parents were to have lifetime rights to residence, and this must have created difficult and cramped living conditions. Few of the settlements examined from the notarial archives in the decade before the census of 1811 provided lump sums which would have been adequate to purchase even minimal town housing outright. Also, in many cases parents promised sums of money, but, at first, only provided an annual 5 percent interest payment for 4 or 5 years. Such sums may have been adequate to provide house rents in the early years of a marriage. Rarely did parents promise more than 100 ducats to either party to a marriage; sums between 40 and 60 ducats were more common, and these were often specified in the value of land being passed on, rather than in cash. Of course, debts could be incurred to support purchase of town houses, but beginning a marriage deeply in debt in those hard times must have been an unwelcome choice.

Peasants with land, however, had another option and this was moving into an existing rural *trullo*, or constructing a new one. At least small amounts of rural property were, as seen, widely distributed and rural residence would have been an option for many. *Trulli* which had been simple temporary shelters could be readily expanded into permanent housing, especially considering the small size of the rural dwellings which parents promised to their sons. One who walks the countryside and takes pleasure in exploring abandoned *trulli* finds that each one has a history of expansion; they seem to have grown almost as if they had been cells dividing, and clues such as steps between adjacent floor surfaces survive to tell this tale. The crowded nature of town housing precluded this sort of expansion.

The inheritance of land also meant the inheritance of a surface upon which to construct a *trullo*. Construction of a town house must have meant purchase of land at a considerable price. Unfortunately, no records about the costs of construction of rural *trulli* or urban housing during this era survive.[6] But given their relative values, it must have been cheaper to build the former, especially since stone for rural houses was often quarried on site in the process of excavating the cistern or transforming property into vineyards. In addition, rectilinear wall masonry in town relied more fully upon square dressed mortared stone, but the free-form *trulli* of this early era were built with techniques which resembled those used in rural walls which were constructed of unmortared stones of unequal sizes.[7] Quarrying, transporting, and dressing the stone for the former also must have been more expensive.

Of course, because population expansion was general to the region, other Apulian towns faced similar housing shortages and developed *borghi*, but not extensive rural settlement. Above all the choice to move "far from the church bells" depended upon already possessing land in the countryside, or upon the hope that some could be acquired through emphyteusis. This is what is peculiar to Locorotondo. A combination of factors allowed the small proprietors of Locorotondo to weather the crises at the end of the eighteenth century and the beginning of the nineteenth without losing their land, and although the general distribution of wealth continued to be quite unequal, many peasants had at least a small plot. During the eighteenth century some settled rural population already existed in at least the *jazzèlere* associated with San Marco and in a few other places, and this pioneer population must have served as a model for betrothed peasant couples contemplating their choices with respect to the establishment of a household. If a town house was economically impossible, an investment in hard work at breaking the rock strata on a bit of inherited land to form a cistern, and then working alongside a master *trullo* builder to put up a house for a new family was always a possibility. In fact it was a possibility akin to the hope that peasant families could aspire to the capture of land to transform into a vineyard through emphyteusis, and it is secure that both aspirations often went hand in hand.

Considering questions of housing also clarifies the sense of alarm expressed in the peasant removal documents dating to 1827. Not only were peasants slipping away from the control exerted over them by church and town authorities, they were slipping away from potential landlords into independence with respect to housing. In 1811, 179 landlords owned rental housing in Locorotondo. The vast majority of these were ordinary townsmen who owned a single piece of property which was most often adjacent to their own. However, about 17 percent of landlords were elite (as indicated by the application of the titles "Don" or "Signore" to their names). Indeed, almost every prominent family in Locorotondo was a rental property owner, and several, Don Francesco Conti who owned eight houses, Don Francesco de Bernardis, who owned six, and the sisters Papatodero, who rented out four dwellings, were, for a town of Locorotondo's size, real estate magnates. For some of these families rental property was a considerable portion of income, for others only a minor part, but continuing movement of peasants into the countryside threatened that income, whatever it was – hence the fruitless attempt to move peasants back to town.

Rural housing was taxed at a considerably lower rate than urban housing, but this would have attracted householders into the countryside only after the Napoleonic tax-reform laws under which housing became taxable. Other taxes might, however, have become more readily escapable through residence in the countryside. Control over the exaction of various excise taxes (which became particularly onerous during the second half of the 1790s and contributed to the discontent which led to peasant turbulence in the kingdom through the turn of the century) would have been far more difficult for tax collectors trying to watch over a population dispersed in the countryside. The mayor said as much in 1827 when he noted that tax collection, along with other functions having to do with the "public good," had become "bound up and difficult" as a result of Locorotondo's unusual settlement pattern. Also living in the countryside probably facilitated participation in underground economies such as trade in contraband foodstuffs.[8]

Lastly, another reason for peasants to relocate in the countryside was greater distance from the heated political situation in town. Unfortunately we can only infer this possibility; there are no documents which demonstrate it conclusively. The intensity of politicization and factionalization of life in early nineteenth-century Locorotondo is, however, amply demonstrated by judicial and police records, and other kinds of documents. Throughout the nineteenth and early twentieth centuries, powerful men engaged in feuds which implicated those around them and sometimes resulted in violence.

In essence, in the absence of any other means to assert power, the peasants "voted with their feet" with respect to the local power structure. This, however, would not have been possible without a subsistence base in the countryside, and here again the prevalence of emphyteusis and the widespread distribution of small properties in Locorotondo must be invoked. Political control of the peasantry would not, however, become crucial to the capture of political power until after the franchise was extended in the early twentieth century, and no effective means was established to assert such control until after the inauguration of the Republic of Italy in 1946.

SUMMARY

At the end of the eighteenth century and through the first half of the nineteenth, a number of factors combined to promote the transfer of population from inside the town walls and the newly developing *borghi*, to *trullo* hamlets in the countryside. Very significant among these factors is the fact that peasant small property survived the turmoil of the end of the old regime and the Napoleonic era. Some peasants could move out to land they already owned, when they became pressured by the high cost of town housing. Others could take some on under an emphyteusis arrangement. This was not the case everywhere, as various historians of the period have pointed out. Two things can be seen as contributing to the survival of peasant small property in Locorotondo. First of all, as noted in Chapter 6, the period between 1770 and 1790 saw an expansion of tree crop agriculture particularly in the Terra di Bari. Most of this was coastal expansion of olive groves. Covering the coastal plain with a mono-crop of olive trees pushed viticulture up onto the hillsides and must have stimulated grape production in the upper reaches of Fasano and along the plateau edge of Locorotondo. The high number of Fasanese proprietors cultivating grapes in Locorotondese territory at the time of the Napoleonic cadaster, along with concessions of land to Fasanesi under emphyteusis, suggest an expanding demand for wine along the coast. A second factor in the survival of peasant small property in Locorotondo must have been the existence of a functioning grain bank. One will recall that Locorotondo's grain bank was one of only a handful which made it intact through these times. The *monte* helped provide a safety net for the peasantry of Locorotondo during particularly bad years by loaning both seed, and, as is evident from the records of transactions which can be examined, grain for subsistence in the winter.

A number of factors made it advantageous for the town's land-owning elite to divide and lease estates under emphyteusis. These included escape from tax, management, and risk worries and the guarantee of a relatively steady income from poor karst land which they could not themselves afford to make productive. Of course, emphyteusis *ad meliorandum et pastanandum* would not have been feasible if there had not been demand for wine in the zone, and if the local peasant population had not had some experience in the previous century with viticulture. Elite landowners, who were themselves insufficiently well off to afford the intensive labor involved in planting vineyards, found in emphyteusis a way to meet demand for grape production. During the late 1830s they also found a way out of an unfavorable economic situation through this kind of contract.

The peasantry of Locorotondo took advantage of landowner adaptive strategies to capture pieces of land, and therefore greater possibilities for themselves and their children. The nature of the work of transforming land into vineyards and the advantages of living in the countryside as opposed to paying rent to a landlord in town, as well as higher taxes, propelled peasant families into the countryside in increasing numbers throughout the first half of the nineteenth century. This population movement alarmed the elite of the town and they made, in 1827, an abortive attempt to curb it through force. They seemed unaware that the exodus of the town's peasantry was at least in part an unintended consequence of the actions of those among them who had adopted emphyteusis as an adaptive strategy.

The move to the countryside brought about a separate peasant culture which developed values about work that were quite different from those held by people who remained inside the town walls, and indeed with peasants elsewhere who had less of a stake in land. Work for Locorotondese peasants became the supreme value, and it is not hard to understand why. Intensive work, in combination with land ownership and the emphyteusis contract, brought at least small amounts of prosperity and security, especially in comparison to the bulk of nearby peasant worker populations. The concluding chapters of this book will examine some other important social structural, political, and cultural implications of this separation of peasant from town culture.

Part III

EMERGENT SOCIAL AND POLITICAL PATTERNS

Chapter 8

RURAL SOCIAL STRUCTURE

During the development of the agricultural strategies detailed in the last chapters, the peasantry of Locorotondo also evolved strategies for living socially in the countryside. Only a few glimpses of these are visible in the historical documentation, and a sense of them must be created by working back from the voices of those who can be asked about their own lives and the lives of their parents and elder relatives. Chapter 2 introduced the reader to the unusual nature of the Locorotondese countryside and showed how peasant and post-peasant values strongly center upon the theme of work. It should be clear from the last chapters that those values arose in conjunction with a set of strategies adopted by both elite landowners and peasants which often allowed the latter to make a "step ahead" through hard work. To round out a sense of these adaptive strategies, the questions to be answered in this chapter include: What kinds of structures and institutions did this peasantry evolve? What was the nature of the peasant family? What sorts of conflicts and tensions were a consequence of these adaptive strategies?

The chapter will begin with a detailed description of the formation of households in a particular *jazzeile* in an effort to cast light on cultural norms having to do with inheritance of houses and residence pattern, as well as upon the kinds of conditions and circumstances which could lead to their violation. Then comes a description of household formation and authority structures inherent in the Locorotondese peasant family in the recent past. The discussion will then return to the topic of the *jazzeile* and treat relationships with neighbors, a poignant theme in everyday country life. The discussion will focus upon Locorotondo's peasant cultural system during the first half of this century – a period by which the adaptive strategy of dispersed settlement, and small proprietorship had fully formed. Where possible, continuities with the nineteenth century will be documented. Although there have been significant changes in the economic basis of life in the countryside, especially after about 1960, the social structure described in this chapter also shows strong continuities in the postpeasant society of the present.

THE "JAZZEILE"

To understand country social structure one best begins with the *jazzeile*, or rural hamlet. Some *jazzèlere* date back several centuries and result from early settlement of peasants in the countryside. Others result from the division of *masseria* farmyards and include pitched-roof buildings originally intended for the landowner's summer residence, but now taken over by peasant families. Not all rural Locorotondesi live in *jazzèlere*; many live close to each other along roads, but do not share common space as do *jazzeile* dwellers. However, the *jazzeile*, with its advantages and disadvantages, is typical of Locorotondo's countryside situation, and examination of processes of inheritance and household formation in a *jazzeile* illuminates many of the norms and social structural tendencies of general rural culture.

A particular jazzeile

The *jazzeile* in question lies in the northerly reaches of the municipal territory.[1] This hamlet is a collection of seven houses, all but one *trulli*. Owners have recently abandoned several of these and remodeled them to rent to tourists during the summer. Nowadays a paved road runs in front of the *jazzeile* – which consists of a U-shaped collection of buildings scattered about a common space. The area still contains the remnants of a threshing floor, several cisterns, and once contained a four-celled manure enclosure which fronted on the road, a grape squeezing floor, and a cistern for fermenting wine. Residents held common rights in these components, as well as the right to stack firewood in the central space. The settlement does not appear to have been associated with a particular *masseria*, and is located in an area of rural Locorotondo long occupied by small proprietors. There is a *trullo* in the group which bears the date "1879," but it was not necessarily the first building. The *jazzeile*'s name, which bears no relationship to any of the nicknames of families remembered to have lived there, probably refers to a nineteenth-century resident, perhaps the founding family. In fact, a man with a similar nickname owned land in this vicinity according to the *catasto provvisorio*.[2]

A man nicknamed Scardeine (the significance is unsure), who people remember as having come from Martina Franca, built the house dated 1879. Country folk in Locorotondo most often refer to each other by *razze*, nickname, and people often do not know the true surnames of their neighbors. Nicknames are usually inherited in the male line, but there are occasional exceptions to this rule, and since they are part of oral tradition they change. For instance, the son of Serocche (It. *scirocco* – the hot southeastern wind) became known as Maltimpe, "Bad Weather." People may refer to others, especially to adult men, by the nickname alone, or often in combination with a name, kinship term, or the preposition "of" (*de*) meaning "affiliated with," as in "Tonètte Scardeine" "the daughter of Scardeine," or Tonètte de Scardeine." In Locorotondo, unlike certain other Southern Italian contexts, the Island of Pantelleria, for instance, one may use a nickname in the presence of its owner without insult. Some nicknames have colorful meanings and people enjoy their use.[3] Many originated in the course of linguistic playfulness. Others, perhaps because they are combinations of archaic dialect words which have become unrecognizably scrambled together, have lost their meanings.

Scardeine's *trulli* consisted of a complex set of spaces containing stalls, silos, and wine-processing areas, and even a large wine barrel. The *trulli* next door belonged to a contemporary of Scardeine's who went by the nickname Purcheneure ("Black Pig"). Scardeine, at an age of over 60, married a woman whose name no one remembers, and she produced two sons, Cicce (Francesco) and Giuanne (Giovanni). For the marriage of Cicce, the elder son, Scardeine built a house in a nearby zone, and passed on no rights in the *jazzeile* to him. In 1921, at the age of twenty-two, Giuanne, because he was the youngest son, and according to the local rule of ultimogeniture by which youngest sons inherit their parents' houses, took over his father's *trulli* and rights in the *jazzeile*. He married Tonètte (Antonietta) Purcheneure, the girl next door, who died young after bearing two children, Jangiue (Angelo) and Roseine (Rosina).

After Tonètte's death, Giuanne cohabited with Comasie, who came from the other side of the hamlet, and whose husband had abandoned her in favor of another (see below). She brought a child with her. Comasie lived in the *trulli* until her death in 1978 enjoying the *vetedurante* (lifetime habitation rights) left her by Giuanne u Scardeine. His daughter Roseine married out of the *jazzeile* and resides with her husband elsewhere, and Jangiue, who died at middle age in a tragic accident, built a larger house a few hundred meters away, but outside the *jazzeile*, upon his marriage. However, since by default he was the heir to the *trullo*, he maintained rights in the *jazzeile* components – the cisterns, threshing floor, and so on. The building is now split between Janguie's daughters Tonètte and Zèlle (Graziella), such that the former owns the stalls and work spaces, and the latter the living quarters, which she and her husband have remodeled into property to rent to summer sojourners.

"Black Pig's" house, next door, dates to the same era as Scardeine's. The oldest remembered proprietor married a woman nicknamed Scaccioppele ("Artichoke") who produced three girls and a boy. The eldest daughter married elsewhere, and Tonètte, the second daughter, married next door. The boy, who by the rule should have inherited the *trullo*, died young without marrying, so it passed to the youngest daughter Nennèlle, who married Carue (Carlo). This couple produced four girls and a boy and here again the *trullo* was split between two daughters, one of whom rents to tourists. Both daughters enjoy rights to the hamlet's components. Being of the generation which began to find *trullo* architecture too confining, the son chose to build elsewhere.

Another *trullo* belonged to Ciucceridde ("Little donkey"), an approximate contemporary of the sons of the original Scardeine and "Black Pig." He married, but producing no children adopted a girl named Janne (Anna) and made her his heir in exchange for *servetutene* – care for him and his wife in their old age. (It is not clear whether Janne was a relative; such adoptions were often made among nieces and nephews.) Janne, who inherited the *trullo* married Cicce and before she died they had two children. Then Cicce remarried with Lilleine a Cucciaridde ("Little spoon"), his deceased wife's sister. (This marriage met no particular expectation, and does not reflect a rule about the sororate.) His son by Janne died and the daughter lives elsewhere, as does a daughter by Lilleine. Currently the old couple continues to reside in the *trullo*.

Next comes the *trullo* of Uesteine (Agostino), who died an octogenarian just before the author carried out fieldwork. This man married Jannemariggje (Annamaria) and produced two boys and a girl. The elder son built elsewhere, the daughter married the boy next door and resides in the *jazzeile*, and by ultimogeniture Uesteine's *trullo* went to

Giuanne, his younger son. However, Giuanne, discontent with *trullo* living, built a new house in the *jazzeile* where he lives with his wife from a neighboring town and two children. His mother, Jannema-riggje, goes *mési-mési* ("month-month"), rotating among her three children, because she is too feeble to care for herself.

Adjacent to Uesteine's *trullo* is that of Giuannidde u Prieore ("the Prior"), who married the younger daughter of his neighbor. Giuan-nidde inherited the house from his father's sister's husband, who had no children and who adopted him in return for care. Giuannidde's sons had not yet married at the time interviews were conducted.

Last come the *trulli* of Comà ("co-mother") Vetodde. Vetodde's first husband Coleine (Nicola) died, and Giuanne u Teore ("the Bull"), who owned the *trulli*, deserted his wife Comasie and a son (who both went to live with Giuanne u Scardeine in the *trullo* of the Scardeine line), and took up with her. (The desertion of Comasie, and her subsequent cohabitation with Giuanne u Scardeine, must be considered highly atypical in Locorotondese peasant society.) Comà Vetodde had three children by her husband, and four by her companion, all seven of whom moved out of the *jazzeile* leaving the *trullo* abandoned.

Jazzeile patterns

Several principles and tendencies operate in this example. First, all children should live in households separate from each other and from their parents. The proverb: *Do peit jint'a na scarpe nen ce potene stè* (Two feet can't be in the same shoe), underlines the strong value placed upon the formation of nuclear households and neolocal residence. It especially applied to the residences of younger sons because of the rule that they inherit their parents' house and its contents. This dwelling was separated from that of parents by dividing or expanding the household into two separate residences upon the son's marriage. The younger son's inheritance of an established household, and farm headquarters, came in return for caring for parents as they approached the age at which they would begin to circulate among their children, and in compensation for not receiving a new house at marriage like older brothers did. Although, there is some evidence of temporary patrilocal residence from early nineteenth-century documents, any such regular expectation had disappeared by the period remembered by informants.

However, the general rule of male ultimogeniture for parental houses was frequently disrupted. The most obvious cases were those where there were no sons (or where they died before marriage) and the house went to a daughter. In such cases *trulli* passed into lines bearing other patrilineally inherited nicknames and surnames. When couples had no heirs, or when individuals owning houses did not marry, the form of adoption known as *servetutene* (servitude) came into play, the adopted child playing the role of a youngest son (or sometimes daughter) in caring for the adoptive parent in exchange for inheriting the house and its contents and a marriage settlement. Commonly, old people adopted the child of a sibling as an heir in return for servitude (cf. Brettell, 1986: 44–45). The adopted child's parents might welcome this because it relieved them of the burden of providing a marriage settlement, a particularly heavy burden if they had produced many children who would need houses, land, and trousseaus.

Parents were (and are) expected to provide new, or remodeled houses for their other sons, and doing so was a source of pride. Therefore, there was a tendency for *jazzèlere* to contain partial patrilines expressed through younger sons. In the twentieth century elder sons often built elsewhere because of restricted space available in the *jazzeile*. However, in the first formation of *jazzèlere*, some of which was glimpsed in the last chapter, fathers could build sons' houses adjacent to their own, producing little patrilineal enclaves within them. This was probably advantageous with respect to exchanging labor *a vègete* (in turn). However, as time went on, and as ever more distant cousins inherited buildings, the pattern was interrupted and the hamlets of Locorotondo contained more families which considered themselves unrelated. Larger *jazzèlere* contained unrelated families from their beginnings because groups of unrelated men would take on emphyteusis contracts in the same zone.

Examples of provisions for old people besides servitude spring from this *jazzeile*. Typically, parents divided their remaining property when the youngest child married, although usufruct and residence rights for parents continued, especially if they remained able bodied. Houses might be passed in inheritance to youngest sons but parents or in this case, Giuanne u Scardeine's aged companion Comasie, would be given lifetime residence rights – in dialect called *vetedurante*, which derives from a Latin legal term meaning "for the duration of the lifetime of," – which exist in notarial contracts dating to the eighteenth century. In earlier times, when life expectancies were shorter, providing for aging parents would have been a lighter burden for most people.

In peasant Locorotondo, especially before old age pensions became available, children shared the subsistence of their retired parents by providing *mantenemènte*. Each contributed equal portions of grain, fava beans, garbanzo beans, grapes to make wine, and often milk to make cheese. The grain portions were payable upon the end of the agricultural year in mid-August. Now, even though aged parents live on pensions, they expect their children to provide wine, or grapes to make it, and sometimes cheese, because of their concern about consuming "genuine" home-made products. Historical examples of this institution can be found in a few eighteenth-century notarial contracts, and therefore it has considerable time depth among local peasants producing their own subsistence (ASB–AN, 1683–1729: September 9, 1725, for instance).

In the countryside of Locorotondo, but not in the town, an infirm parent "went month–month" (*scève mési-mési*), circulating monthly from child to child. This was a strong expectation. Parents had to be taken care of and provided for out of respect, and in return for the sacrifices they made to establish their children's households. Rarely, if both parents were alive but infirm and caring for both was too much of a burden for single families at a time, they might be split up and circulate separately. Relatively healthy widowers, because their domestic skills were little developed, were more likely to circulate than widows. Country parents scrutinized their sons' marriage choices with the hope that the daughters-in-law would provide loyal and respectful care. This was especially true of women engaged to marry youngest sons who would divide a house with their parents. The circulation of sickly parents among their children is an institution which continues in postpeasant rural Locorotondo. An exception occurs, however, when a parent is too sickly to be moved comfortably. In such cases the parent will move in with one child on a longer-term basis, or a child will provide daily care at the parent's house, especially if it is nearby. That care might rotate. The expectation of going *mési mési* seems to be limited to the Locorotondese countryside. In nearby Fasano, for instance, the community expects youngest daughters to care for their parents.

Proximity with in-laws was sometimes a source of conflict in country neighborhoods, and restraint about mutual criticism had to be exercised by both daughter-in-law and mother-in-law. Gossips held that a girl who married a youngest son knew what was in store for her, and had to live with it. A proverb, also used to talk about neighborhood conflict, *Ce capisce chiù assé se fènge* – "The person who understands more, pretends" – sums up this situation. The saying means that under certain circumstances it is better to be silent, pretending that there has been no offense, when one has been offended and to consider the broader perspective of the consequences of reacting angrily. A daughter-in-law who lived near her husband's parents was expected to behave in such a way. She had to accept the authority of her husband's parents, and not overreact to criticism by her mother-in-law. In some cases encountered among neighbors and informants in rural Locorotondo this had not been easy.

COURTSHIP, MARRIAGE, AND THE FORMATION OF HOUSEHOLDS

Meeting and becoming engaged

Generally, parents did not arrange marriages, but they exercised strong veto powers over their children's choices of partners. They tightly controlled contact between unmarried people of opposite sex, and in the countryside of Locorotondo, often still do. Young men and women first noticed each other in several contexts. Commonly, young men made marriage choices from among familiar neighbor girls in a *jazzeile* or in their country neighborhoods. The first meeting might also take place in the context of market, Sunday Mass, or a saint's festival in the town. Another especially common context to meet was at a country dance.

   With the express purpose of providing a context for single young people to meet, parents provided dance parties for their daughters, often in the context of Carnival, but also for other holidays (Cardone, 1980: 40–43). Neighbor families were invited, and girls came chaperoned by their mothers. Boys roamed the countryside attending dances, especially during Carnival when there were likely to be many of them. Engaged girls let their fiancés know, and word about the whereabouts of festivities would spread among young men encountering each other at crossroads (nowadays, at country bars). Before the advent of other forms of evening entertainment, notably television, country dances were frequent, and single men could find one nearly every night, especially if they owned bicycles, or later cars and scooters, to take them considerable distances from home, even into neighboring town territories.

Dancing at such functions was mostly for the benefit of the unmarried young and was tightly controlled by a man acting as dance master, whose task it was to exclude rowdy youths (fights were a common possibility), and act as a master of ceremonies. Parents closely chaperoned behavior, and because the space inside a *trullo* was tight, young men went in to dance only once, and then had to stand outside. People who are now middle-aged recall that they danced with their partners silently with serious expressions – the audience present frowned upon talk between unattached partners. Males expressed interest in individual young women as potential fiancées through choice of dance partner alone, not in words.

In these contexts, and in situations, such as market, which drew peasants to town, young men and women who lived considerable distances apart in the rural territory, or in neighboring towns, became mutually interested. Therefore, although there was some tendency for men, especially younger sons, to set up their households in their father's *contrada*, either in the *jazzeile*, or on a separate, but nearby, piece of family land, there was also a tendency for wives to come from a distance of many kilometers, producing patterns of affinal kinship relations which extended over the landscape, sometimes into neighboring communes, as well as scattering the land holdings of households over a wide territory.

In another context, the author has pointed out that scattering of household fields over the landscape has considerable advantage in reducing risk to crops either because of differences in microclimate, or simply because of reduction to exposure to randomly striking disaster such as hail storms (Galt, 1979). The latter are a considerable problem on the Murgia dei Trulli, and institutions which assured the scattering of a family's fields, protected the crops from total loss, because hail strikes in a patchy and randomly unpredictable manner.[4] Widespread affinal kinship connections also provided geographically broader social networks. This meant that people had access to information and potential patronage connections at a distance from their home *contrade*, and this affected their employment possibilities, and their ability to approach elite townsmen for favors.

People considered talk between single men and women a highly significant sign of mutual interest. Even now informants often

describe a pair involved in courtship as "speaking to one another."
Once first interest had been shown, the suitor would begin the first
phase of courting – *se gire de fore fore* – circulating outside the girl's
gate. The couple might also communicate with secret notes delivered
by friends, or even unofficially, without a stamp, as a favor by the
postman. This could go on for many weeks while parents decided
whether they approved of the courtship moving ahead. Gradually the
suitor began to talk furtively to the girl through her gate, and then,
after a while, more intimately after entering the courtyard. Parents
who approved would invite him inside their house and this was a
significant step. Other times, suitors gained entrance to the courtyard
with an excuse like a deflated bicycle tire and the need to borrow a
pump, and struck up an acquaintane with a girl's father with the hope
of talking to her. The proposal, as related by several informants,
consisted of the laconic question *"Me vui a meé?"* ("Do you want
me?"). Or, indeed, a father, upon having been asked for his daughter's hand with words such as "I have the pleasure of coming into
your house because I want your daughter," might ask the latter, "Do
you want him, yes or no?" Once engaged, people considered talk
between the girl and any other single male, at a dance, or otherwise,
under even potential public scrutiny, as betrayal of her fiancé, and
this could lead to a ruptured engagement which did the girl's
reputation little good because people would suspect her *onestà*. The
concept of "honesty" included the idea of sexual loyalty to the future
husband, as well as respect for his reputation and that of his family;
both could be damaged if she were not "honest". However, at this
stage sexual loyalty was only a potential for the future, not usually a
fact, because engaged couples were expected to remain chaste in their
relationship, and indeed careful chaperoning saw to this, for the most
part. Engaged girls, interested in preserving their reputations, thus
pretended not to hear any flirtatious talk from other men.

A ruptured engagement perpetrated by a boy who too easily
fraternized with other girls, or who broke off with one fiancée to
contract marriage with another, could lead to dire consequences.
Jilted fiancées committed two murders during the late nineteenth
century.[5] In one of these the victim visited his betrothed and her
parents to inform them that he had taken up with another girl and to
ask that he be let out of the agreement. According to the police
record, the jilted girl, with some help from her parents, one suspects,
became enraged and hacked him to death with knives, hatchets, and

pruning hooks! More commonly, the young man who jilted his
fiancée faced the possibility of magical retaliation of two kinds: a
harmful, or even lethal, spell purchased from a local sorcerer, or the
curse of either the jilted girl or her mother (see below). Belief in the
efficacy of magic was, and, among older people, still is, strong in the
countryside and served as a check on such risky behavior. There was
also the danger that a girl who desired a particular partner would buy
a love potion from a sorcerer and administer it secretly to the
unsuspecting youth in a cup of coffee or a glass of wine. Mothers in
Locorotondo's rural zones warned their sons about consuming
anything at houses in which there were single girls in whom they had
no interest.

By the time the "talking" culminated in a formal proposal, both
sets of parents had separately considered the match and arrived at a
conclusion about whether the engagement should proceed. Information the girl's brothers (if any) gathered about the suitor could be
important, because they had networks which extended generationally
and could usually find out about his character. People were supposed
to marry others of about equal property, and certainly no less. Other
informants stress that they married for property considerations, but
the personal qualities of the individuals considering marriage were
also extremely important. Most significant, of course, was their
honesty and capacity for hard work. Individuals who people considered lazy or wasteful were not welcome marriage partners, or sons-
and daughters-in-law. Such individuals merited the dialect label
cazzecarne, which might best be rendered into English as "flesh butt."
Most specifically, people viewed too much concern with luxuries,
comforts, or expensive leisure activities on the part of either partner
to an engagement, negatively. A proverb which deplored such
qualities in women was *Fèmmene pumpeose i tèrre de vasceine
portene l'umme a ruveine* – "Women who put on airs (with clothing
or cosmetics) and land on a slope bring a man to ruin." A young man
who spent too much time or too many resources on hunting, which,
given local depletion of game, could only be seen as a non-productive
activity, would be examined skeptically as a potential son-in-law.

However, parents were interested in marrying off daughters
quickly, or at least as quickly as the need to accumulate dowries
would permit. Several proverbs underline this: *A fèmmene jé na
cambièle – quanne chiù subete a po scangé megghi'è* – "Daughters are
like IOU's, the sooner you pay them off, the better." *A fèmmene jé*

come a votte de meire, na volte se sciute a acite – "Daughters are like barrels of wine, someday they will turn to vinegar." These proverbs stress the local perception that as time went on women became less physically attractive, or had more opportunity to lose their virginity. People considered it generally important for sisters to marry before their brothers. The latter looked after their sisters' welfare and behavior, and protected their honor. A brother kept an eye on his sister's fiancé to be sure that he was loyal to her. Importantly, single brothers contributed their income to household finances and helped sustain the expense of girls' dowries.

Parental authority was important in determining marriage choices, but informants note that their vehement objections could easily backfire and produce an elopement (*sceneute*) in which the couple would flee together, remain away overnight, and be forced to marry. Elopement might also result from the frustration of a long engagement produced by the need to accumulate goods. Those involved celebrated their marriages in the basement of the church without the ritual and ceremony of proper weddings, and with the bride dressed ordinarily. Gossips often blamed overly rigid parents for the impetuous actions of their eloping children. Having a daughter run off with her fiancé damaged parent's reputations. The consequences of such rigidity are expressed in the country folktale about St. Lucy in which an overly rigid father overreacts to his daughter's choice of fiancés. Recall that St. Lucy was martyred by having her eyes plucked out, and that statues of her commonly portray her holding her eyes before her in a dish, but also with her eyes in their sockets.

That one [St. Lucy] was being courted by a boy. St. Lucy's father didn't want that boy. So he said, 'You will not look at that boy. I don't want him.' 'But I want him!' she said. Friend [*cumpá*], he had the eyesight torn from his daughter. Didn't he! He had both of her eyes torn out. But after her eyes had been torn out St. Lucy went to bed. The next morning . . . you've seen how St. Lucy holds her eyes in a plate, like this [informant pantomimes holding a plate in front of her body] . . . the statue of St. Lucy . . . and she has other eyes. As many times as the father tore out her eyes they always grew back. And then she became a saint. He said, 'She is a saint,' said the father, 'if I tear out her eyes and they grow back afterwards!'[6]

Engagement became official when the girl's parents invited the suitor's parents to a dinner at which he gave his fiancée a small gold neck chain, but not an engagement ring – a recent innovation borrowed from international culture. Negotiations about the marriage settlements began between the two sets of parents. Normally this was not officially recorded among peasants, but parents took care to verbally establish a parity in the items given on both sides – a house and land from the groom's parents, and land and money from the bride's. Men brought the simple furnishings for the house, women brought the bed, and bedding, and cooking utensils. Parents considered the trousseau separately because it consisted exclusively of things for the bride's use.[7]

The period of engagement

Parents bore the expense of providing children with marriage settlements, but one must also remember that both sons and daughters turned over all their earnings before marriage to their fathers, who disbursed money for their minimal daily needs, and added the rest to household finances to meet family needs. Typically before marriage, and before being officially settled with land, sons and daughters worked as day laborers in the fields and vineyards of others, as well as helping out with the cultivation of family land. Both traveled long distances to work cereal harvests (see Chapter 2). (Whether men and women ceased doing day labor after their marriages varied, of course, with the amount of land they had to cultivate independently.) Even now many fathers insist that their sons' and daughters' earnings be pooled with other household incomes. This continues to be the case under new economic circumstances in which younger people have left agricultural jobs and taken up the "new" artisan trades, or undertaken middle-class occupations such as teaching school.

A man usually built or remodeled his son's house with the help and supervision of a *trullo* builder, but also with large amounts of male family labor. Brothers expected each other's help. In the last historical phase of *trullo* construction, until just after the Second World War, the minimum dwelling which parents supplied to a marrying son consisted of a central room, a bedroom, and a kitchen – this contained a hearth, wall niches for storage, and often wooden benches built onto the wall near the hearth which could be used to bed down children. The mason often built closed door arches into the walls for the future addition of rooms as they might be needed either to fit a growing family, or to ease eventual division of the house with the younger son. In addition some stalls and other outbuildings were provided. Most *trulli*, especially along roads, also had a walled yard in front with a gate.

Rigid rules and expectations circumscribed the period of engagement. Its length depended upon factors such as whether the man involved had done military service and whether he had a house. Generally, engagements lasted two to three years but could often last more. One man, who married in 1933, related that his engagement had lasted fully six years, and that during that time he and his wife to be never once walked alone together. During engagement, young men expected to visit their fiancées and their parents twice weekly on Thursdays and on Sundays. In the countryside and in the town, until recently, fiancés never went out in public together alone, and on the way to country dances walked ahead of the girl's parents in their full sight. Older informants recall a few stolen words on Sundays in town when the girl's mother was not looking, or at the girl's house when her mother was busy feeding animals. They had little opportunity to come to know each other well before marriage outside the rigidly structured expectations of being engaged. There were also rigid expectations about gift giving between fiancés at Christmas, New Years, and Easter. Girls gave gifts of gold to their fiancés at Christmas, and the boys' reciprocated at New Years – this was known as the *strinne*. At Christmas engaged girls gave their future husbands a sweet known as *torrone*, consisting of almonds candied into a large ring, and at Easter they gave their future mothers-in-law large frosted dough rings which had eggs, attached with dough strips, baked whole on them. On Palm Sunday, it was again the turn of the boy to give his betrothed a gift, and she reciprocated, often with an article of clothing, on Easter Sunday.

The families celebrated the marriage in several phases. The first, called *u matrimonie* consisted of a dinner celebrated among the relatives of the couple a week before the Sunday scheduled for the wedding in church. On the appointed day, after the church wedding took place, there was another dinner, known as the *sponsalizie*. A family member drove the couple home in a buggy from the Church of San Giorgio in town, and along the way people who knew them would hang their best bedspreads and quilts on lines or on bamboo poles to acknowledge the event. The couple reciprocated by stopping to give out sweets as favors. Only family members were guests at the wedding dinners, and they had to bring small gifts such as cups and saucers, or items of crockery. Meat was to be served at these dinners. One elderly woman noted that hers had been an especially poor wedding and her brothers had hunted hedgehogs for the meat course.

Richer families served chicken, rabbit, or kid. For about a month after the couple married, but after a three day period of seclusion, friends made evening visits bringing small gifts and the couple provided them with sweets and drinks. In the middle 1960s country people began to adopt the more national and middle-class custom of holding a single lavish wedding dinner in a restaurant to which a wider range of guests would be invited.

Friends interrupted the wedding night with pranks: the bride's girl friends would put sugar between the sheets when they ceremonially prepared the bed a week before the wedding day; revelers lowered a cat down the chimney with its head tied in a bag so that it would howl. Groups of friends would stand outside the couple's door and serenade them to the accompaniment of an accordion, and the newlyweds would, by local custom applicable to all serenades, be obliged to open up and invite them in for sweets and wine or liqueur. First thing in the morning, the mother of the groom went to inspect the wedding sheets for signs of the bride's lost virginity. It was a source of pride if they were found, but no informants mentioned any particularly dire consequences if they were not, although theoretically the groom could send the woman back to her parents. The mothers made no display of the bloodied sheets.

FAMILY SIZE AND LAND

Number of children

The author, when he began to consider the questions for the family interviews to be conducted in rural Locorotondo, consulted with his field assistant about how best to ask people, particularly older people, about how many children they thought were appropriate in a family. The latter felt that this question would be found meaningless by many peasant informants because they did not consider the question of exerting control over fertility, and that it might be more reasonable to ask if it was appropriate to have children at all. In essence he said that the only decision to be made was whether to have children, the number which came was not something people could decide.

This fatalistic view does not operate in postpeasant rural Locorotondo. Changing family size is clearly illustrated in Figure 8.1, in which the number of children produced by 69 women assumed to have completed child bearing (age 47 and above) is graphed alongside

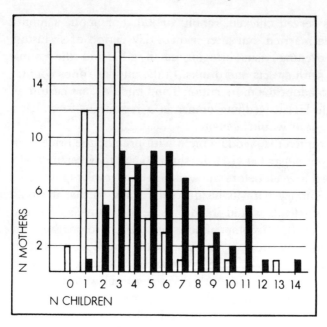

Fig. 8.1. Number of children born to all women older than the median age in the
Locorotondo sample survey (white bars) contrasted with the number of
children born to the mothers of those women (black bars). (Source:
1982 Locorontondo Sample Survey)

the family sizes produced by the mothers of those women.[8] The 69
women were born between 1897 and 1934, and therefore well within
the end of the peasant era. It can be assumed that their mothers and
fathers produced children operating by expectations relevant to the
peasant adaptive strategies discussed in this and the last chapter.
Modern completed family size, as reflected by the 1982 survey, shows
strong modal values for two- and three-child families (mean equals
3.29, standard deviation equals 2.47). This is a response to increasing
costs of raising children (which include increasing educational expectations, and more expensive diets, among other things), coupled with
the decline of viable peasant and *masseria* agriculture, and therefore
the necessity for farm labor either to help out on family land, or to be
sold on the labor market to supplement household incomes.

Early twentieth-century peasant families, and by assumption, those
of the preceding century, were often large. The mean family size
produced by the older generation of mothers was 5.53 (standard
deviation 3.55). Families which produced 5 or 6 children were most
common. The interview question which produced these figures asked

for "children ever born," and because the answer depended upon recall, children who died very young may have been underreported by informants. Conventional infant mortality rate during the pre-war decades of the twentieth century for all Locorotondo was probably high. Unfortunately adequate data for only one year survive from which to calculate it, and the rate for that year (1936) was 135.6 first-year infant deaths per 1,000 births – or a ratio of 1 death per 7 births. Most of these deaths resulted from either intestinal or respiratory diseases, or from malnutrition.[9] Such levels of infant and child mortality were probably high enough to keep parents producing children to insure the survival of some of them – the classic explanation of high fertility.

As previous work on the Island of Pantelleria demonstrated, ignorance of birth control possibilities can neither be assumed or directly blamed for large families, and not controlling births must, therefore, be seen as a choice, even if unconscious (Galt and Smith, 1979). Children were money earners from a young age and they supplied labor to the family enterprise, and therefore peasant families considered them a blessing and did not seek to limit their births. The only institutionally operating check on fertility was late marriage brought about by the necessity to accumulate dowry goods and other resources to establish a household. The mean age at marriage for the sample of 69 women over 47 was 26.6 years. Men married in their late twenties or early thirties. Had women married earlier, of course, they would have produced larger families. Late age at marriage also had the advantage of keeping vigorous adults in their parents' households to work family land and to pitch in collectively to amass savings for marriage settlements. The peasant world view in rural Locorotondo assumed the possibility that resources could be gained through hard work, that somehow children would be taken care of, and that their labor could be invested in the process.

Children and land

Ideally, a prudent father began to think about settlements to be made for children when they were young – perhaps eight years old. He began to earmark fields for specific children, and to consider how to acquire more land, if necessary, to provide adequate landholdings to the new households which would form. Obviously the more children he had, the more these considerations became a burden. A local country proverb says, *"Sparte Napule e devènte casèdde"* – "Divide

Naples and it becomes a *trullo*." The sense is that even a great property can become insignificant if divided too much. The author has argued that the peasantry of the Island of Pantelleria solved this problem by limiting births (Galt, 1979; Galt/Smith, 1979), but it is difficult to make such a case for Locorotondo where large peasant families were common.[10] However, the processes of division of estates which took place sporadically over the nineteenth and early twentieth century allowed the peasantry to think of the countryside as a resource which, from their perspective, expanded from time to time, as land which had been locked up in medium estates became available. The institution of emphyteusis allowed peasant fathers to achieve partial solutions to the problem of providing for families which expanded beyond levels at which children could be given viable landholdings solely from already existing family patrimonies. New households could at least be begun, and through a combination of savings from wage labor either locally, or in an emigrant situation, and the ready possibility of emphyteusis before the First World War, and of purchase later, parents and children perceived a chance to acquire adequate amounts of land.

The experience of particular families illustrates this point. A couple, Francesco and Angela, both born in 1892, married in 1919. Francesco brought a bit over 1.5 *tomoli* (about 1.3 hectares) to the new household, and his wife brought 2 *tomoli* (1.7 hectares) of vineyards. Thinking of his children, Francesco bought another 4.5 *tomoli* of land making 8 in all. The couple produced four children, two girls, Giulia and Angela, and two boys, Francesco and Giorgio, and was able to give each a start with 2 *tomoli*, as much as their mother had brought to her marriage. Each child married someone who brought about the same amount of land to the match, therefore reconstituting four farm enterprises of about the same size as their parents' settlements at marriage.

In another case, this one reported by Calella, another Francesco, born in 1864, married Anna, born five years later. This Francesco brought 6 *stoppelli* (0.64 hectares) of land in cereal fields and vineyards to the match, but his wife brought nothing but her trousseau. The land was burdened with an emphyteutic rent of 21.25 lire a year. Francesco and Anna had their work cut out for them to provide for the children which would come and they both labored hard for agricultural wages. Some years after the marriage, probably upon the marriage of his youngest brother, Francesco's father passed on to them another 7 *stoppelli* (0.75 hectares) located next to the original marriage settlement – there was an emphyteutic rent of 28 lire involved here as well. Still later Francesco borrowed money from his sister and bought another 7 *stoppelli*, also subject to emphyteutic rent, this too adjacent to the other parcels. Saving their earnings from these lands and from wage labor, the couple managed to enfranchise the land and repay Francesco's sister, but as they had started to produce children, the need to amass more land became apparent. From their savings, they were able to buy 3 more hectares of land, which they transformed into vineyards, and, in 1929, they bought a house in town. Francesco and Anna produced five children and gave each 1 *tomolo* of land (0.85 hectare) upon marriage, reserving for themselves just over a *tomolo*, which upon their definitive retirement from the fields would be further divided among their children (Calella, 1941: 163–165).

These cases exemplify the proper strategy expected of parents. Certainly not all were as successful. However, a comparison of the distribution of enterprise sizes as reported in the *catasto provvisorio* and in the cadaster of 1929 (there is no good cross-sectional data between those years) indicates that over the nineteenth century the peasantry of Locorotondo managed to increase the average peasant family holding instead of fragmenting it. The early nineteenth-century mean for farm enterprises was 1.04 hectares, about one-third of the 1929 mean of 3.01 hectares, and the mode in the earlier distribution fell in the less than 0.26 hectare range (832 enterprises). The early twentieth-century mode fell in the range between 1 and 3 hectares. Therefore the mean property size increased despite increases in population. This implied, of course, the shrinking of larger estates and the accomplishment of a more uniform distribution of land as reflected in the Lorenz curve at Figure 2.2.

Early nineteenth-century properies were more fragmented, and tiny properties were more numerous; those of the early twentieth century were generally small, but peasant properties were likely to be more viable. The larger peasant properties of the early twentieth century had been constituted by judicious application of marriage strategies, emphyteutic lease, and purchase through savings (see Figure 8.2). Over the long run, the operation of partible inheritance did not necessarily lead to reduction of household properties, at least in terms of total land surface area. In combination with the marriage choice institutions described above, it probably did, however, operate to

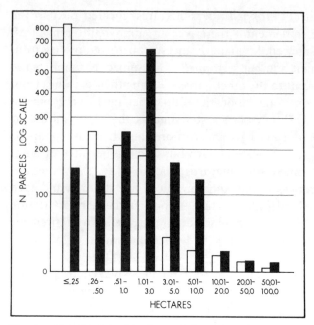

Fig. 8.2. Distribution of land parcels by size category for Locorotondo in 1816
(white bars) and 1929 (black bars). Size categories standardized on the
1929 cadaster. (Source: ASB-CP, 1816; ISTAT, 1933)

scatter fields and vineyards owned by single households over a wider
area, and to fragment them into more isolated fields.

Since the 1929 cadaster there is evidence that mean farm enterprise
landholding size has decreased. The 1970 agricultural census reports
data from which a mean of 2.34 is calculable, with the mode in the
group below 1 hectare. The non-profitability of viticulture coupled
with industrial opportunities, local and elsewhere, has led families to
pay less attention to the problem of acquiring and maintaining viable
family landholdings. They no longer assume that children must be
provided adequate patrimonies because agriculture no longer forms
the central basis of their livelihoods. The key to their children's future
is education, at least through middle school, and then perhaps
through a trade high school. There is no longer an agricultural reason
to produce many children, and those brought into the world are more
expensive to provide for, not only in terms of education, but also
because, less isolated than their ancestors from the broader world,
they demand more, and their parents find it difficult to deny them
things, such as vehicles, television sets, and toys, which are now

perceived as essential parts of the national lifestyle. The strategy of acquiring land to pass on to children, except perhaps as a place to build a house, no longer makes sense, and erosion of landholdings has taken place through division.

PARENTS, CHILDREN, AND AUTHORITY

Parental authority and the household economy

When interviewing older informants about the nature of family life during their childhoods it becomes clear that there have been significant changes in the nature of parental authority. Participant observation of the treatment of children in rural postpeasant Locoro-tondo leads to the conclusion that the current pattern is one of considerable indulgence and affection. This was not true for those socialized to be small proprietor peasants. Parents expected hard work, thrift, obedience, and honesty of children, and when they disobeyed, especially disobeyed their fathers, the punishments could be severe. The disloyalty of older, even married children, toward their parents harmed their reputations, and there were even supernatural consequences. Now, because of the economic changes outlined in Chapter 2, children have much greater autonomy about what they will do with their lives. They need to be socialized for hard work, and they are through the example of their parents, but unquestioning obedience to fatherly authority is no longer so central, because fathers have less to do with setting their children up to make a living when they marry, although there are still strong expectations that they will provide houses. Also, as one old man put it, children who now grow up more "active," by which he meant more autonomous, are less likely to be duped by others.

The older adaptive pattern required a family unit which cooperated and supplied massive amounts of labor for the common goal of making an economic step ahead and providing for the new households which would spring from it. Locorotondese rural social structure responded by centralizing parental authority in the father and by making obedience to his desires extremely important. A local folk metaphor compares the father's role to the axle of a cart in its centrality and indispensability. Ultimately, it was up to him to organize the household economy – to allocate labor to family lands, or to wage producing activities, and to decide how to spend, save, or invest the money which accumulated from these activities. It was also up to him to make wise decisions about the acquisition of new land through emphyteusis (in the nineteenth century), or purchase, and to make sure that his children married advantageously with respect to property. These managerial responsibilities required a high degree of authority. With respect to the marriage of his children it meant that he had to be able to exert his will (with daughters through his wife) over children who looked as though they were heading toward a disadvantageous marriage, without precipitating an elopement. It was also necessary that he set a good example for his children about work. Authority to make such decisions centered on fathers, but as in the fields, husbands and wives were teams and decisions were at least discussed between them.

Disobedient children risked physical punishment. Fathers punished sons and mothers punished daughters, and the threat of such punishment could last until children married and formed their own households. A punishment mentioned by several elderly informants was binding children to trees, or inside the house to the iron bed-frame supports. One informant recalled a case in which a boy had stolen, and later sold, the wedding ring of a neighbor woman. His father questioned him about it, and hearing only denials beat him with a wet knotted rope. After dinner there were more denials which resulted in another beating, after which the boy's father tied him up outside next to the family dog and told him that he could come in only when he confessed. After two nights of such exposure, the boy gave in, recovered the ring, and returned it.

Informants also noted that although there was a threat of corporal punishment, once children began to be socialized, a stern glance from a parent sufficed to assure obedience. Furthermore, justified punishment by others, either in school, or by close relatives, often met with more punishment by parents. Parents who faced the worry of bending their children's wills toward the hard and disciplined lives they would face in Locorotondo's countryside, felt such treatment, sometimes child abuse by current Locorotondese standards, was necessary. No informants who grew up with such treatment talked with resentment – in fact, they recalled it as an expression of parental concern about their growing up properly. As a rule harsh punishment does not seem to have been arbitrary, capricious, or the result of parental frustration. Listening to the older generation of Locorotondese country people, one has the impression that children learned obedience and learned it well. In response to an interview question about whether children would criticize their parents an old man responded, "maybe once, but never twice."

However, the community did not expect loyalty and obedience to parents if the path they followed did not conform to cultural norms. In the late 1940s one young man was forced to migrate to Switzerland because his father demanded that he join his gang of livestock rustlers. People remember that the son refused saying, "I won't lead your life!" His father threw him out of the house, but the neighborhood respected the young man's decision. In the value system of rural Locorotondo people thought honesty should take precedence over strict obedience.

As with the question of ruptured engagement, there were magical sanctions surrounding questions of extreme disobedience or disloyalty by older children toward parents. The curse of a wronged parent was particularly potent, and speaking generally, the curses of powerless people, such as sickly widows, were most powerful. Curses, (*i jasteime*) were, and among the oldest are, taken very seriously, and not issued casually. (An unjustified curse might visit the disaster wished on another back on the initiator.) For truly villainous mistreatment or neglect of parents, children might also be subjected to God's direct retribution – known as *a malepotènse de Diggje* (the harmful power of God). God, they feared, would punish them while they still lived, not only in eternity. A context in which such earthly divine retribution was believed to operate, for instance, was when a son refused to take care of an aged and sick parent after the latter had given him a share in the family patrimony. An informant reported an example of a curse aimed at a daughter who, after running away with a man not to her parents' liking, stole all their furniture and food. She died soon after, and her lover went bankrupt; the hamlet considered this the result of her father's curse.[11]

Man by the shovel and woman by the spoon

An often quoted proverb sums up the division of domains within the family between men and women in rural Locorotondo: *L'umme pé a péle i fèmmene pé a cucchière* – "The man by the shovel, the woman by the spoon." Each equally had a domain in life, particularly with respect to work, as each had a characteristic tool which in form, but not in size, resembled that of the other. The metaphor should not, however, be taken too far because women's roles in agricultural work often took them outside the household where they literally wielded the spoon. (The use of the shovel image is also figurative; men were more likely to move dirt with their large hoes than with shovels or spades.) Agricultural activities were subject to strict expectations about the sexual division of labor, and the proverb could also be used to underline this.[12] The proverb's truer sense is more that all is right when husbands and wives behave according to proper cultural expectations and do their complementary jobs, thereby forming a team to sustain the household.

For a woman, such expectations principally revolved around hard work, but also included the qualities of thrift, honesty, and loyalty to her husband. A good wife managed the household well by conserving resources and avoiding any temptation to spend money on luxuries. Families bought provisions on Sundays when they went to town to market and to attend Mass, and a woman who knew how to bargain well was admired. In peasant times, however, the ideal was to attain as much household self-sufficiency as possible, and purchased food items were limited to a few staples like coffee, sugar, and salt. Peasant households produced and processed almost everything consumed, including oil, cheese, wheat, favas, and, of course, wine, and this was a source of pride. Cheese, especially, was a visible symbol of peasant prosperity. Women still make it in a cauldron in the hearth and then press the curds into basketry forms. Cheese was aged, in the open, on a shelf high over an interior door in the central room of the *trullo*, and the row of cheeses was immediately apparent to anyone entering. Such a row was a rural marker of prosperity and a target of envy for the hungry artisan townsmen.

Subsistence, then, also followed the shovel/spoon proverb and was a matter of team work, men and women carried out complementary tasks in growing and harvesting grapes and men made wine (although women boiled the must into the syrup used to bring up the alcohol content). Men and women cultivated and harvested wheat and barley, men took the grain to the mill and women made it into loaves and baked them. Women gardened. Men and women cared for olive trees; women harvested olives, and men took care of getting them pressed for oil. Women tended animals, spun and wove woolen cloth, and made cheese. The central staple in the diet, fava beans, was cultivated and harvested by both sexes, and shelled and cooked by women. Many rural households continue many of these subsistence activities now, although there is less emphasis on fava production, and no household produces its own textiles any longer.

Belmonte, writing of Naples, has noted the emphasis placed upon food in the family, and his discussion of family roles characterizes the Neapolitan mother's role as one in which she expressed love for her family through the provision of abundant tasty food (1979: 88–89). Although, this could now be said of the Locorotondese postpeasant family with its greater income, and of town households, the limited traditional diet consisting mostly of puréed fava beans, pasta, fresh vegetables, cheese, wine, nuts, figs, and bread did not lend itself to such expression. The diet, and the chores of cooking it on a daily basis, were monotonous in the peasant household, except on a few festive occasions during the year at which a more abundant table was presented. If mothers expressed love through food, it was probably on these occasions, and particularly through the holiday pastries and special foods appropriate to them. Rather, what was expressed at daily meals was the reward of husband and wife team cooperation – if each carried out the expected complimentary tasks – "the man by the shovel, the woman by the spoon" – the household knew peasant prosperity and a degree of security.

Household chores consisted of cooking and cleaning. The Locorotondesi place a high value upon cleanliness and maintaining this was a female task. Women scrubbed the stone floor slabs of the *trullo* once a week and, in a few families, whitewashed walls weekly. In others, they completely renewed the whitewash, inside and out, once a year and touched up before significant religious holidays. Women laid the fire in the hearth, and with their daughters, did almost all the cooking chores. Men often knew how to cook a little, and in some families the father stayed home from Mass and market on Sunday morning to watch the house – an unguarded house on Sunday was an invitation to thieves – and to prepare the sauce for pasta. However, when outsiders were present in the home, men were (and are) careful to make sure that domestic chores and courtesies, such as serving guests with expected refreshments, were carried out by females. So strong is the latter expectation that after an interview, one rather lame old man spent five minutes on his feet finding his daughter so that she could come and serve liqueur from a bottle which had been sitting on a tray with glasses within an arm's reach of his chair.

It is difficult enough for an outsider to assess the sentiments expressed in families on the basis of participant observation, and, obviously, it is extremely difficult to make such assessments for the unobservable past. Barbagli bases a discussion of change in affect and authority in the north Italian family on changes in the application of personal pronouns inside the family. Briefly, he argues that around the turn of the century, among peasants, there began to be shifts away from formal pronouns addressed towards parents (*voi*, in Italian) toward an equal application of the familiar (*tu*) among all family members. This, he further argues, reflects changes in parental authority and distance toward greater closeness and affect, and lags behind similar changes among higher-class Northern Italians which began in the early nineteenth century (Barbagli, 1984). Among Locorotondo's country peasants there is no memory of change in the use of personal pronouns used to address parents, in Locorotondese dialect the familiar form (*tègue*) is used with almost everyone.[13] But the emphasis on parental authority, both that of mothers and of fathers, suggests that in peasant Locorotondo, discipline came before affection. An octogenarian priest of local origins confirmed this when he volunteered that in peasant times parents, both mothers and fathers, showed more concern for the socialization of children than open affection toward them.

COUNTRY NEIGHBORS

Importance of neighbors

Rural informants in Locorotondo agree that neighbors, whether kinsmen or not, are extremely important to them; sometimes they are more important than kinsmen for the immediate help they can render in times of need. Living in the country, whether in isolation or in the *jazzeile*, necessitated reliance on neighbors. The countryside was not always safe, and friendly neighbors helped guarantee some security. Hence the elaboration of neighborly expectations in Locorotondese country culture was part of the adaptive strategy for living in a dispersed settlement pattern. However, country institutions, especially the *jazzeile*, created situations in which conflict between neighbors arose often, and states of social distance developed. Such conflict can be discerned as far back as the early nineteenth century through police and judicial records and the early eighteenth in notarial contracts (see Chapter 4). This section will discuss these contradictory tendencies, and, further, will deal with the means by which

Locorotondese country people attempt to define, contain, and remedy neighborhood conflict.

The importance of country neighbors to each other made the threat of quarrel especially poignant.[14] Kinsmen might not live nearby because of the patterns of household establishment, and Locorotondese countrymen felt strongly about being able to call upon their neighbors for various kinds of help. Refusal of help to a neighbor was a serious affront. A proverb says: *A regeine stè suggètte o veceine* – "The queen is the subject of her neighbor." Neighbors exchanged work in the fields when tasks pressed upon them. They also provided each other with child care, food items, loans of money, care for the sick, transportation, surveillance of vacant houses, tools, errands, and company. The closeness of neighborly relations was underlined by the expectation that neighbors wash and dress each other's dead for funerals, and cook meals for each other during the first phases of mourning. Sometimes neighbors had to be called upon in emergency situations to fetch a doctor or to help with lambing or calving. The latter, in particular, required the mobilization of help at a moment's notice.

Mutual help was a matter of delayed reciprocity operating much like the classic horizontal dyadic contract described by Foster (Foster, 1961). Like so many other institutions in rural Locorotondese life, an often quoted proverb summed it up: *Quanne pannere vè i viène amecizze se mantiène* – "When the basket goes back and forth, friendship holds." Exchange, even of tokens (a few almond cookies out of a batch, for instance) held relationships together by creating affective ties and assuring aid in case of eventual need. Local speech recognizes reciprocity for a favor with the expression *se lué l'obbeche* – "lifting obligation." Between households which are close this need not happen immediately, but between individuals who were not so close at least a gesture, in the form of an offer of immediate reciprocation, or even payment, to "lift obligation," might be expected, but usually refused. Such an offer and its customary refusal underlined the importance of the relationship cemented through delayed reciprocity.

Country life in the *jazzeile* depended upon the sharing of certain resources held in common by those who lived around it. Such rights included use of features such as the threshing floor, cistern, or grape-squeezing facilities. Each *jazzeile* contained a large cistern and several kinds of rights were attached to it – the right to water animals at the trough, and a lesser right, *u dritte d'a cantere*, the right to draw small amounts of water (the contents of a *cantere*, or pitcher) for slaking one's thirst or washing. In addition, neighbors recognized rights to use the common space in certain ways. These included rights regarding the tethering and passage of herd animals, rights about courtyard animals, and rights having to do with the stacking of firewood. In essence the *jazzeile* was a common farmyard, and served small proprietor peasants as the farmyard of a *masseria* headquarters served the *massari* of the larger landowners. Common ownership meant that individual smallholder households did not have to make individual investments of energy, cash, or land to provide themselves with such essential facilities. Policy about the use of the facilities in a *jazzeile* had to be agreed upon unanimously by all those having rights. Such rights were, as seen from notarial acts dating as early as the first quarter of the eighteenth century, formally acknowledged when property on a *jazzeile* was bought, sold, or inherited, and were written into contracts.

For those who did not live in *jazzèlere* there were also certain common rights which pertained. Not all fields fronted on public roads and not all roads were public. This meant that rights of passage to fields through the fields and household yards of others had to be defined carefully, and such definitions included stipulations about whether animals could be moved through the property, or only people going to work in their fields. Generally speaking, one who had to cross another's property to reach a field or a pasture had the right of *passe i cameine*, to pass through and keep walking without stopping or touching anything.

Sources of conflict among neighbors

The situation in the *jazzeile* contained inherent tensions because highly independent small proprietors, who had their own lands and their own family interests to concern them, also faced the necessity of sharing certain significant resources. Quarrels occurred among neighbors over precedence in the use of threshing floors or grape-crushing basins (which should, according to one informant be established by drawing lots), damage to property, straying animals, distribution of commonly owned firewood and refusal to sell unused properties between neighbors, among other things. In addition social affronts toward neighbors, such as failure to invite them to dances, refusal to provide help when requested, non-attendance at their funeral, or remonstrating their children too harshly, could also lead to quarrels.

The complexity of these common-use rights often provided an excuse or a reason for the eruption of trouble between neighbors, and quarrels particularly between fellow *jazzeile* dwellers, are proverbial in Locorotondo's countryside and have been common over the historical span in which dispersed settlement has existed. For instance, a case which would seem comic, if it had not ended in injury, was tried before the town magistrate on August 20, 1845. Giovanni Pinto lived with several sons in a *jazzeile* in the *contrada* Tuttulmo where there was a commonly owned bread oven. He had a son, Angelantonio, who did not live in the *jazzeile* and who had no rights in the oven's use. Early that morning the son had the oven lighted to bake bread, and his father caught him and dowsed the fire with a nearby vessel of water. A fight ensued between the two in which they began dumping water on each other, but ended when Angelantonio broke the vessel and his brother Tommaso, who had joined in, threw a jagged pot sherd at him, causing a slight head wound. Tommaso received a sentence of two months of "correctional exile" (ASB-PSP, 1819–1857). The sentences of the local magistrate during the early nineteenth century, from which this case comes, contain many small quarrels which led to minor injuries, often the result of rock throwing. Conflict between neighbors is still common, but no longer commonly leads to blows; social distance, anonymous denunciations to the town authorities of alleged construction abuses, and protracted law suits are more common outcomes.

The importance of the neighbor relationship in rural Locorotondo led to a special concern with classifying states of estrangement between neighbors which implied regular expectations about behavior so that more open quarreling would not break out. Moreover, several means of resolving conflict existed. There was a four-level terminology for talking about bad feelings between neighbors. For those around them, and for the neighbors themselves, establishing where in this hierarchy a particular quarrel lay allowed adjustment of behavior so as to prevent further conflict. The category of estrangement could be judged by observing those involved because each category implied certain observable behaviors.

The first level of estrangement was labeled *se fènge* – literally, "one pretends." This comes from the saying, reported above, "The person who understands more pretends." Neighbors who became annoyed at each other tried to keep it to themselves if they felt that airing the annoyance would lead to unwelcome consequences and an escalation of conflict. A common circumstance in which this strategy was applied was when neighbor children came to words or blows in an argument, and parents felt tempted to support them. People thought that ignoring the incident was the best policy because words between adults could lead to serious conflict at the same time hostilities blew over between children. The proverb allowed each party to the controversy to assume that he or she understood the possible consequences of open conflict better than the other. The proverb's use allowed people to buy off their ruffled honor with the assumption of greater wisdom.

The next higher level of conflict was labeled: *agnune a chés* – "each at home." Other neighbors read this stage in the behavior of the conflicting parties if their interaction became reduced to short conversations in public, and all efforts to exchange visits, which are important to neighbors on good terms, ceased. Behavior in a *jazzeile* was instantly read and interpreted by neighbors, and the fact that formerly friendly families no longer entered each other's doors was obvious to all. A degree beyond this was *care i cameine* – "greet and walk on." The word *care* is the dialect way of giving the Italian greeting *ciao* – a familiar word meaning both hello and goodbye. In this stage individuals only muttered greetings, exchanging no conversation. Neighbors reached such a stage when one or both suspected the other of malicious gossip, or of having broken a confidence, and there was no longer trust between them. Informants said that each of these states of estrangement might pass with time.

Country folk labeled the final and most serious level of estrangement as *nen se trèmende chiù m'bacce* – "they no longer look each other in the face." This consisted of complete avoidance. A pair of neighbors in this state would look away if they happened to pass each other on the road. Efforts would also be made to avoid even that. One individual with whom the author often found himself in a car, would drive very quickly by the house of a neighbor with whom his father was in this state of hostility so as to avoid any possible contact. Complete avoidance behavior was less likely to be healed by the passage of time, and states of avoidance exist in the countryside now which have lasted for decades and shown no signs of extinction.

Distance between neighbors in a *jazzeile* disturbed the regular social life of the community – other neighbors had to tread lightly and put up with the avoidances of quarreling individuals. Sometimes they would attempt to make peace by going to both parties to talk them into reconciliation. Some rural neighborhoods had particular individuals who were adept at the diplomacy necessary to bring about reconciliations between distanced neighbors, and who were appealed to by other residents to do so. Other times, one party to a feud would attempt to end it by "putting himself under" (*se scaffe sotte*) the other – by giving in to bring about peace. In essence, this was a more serious instance of the philosophy expressed in the phrase "one pretends."

If both parties to the fight were willing, there was also a ritualized way of making peace without negotiations. This continues to be important. On Palm Sunday families went to church carrying bundles of olive branches and piled them inside to be blessed by the priest. Individuals then used these sanctified branches (called "palms" even though they were always from olive trees) in several ways. They made trips to each field and each building they owned and affixed an olive branch there to insure protection and a good crop. They also placed branches inside the house, especially in the bedrooms. Also, and very importantly, blessed twigs were exchanged with friends and neighbors to underline the openness and healthy nature of relationships. Upon receiving sprigs people thanked each other and brought them to their lips in a kissing gesture. Also the twig one received in exchange for one's own was soon exchanged for another from another person, so the exchanges were not merely dyadic, but generalized – a single olive sprig touched the hands of many in the community as it went from person to person all day long. That the twigs were imbued with transcendent power, ritually solidified relationships. Transcendence came not only from their having been blessed by a priest, but also from the folk belief that during the flight into Egypt, Jesus and Mary, after having failed to find refuge in a field of fava plants, entered inside an olive tree which opened for them on the child's command. (This is why olive trees have split trunks, and fava plants have thorns.) The ritual, of course, annually renewed local community relationships symbolically.

A special aspect of the Palm Sunday exchange of olive sprigs was that a person who wished to end a feud with another could offer the latter a "palm," and if the latter accepted it and reciprocated, things were automatically patched up without an exchange of words and with no humiliation to either side. Go-betweens would urge attempts at peace making and try to pave the way. The community expected the younger of two enemies to offer the twig. If the olive sprig was offered and refused, the pair remained estranged, but with the passage of time further attempts might be made on later Palm Sundays. Thus transcendent power could be used to mend rifts between neighbors. The ideal of community was (and is) a powerful one among Locorotondo's peasant neighbors, and, as the next chapter will show, the peasant community was further delineated with respect to those of the town.

Chapter 9

TOWN AND COUNTRY

Having dealt with social structures and processes internal to rural society in Locorotondo, it is now appropriate to turn to questions of the relations of that society with the town and, through it, with broader levels of social and political organization and various institutions in Italian society. Such relationships have changed during the post Second World War era, and rural society in Locorotondo in the early 1980s consisted of people having a variety of ways of relating to the town and urban worlds. Attitudes among many, including the older generations of country dwellers, appeared to differ little from the kinds of diffident attitudes town, and some country, people suggested were common before the significant changes of the late 1950s and early 1960s. Other people, some of them older but most of them representatives of newer more cosmopolitan generations of country-raised folk, are clearly much more at home operating in the town and urban worlds.

This chapter will first explore the question of peasant education and exposure to information coming from urban centers. It will also deal with peasant attitudes toward the town population of Locorotondo and, vice versa, artisan attitudes toward the peasantry. Lastly, the discussion will show how political relationships between town and country evolved during this century, most particularly after the Second World War, when the new republican government and broadly extended franchise created intense rivalries for electoral support and the need for men of power to invent new strategies to ensure peasant votes.

EDUCATION AND THE DIFFUSION OF INFORMATION

To understand the world of the peasant countryside and its relationships with political forces, one must understand the degree to which men and women have been educated and exposed to various stimuli

Table 9.1. *Mean years of schooling by age cohort of adult generation individuals in the Locorotondo sample survey, winter 1982. F for males = 10.96, and for females 16.65. The group means are significantly different at less than the 0.001 level.*

Age cohort	Men			Women		
	mean	stand. dev.	N	mean	stand. dev.	N
20–29	8.00	2.87	10	6.71	2.54	17
30–39	7.00	3.11	18	4.77	2.05	22
40–49	5.13	1.94	30	3.47	1.34	32
50–59	4.26	4.27	30	3.21	1.13	28
60–69	3.88	1.60	24	2.73	1.44	15
70–79	1.88	2.71	9	1.43	1.99	7
80–89	1.80	1.64	5	0.00	0.00	5
90–99	0.00	0.00	1	—	—	0

and influences from the world outside the Locorotondo hinterlands. What education reached the current adult generations of Locorotondo came through a variety of sources: formal schooling, paid tutoring, adult night schools, the broadcast media and military training. From the Locorotondo Sample Survey it is apparent that age and years of schooling vary inversely (See Table 9.1). Men between 20 and 29 years of age in 1982 averaged 8 years of education (schooling through middle school), but moving to the 40 to 49 year old cohort that average dropped to a bit over 5 years. Men between the ages of 50 and 69 had a mean of around 4 years of elementary schooling, and those 70 and over typically had a bit under 2 years. Women in each of the age cohorts had about one year less than the men in corresponding cohorts.

However, schooling for Locorotondese peasant children has not always been of the best quality, and most country parents did not concern themselves highly with their children's academic achievement. At the dawn of the twentieth century the number of peasants who could read and write, or speak the national language with ease, must have been very small because elementary education was severely limited in the countryside. The central elementary school building in the historical center was not completed until 1924, and before then school was taught in cramped improvised quarters. At the turn of the century, rural schools were non-existent, except for one begun independently, but then officially recognized, in the *contrada* of San Marco. In addition, there were a few men in the countryside who taught reading in the evening and charged each pupil by the week (Palmisano, 1986: 70). By 1908 there were three rural schools, but few children in that era completed more than three grades of elementary school (Palmisano, 1986: 34). Parents considered children's wage labor, or their work in family fields, to be more valuable than their completion of more education. During the post-war era, and until recently, teachers from other regions of Italy, who because they were unfamiliar with the local dialect had trouble dealing with the problem of teaching children Italian as a second language, staffed rural schools. Classes containing more than one grade were also common. Compulsory education through middle school was legislated nationally only in 1962. Therefore, years of formal schooling is not necessarily a good measure of mastery of basic literacy in what is essentially a foreign language in a community in which most daily affairs in town and countryside are still carried out in a local dialect which is distinctly different from Italian and not mutually intelligible with it. With respect to literacy and comprehension of the national language, men have had the advantage, because most have done military service elsewhere and have had to interact with other men from all over Italy on a daily basis. It is not common to find elderly men who cannot express themselves to some degree in the national language, although there is often significant linguistic interference from dialect. Among older women, on the other hand, it is common to find individuals who are totally unable to speak Italian.

The penetration of radio and television has had significant effects upon comprehension of spoken Italian for many, and those who have grown up with radios and televisions in the household grasp the national language well. These are the same generations, moreover, which have been exposed to middle-school education. Currently there is considerable parental concern with the quality of children's educations at least through the eighth grade, and many parents take pains to speak Italian to their children in the home so that they will arrive at school fluent. In 1982 it was common to observe country children, even of pre-school age, speaking to each other in Italian, not dialect. Already there are local intellectuals who worry about the eventual loss of dialect, at least in its "pure" form.

Many peasants' lack of language facility and literacy limited their access to information emanating from administrative centers, such as the municipal and provincial levels of government. Information diffused by word of mouth, often subject to distortion, as it passed from family to family through faulty understandings. Participation in town events, such as saints' festivals and the Sunday Mass brought country folk closer to sources of information like posters, but these were written in Italian "bureaucratese," and not always accessible. Other events, such as political rallies, or the annual membership meeting of the cooperative winery, were also potential founts of information. The cooperative has been especially important for the dissemination of knowledge about viticultural techniques and information about how to prevent crop disease (see below).

Because of widespread functional illiteracy, certain figures in the countryside who could read and write assumed importance in making links between the rural and official worlds. Especially important were rural postmen, who not only delivered the stamped mail, but also often helped with its reading and writing. The postman was a source of information about goings on in the town, and a source of advice about dealing with official forms and bureaucratic details. It is no accident that in several cases in the zone of the *trulli*, postmen came to occupy the position of local union ombudsman (see below). Other more literate, or at least more verbal, men came to occupy central positions in the hamlets of Locorotondo as well. People turned to them for help with bureaucratic matters. Such men played the role of *capocontrada* – hamlet head – which fell to them because of their superior verbal skills and self-confidence, and political parties and union organizations eventually exploited the role in their attempts to capture the loyalty of rural Locorotondesi.

REGULAR AND IRREGULAR CONTACTS WITH TOWNSMEN

There was a furtive quality about peasant contact with the town, which occurred mostly during market, Mass, festivals, negotiations for wage labor, or business errands. Country dwellers refer to themselves as *nègue de feuore* ("we from outside") and they talk about having felt like outsiders in the town. Townsmen instantly identified them by their patched homespun clothing, their shoes blackened with soot from the kettle, and their deeply tanned brows. Those who grew up in the countryside close to the town and attended the central school, or ran town errands for their parents, have childhood memories of being bullied by gangs of artisan boys who would corner them and demand to be brought food such as dried figs. Peasant adults remember being accused of smelling like animals, sweat, and onions by such bullies, and an oral account portrayed hostile town adolescents waiting for people "from outside" to step from the cafe in the main square to knock the ice cream off their cones.

There is in the town a genre of anecdote which concerns jokes put over on peasants by artisans remembered for their qualities as tricksters. For instance, a recently published narrative recounts the story of Tetè and Tutuccio, the two town characters fondly remembered (by townspeople) from the first three decades of this century, who one day descended into the countryside to steal figs. They were caught sticky fingered by the fig tree's owner, a peasant named Cosimo, who upbraided them for the theft. Tetè and Tutuccio cleverly replied that the peasant had better retract his accusation because they were collecting cicadas in the tree to sell to the pharmacist; he would pay ten (pre-Second World War) lire per insect to make pills that would restore a person's lost youth. Cosimo, seeing an opportunity, told them to eat as many figs as they wanted, but to leave him the cicadas. After they left satiated with ripe figs, he caught 300 insects and went home to show them to his wife; together they schemed about building a new house with the money. The next day Cosimo took his insects in a covered basket to the pharmacist, who, because figs were ripe just then, thought he was receiving a nice snack. Stealing a moment away from his customers, he took the basket, indicating that the peasant should return for it later, and went into the back room for a moment to stuff his mouth with figs. Of course, when he removed the cloth the cicadas swarmed out, some escaping out the door, and others taking refuge on the ceiling above the customers' heads or among jars of medicine. When the hapless Cosimo returned for what he thought would be his 3,000 lire, he was forced to make a fool of himself confessing to the pharmacist how he had been duped by Tetè the shoemaker and his friend the redoubtable Tutuccio (Ancona, 1988: 118–20).

Peasants, from their own accounts and from the observations of townsmen, experienced the town as an alien environment. A rural informant related that during holidays peasant families appreciated the outdoor food stands where they could see what was for sale, and the vendor would shout prices, because in cafes they often did not know how to ask for things and risked ridicule. This also applied to the stalls set up during weekly market day. Sometimes, the same informant recalled, there was not enough cash at home to allocate toward snacks during a festival and peasant mothers would toast some almonds and send their children to town with them so others would think that they had been bought from a stand. This saved face.

Peasants forced to deal with the town bureaucracy armed themselves with gifts of food for the clerk they would have to see. This was not so much a direct bribe, but a token in a continuing patron–client relationship. A proverb, *U monache a jèsse ceccante p'avè* – "The monk must be a religious beggar to receive" – expresses the notion that the peasant must humiliate himself in the face of greater authority to get what he needs. (The missing context is that of the *quèstue*, door to door mendicancy undertaken to raise money for festivals.) Part of this humiliation came, according to Locorotondese peasant values, merely in asking for something from someone else, particularly a townsman, because it might create the impression that one was not self-sufficient. This constituted violation of a primary value in the countryside. The rest of course, came simply with having to play a subservient role. The following proverbial dialogue invoked by country people, which asserts that not even Christ showed compassion toward the peasantry, expressed their sense that few in town had much interest in peasant welfare:

Disse a Semeone Criste,	Said Christ to Simon,
'Ajeute l'artiste.'	'Help the artisan.'
Respunne Semeone,	Answered Simon,
'I chire de feuore?'	'And the peasants?'
Respunne Criste,	Answered Christ,
'S'ajeutene da seole.'	'Let'em help themselves.'

Artisan adults often describe their childhoods as hungry times. Their envy for the peasants' food production has been noted, and hungry town boys did descend into the countryside to steal fruit and nuts from trees. Peasants saw artisans (sometimes called *i murte de feme de pais* – "the dead-from-hunger from town") as voracious exploiters who came to take what they could from the peasant's larder without repaying generosity. Several proverbs express this notion, for instance, *Chire de jinte o pais so cume a scheope* – "Those from inside the town are like brooms." They sweep away food. Another proverb says, *Ce vè a na cheése i nan si metteéte, cume vè, si trateéte . . .* "If you go to a house uninvited, as you go, so shall you be treated." Peasants directed this in the third person at town dwellers who came to visit and expected to be fed. They also extended this notion to those few artisans who owned *trulli* and spent time in them during the summer. These individuals would sometimes organize dances among family members and friends, as was the custom in town, but invite local peasant girls, specifically excluding rural boys who in the country-dance tradition expected to be allowed entrance as they roamed from party to party. This led to pranks and reprisals by the latter.

Certain areas of the countryside, the eastern third of the municipality in particular, contained, and still contain, intact middle-sized estates. The peasant populations of such zones were neighbors of the landowning families, and have richer experiences of interaction with such gentry. These range from folk memories, sometimes intertwined with legends about such things as treasure chests guarded by serpents kept in estate building, to recollections of actual events. Peasant informants do not have pleasant memories of their gentlemanly neighbors, whom they accused with great hostility of having taken advantage of their ancestors, and whom they remembered as treating them like beasts. Folk memory, which is usually vague about dating, notes instances in which landowners talked hungry small proprietors into selling their land for "a loaf of bread", or "some beans", or changed cadastral entries to deprive them of a field. Many townsmen and peasants believe that one of the town's most prominent families acquired its wealth with help from bandits "in the old days." Folk memory therefore preserves, albeit in a vague and class self-serving way, an early nineteenth-century connection between Ciro Annichia-rico, the scourge of this part of Apulia during and just after the Napoleonic era, and the highest local elite class, which is in fact documentable in archives.[1] Within living memory, individuals recall being denied work when their families were hungry, or being told summarily to leave for what they considered a trivial reason, such as asking for time off to conduct business in town. Class hatred of the local gentry still runs deeply among many of peasant orgin, although some members of the class – those involved in the formation of the cooperative winery for instance – fare much better than others.

Interestingly, before the watershed of the 1960s when the *masserie* were more profitable and the position of *massaro* was highly desirable, large landowners, especially those whose larger estates were located in the eastern end of the municipality, had preferences for hiring their overseers from communities other than Locorotondo.

The reason informants among them give for this practice is that the local peasantry had little familiarity with animal husbandry. This does not ring true as most households had animals and there were shepherds in the peasant community. One rather suspects that the practice also had management advantages because such *massari* would be less connected locally and therefore less likely to coddle local workers. Arlacchi makes a similar argument about the management of the much larger estates of the Crotonese area in Calabria (1980: 178–180). Agricultural worker informants admit that they did hired work for landowners, especially the more arrogant among them, with less care than work done for neighboring small proprietors.

A rural man related the tale of a neighbor who was given the task of feeding his gentlemanly employer's dog while the latter went off on his honeymoon. The dog was to be given a half kilogram of meat daily over a period of several weeks – this was, of course, many times the quantity of meat the peasant would eat in a year. Cleverly he taught the dog (which howled at first) to eat onions and bran, and feasted upon the meat with his family and friends. When the boss returned the peasant told him he had taught the dog to eat onions and demonstrated how the dog would gobble them. Then he admonished the owner that he had no right to lord it over peasants and to think that he was more *dritte* (upright) than others. All people are "picked from the same plant," said the teller of the tale, it is only that some have more possibilities than others.

The countrymen of Locorotondo admit that it is natural that there are richer and poorer people – a man's career in the countryside included the ideal of trying to build a more productive enterprise – but strongly deny that this creates fundamental differences in the value of individuals. They especially criticize the leisurely ways of the rich, using proverbs such as, *Ce beune ui paré l'ossere i a pèdde t'onne a dolé* – "If you want to look good, your bones and feet must hurt you." This means that only those who have prospered through hard work and sacrifice deserve true esteem: inherited or ill-gotten wealth are not respectable.

INSTITUTIONS AND POLITICS

Pre-Second World War politics and the countryside

The division of Locorotondo's population into a rural sector and a town sector has long presented political and administrative problems for its men of power. During the third decade of the nineteenth century that class made a vain attempt to recover political, economic, and administrative control over the peasant population, then fully in the process of moving out into the countryside, by trying to have it forced back within the town walls. After that failed attempt, the peasantry as a class little interested town politicians and power brokers. In Locorotondo's nineteenth-century political documents – communications about appointment to office, composition of the town council, surveillance reports about subversive activities such as *Carboneria* membership, and many anonymous letters generated about these and other matters – the peasant population counted for little with respect to the political ambitions and frustrations of aspirants to power.[2] Except for the peasant removal correspondence of 1827, rurally dwelling peasants were largely invisible in such documents, even though they constituted two-thirds of the town's population by mid-century. Contenders for membership in the governing class of Locorotondo included the elite landowners, the professionals, and a few artisans, but no peasants. All throughout the nineteenth century and well into the twentieth, beginning with the period of secret societies, such as the *Carboneria*, in the years before 1820, the powerful and the less powerful in town engaged in sometimes vicious factional struggles. The local peasantry counted little in such internal warfare. In fact, because they lived rurally they were probably spared the full brunt of it during certain times, such as the several decades before the First World War when the town was sharply divided into two warring political factions called the Beduins and the Senussi, and people remember that town streets were not always safe at night.

During most of the nineteenth century, control exerted over the countryside was a matter of policing and tax collection, particularly during the dire period of brigandage, just after the Unification of Italy. Throughout the later nineteenth century there was little need to exert much political control over rural Locorotondo's population because, until the broad extension of suffrage to all males over 21 in 1912, few in the countryside met the income or literacy requirements to vote. Those whose votes had to be secured were mostly close at hand within the historical center and surrounding neighborhoods of the town.

Many country families, of course, had recourse to patron–client ties with powerful town individuals, and such ties figured among the sources of power enjoyed by these people. During the nineteenth and twentieth centuries patron–client connections frequently operated between landowners and their *massari* and hired employees. Peasants saw certain doctors as more concerned and approached them as potential godparents to children. Before the extension of suffrage, and during the fascist era when electoral politics were nullified, people of power in the town had little use for the support of most peasants and therefore, unless they felt a certain compassion, little reason to do them favors. Also, pension and other welfare systems developed little until after the Second World War, and peasants did not face the extraordinarily complex bureaucracies they would later. They had somewhat less need for patrons and help with paperwork, and often the advice of the postman sufficed. The well-ensconced one-man mayoral regime which ruled in the municipality from 1902 until 1928 could be assured the peasant vote after 1912 and before 1926, because it represented a strongly established power against which it would have been foolish to turn. However, peasants did have to turn to the municipal hall for such necessities as shotgun permits, certificates of good conduct, and other personal documents, and these could be delayed or denied. In general politics little interested those of the countryside, who, according to an account of local peasant life early in the century, declared proverbially on the subject that, *Le chiacchiere no riempiono la pancia* – "Chit chat (political ideas and maneuvers) doesn't fill your stomach" (Palmisano, 1986: 54).

Since the peasant strategy for improving conditions was largely an individual one in which success came through increasing work and practicing self-denial, collective political movements were never very interesting in the countryside. The early resolution of the question of common lands during the Napoleonic decade, and widespread peasant landownership, meant that collective peasant political or militant activity which focused upon these issues, found again and again in other southern towns, was absent in Locorotondo. Notably, even during the time of the great anarcho-syndicalist peasant worker upheavals in the northern reaches of Apulia in the early decades of this century (cf. Snowden, 1986), no organization of peasant workers developed in Locorotondo. Locorotondo's country dwellers never saw much to gain from organized collective political action. On April 3, 1930, in Martina Franca, 4,000 local peasants, among them some

Locorotondesi, stormed offices and burned tax registers because new excise taxes threatened their incomes, already made precarious by a 50 percent decrease in the price of grapes that year; but this, of course, was a short-lived mob action, inspired by desperation, which led to no further organization, which, in any case, would have been illegal and very dangerous under the fascist regime (Palasciano, 1986: 29–30).

Leftist artisans in Locorotondo, whose interests and world views were divorced from those of the peasantry, never made much effort to organize in the countryside.[3] Masons and construction workers were at the core of Locorotondo's small leftist movement. They were among the first to be exposed to more organized forms of management because external contractors hired them to build larger public and private projects – the Bari-Martina Franca railway which was begun around 1900, for instance. There were strikes for higher wages and a ten-hour work day among the 900 workers (including those from Locorotondo), some of whom adhered to a newly formed League of Masons. Between 1900 and the First World War many manual laborers from Locorotondo and neighboring towns emigrated via the city of Trieste to cities in the Austro-Hungarian Empire for work, leaving in the spring and returning just before Christmas. Exposure of migrants to labor conditions in more industrialized parts of Europe transplanted radical ideas to Locorotondo.

However, because there lacked industries employing more than a handful of workers, labor union activity only developed further in conjunction with periodic and short-lived public works projects such as the construction of the Apulian aqueduct in 1912, and the construction of the central school in 1921–1922. This sporadic employment pattern killed the League of Masons. In 1920, 20 artisans and construction workers led by a local barber founded Locorotondo's first Socialist Party chapter. Ephemeral labor victories were won, but because of sporadic employment and fascist suppression, they did not become institutionalized, and dawn to dusk workdays persisted well into the 1950s. Lack of understanding of, or sympathy with, peasant culture, and the small proprietor nature of the latter, kept the radical artisan core from attempting to include country dwellers as a part of its political program, and the left in Locorotondo has always remained weak because of the peasant majority among the commune's working classes.

The cooperatives

On the other hand, collective activity, when perceived as directly in their economic interests, has received a following among some members of the peasantry. The most important local collective institution involving country people – the *Cantina Sociale di Locorotondo*, the cooperative winery – was not, however, founded as a peasant initiative. Rather, its founder Don Sigismondo Calella, was a local banker, landowner, and intellectual, whose rural fascist ideology envisioned an Italian countryside populated by small proprietors working in concert with larger capitalistic interests, thereby reducing the threat of class conflict between estate owners and landless workers. Fascist ideologies of the time clearly influenced him, but his experience of the Locorotondese countryside also shaped his thinking. Calella extolled the virtues of Locorotondo's small proprietor peasantry in a book in which he advocated the local emphyteusis contract as a model for agricultural development elsewhere in the south (Calella, 1941).

As a result of the viticultural crises of 1929 and 1930, which culminated in the riot in Martina Franca and smaller demonstrations of frustration in other local towns, including Locorotondo, fascist provincial authorities established a fund for the development of local viticulture and especially the establishment of cooperatives. Taking the initiative, Calella, with 18 others, began an experimental cooperative for the harvests of 1931. Only four charter members were peasant small proprietors. The other vineyard owners were professionals or larger proprietors, along with several artisans, and a priest. (In fact, throughout the years of its existence, the largest single portion of grapes brought in for processing each season has been that produced by one of the local landowning families.) The first year demonstrated that, by holding wine until prices rose, a better price could be paid to the grower than he could normally receive if he sold just after the harvest. Calella's dream was to establish a large winery which would not only store wine, but also produce a high-quality product for sale in the market using the best oenological methods. (This dream was not fully realized until the 1970s when cooperative bottled white wine from Locorotondo began to find a market because it had been officially declared a DOC wine.) On September 18, 1932, the original eighteen members officially constituted the cooperative, using the constitutions of northern cooperative wineries as models for its statutes. Calella provided financing for the initiative from his bank along with provincial funding, and, in a move which caused some controversy, sold his own winery to the cooperative at what he felt was a fair price. Locorotondo's establishment was the first such cooperative in the province, and inspired the founding of another soon after among grape growers in the nearby town of Castellana Grotte (Palasciano, 1986, Pastore, 1960: 42–50). Calella published a pamphlet exhorting Locorotondo's small proprietors to join up, which concluded with the words:

To work, then, and with full confidence. A cooperative is being formed in Locorotondo; it will bring good and will certainly help grape growers to survive the grave damages of the crisis through which they are passing. But even when the sad moments have been passed, it will always be a fount of utility. Grape growers unite! United you will be stronger! Don't be stopped by the difficulties which will be encountered at first, neither should you lend your ears too easily to know-it-alls and professional denigrators. The choice of directors must be your constant concern alone; upon them depends the success of the institution and upon them and exclusively upon them, the final result. Remember with cooperation even small things become grand. (quoted in Pastore, 1960: 47)

Adhesion to the cooperative, although enthusiastic at first (by the second year there were 147 members), met complication because of hard times and the necessity felt by many small proprietors to sell their grapes, or home produced wine, immediately upon harvest to meet debts, even if this meant a lower price than could be had eventually if grapes were consigned to the cooperative. In part, lack of trust in the cooperative also can be ascribed to financial crises and suspicions about administrative malpractice which resulted in the nomination, on three occasions (1934, 1937, and 1944), of prefectural commissions to sort out its affairs, and to provide refunds to members. After an initial oscillation, membership remained below 100 enterprises until the early 1950s. Then membership began to increase slowly through the ensuing decades such that by 1986 it had reached 1,300 members. No legal irregularities have been experienced since 1944 (table in Pastore, 1960, Palasciano, 1986: 40).

Most grape producers in the Locorotondese countryside sell to the cooperative if they produce enough grapes to sell on the market. In the Locorotondo sample survey of 1982, of the 81 households which produced grapes 47, or 58 percent, sold their product to the cooperative and only 8 sold to private wineries, or directly to the vermouth companies. The other 26 households produced solely for home production and consumption.

After its founding, local gentlemen and professionals managed the cooperative winery, and decision making has never operated on a collective management model. The annual meeting in 1981 consisted of the reading of several annual financial reports and a speech by the president (who is also a popular political figure among country households) about the year's production and plans for the future. No comments came from the membership about the reports or the speech, even though they were elicited, and there was a unanimous vote to accept the former. The production of wine on an industrial scale, and its marketing are matters which are, according to the winery's management, beyond the understanding of most of the members. Since the cooperative now bottles fine wine which its managers hope will find a wide market, perhaps eventually throughout the European Community, most members agree. The management also claims that many of the members are reticent about investing the cooperative's profits in future expansion. A manager commented that the members are reluctant to turn over their entire production of grapes to the winery. It would make greater economic sense for the members to consign all their grapes and then buy wine from the cooperative at a discount, but because it is necessary to add a preservative to the cooperative's wine, they regard it as less than "genuine" and persist in producing their own for home consumption. Much of the job of managing the operation consists of convincing the membership of the wisdom of management decisions. Objection to such decisions does not occur upon formal occasions, but instead in more informal conversations.

In many ways the cooperative winery is the most positive connection between town and country. Even the label of the wine bottles expresses the connection – there is a sketch of the skyline of the town and an inset coat of arms bearing the images of a peasant man and woman, with grape vines rampant, and a motto below, which reads *Nobiltà Contadina*, peasant nobility. Clearly, most people in Locorotondo see the cooperative and its current efforts to market quality as the only hope for Locorotondese viticulture. In both town and country there is a strong awareness that unless a strategy can be found which will financially reward younger men for keeping family vineyards in production, Bianco di Locorotondo wine will never be produced in enough quantity to be marketed widely. Among the Locorotondesi there is pride in the local wine and in the cooperative, and many families, in both town and country, proudly hang its colorful annual calendar in their homes. Country people remember Don Sigismondo Calella as a person who made sacrifices in their interests, and most describe later presidents as acting in the peasants' interests as well as their own.

The cooperative model has diffused to several other economic activities. Notably Locorotondo boasts a cooperative savings bank, *La Cassa Rurale ed Artigiana Locorotondo*, which competes with the town's branch of the Bank of Naples. Many of the same individuals who founded the cooperative winery helped found it, and its success rests squarely on the ample savings accounts of the rural population. Further, there are two collectively owned olive oil presses, one located centrally in the town and the other located in the village of San Marco. Most households which produce oil belong to one or the other of these cooperatives and take their yearly crop to it to be pressed for home consumption. Few households produce enough oil from their trees to consider selling it. There is also a cooperative operated by truck drivers, many of whom are of rural origin, to provide maintenance and servicing for vehicles. In 1986 a cooperative of *trullo* owners, mostly rural families, was incorporated to provide a collective means of advertising and organizing the rental of remodeled *trulli* to summer tourists. The Anti-hail Consortium should also be signaled here as a successful cooperative effort among local rural folk, although its membership extends all the way into Basilicata. This diffusion of cooperative activities reflects the success of the cooperative winery as a model, and the growth of the latter probably reflects the greater levels of education which have become frequent during the past several decades among those who dwell in the country, alongside its promise of general economic success.

Social welfare, rural Locorotondo, and politics

Modern political connections between town and country cannot be understood without gaining a sense of the social welfare systems which affect country dwellers. The expansion of such systems was intrinsically linked with the consolidation of political power, particularly for the Christian Democratic Party (hereafter DC), throughout Italy during the post-war era (Clark, 1984: 348–373). Those which are most relevant to the Locorotondese country dwellers are the various benefits – unemployment compensation, medical insurance, disability pensions, family checks, and retirement – for which people qualify as members of the two official rural occupational categories. These categories are the *coltivatori diretti*, "direct cultivators," and the *braccianti agricoli*, "agricultural laborers." The former category includes, in theory, individuals who are small proprietors or renters, and who employ family and hired labor to work their lands. The latter category is reserved for those who primarily earn their livings working on the land for wages.

Locorotondese informants recognize that many rural families would fit into the other category, but, in fact, most families declare their members to be *braccianti*. In the 1982 rural sample survey, which was conducted in 127 households, about 60 percent of all household heads declared themselves to be *braccianti*, but only 6.3 percent claimed the *coltivatore diretto* status. Most of the rest were involved in one way or another in the construction industry. (Many of their wives and daughters, however, declared themselves members of the *bracciante* category.) People employ this strategy because *coltivatori diretti* must pay part of their incomes into a locally managed mutual fund out of which they receive their benefits. Theoretically employers pay a contribution toward the benefits of *braccianti*. Currently the latter is not always the case, and to receive benefits a *bracciante* usually ends up developing a strategy for making up the difference between the minimum necessary number of days one must be hired and for which one must have benefit contributions, and the actual number of days officially declared by employers.

Much of the agricultural labor force of the coastal plains around the cities of Monopoli and Fasano, where there are vast olive groves and extensive truck gardens, consists of adolescent girls hired through the *caporale* – labor contractor – system, which many consider an unfair labor practice. According to law, when an employer hires an agricultural worker for a day's work, he is obliged to go through the employment office, and file a *foglio d'ingaggio*, an employment form, and pay the legal contribution toward the worker's benefits. In practice, however, growers on the Barese coastal plain and the Metaponto area in the Province of Taranto arrange for female labor directly with labor contractors, who file many fewer forms than the actual number of days the women work. This saves the grower money and profits the labor contractors who charge for their services. Such men are responsible for delivering the workers to the fields and supervising their work. They are also held responsible by the girls' parents for watching over them while they are away from home. Such workers are rarely aware of who owns the fields in which they are working, so extensive is the contractor's mediation between them and the proprietor.

To be entitled to benefits in the *bracciante agricolo* occupational category, a girl must log 51 work days with the employment office and sometimes, although they work considerably more, girls find they have not been credited with this minimum. In one case, a young woman worked over 300 days in a year for a contractor and found that she was not credited at the employment office with even the minimum. She had to adopt the strategy of paying an uncle enough money so that he could, in turn, file enough labor forms for her, declaring that she had worked for him, so that she could maintain her status as a *bracciante* and the fringe benefits due her. Since *caporali* are friends, relatives, and neighbors of the families of the girls they hire, and since those families see them in the role of trusted chaperone, these families rarely complain to the union offices (CISL and CGIL). When there are grievances, they can usually be headed off by the contractors through patron–client relationships with employment office personnel or, sometimes within the unions themselves.

The pattern of having to pay for one's own employment benefits through such procedures is repeated on the *murgia* itself. Those men who work for others in the fields, and women who are hired during the grape harvest, the most labor intensive time of year, do not expect employers in the rural population to pay all of their contributions because they are aware that their neighbors, relatives, and friends can ill-afford to hire labor at all. In fact, families often arrange to exchange labor with each other without charge (*a vègete* – "in turn").

The increased incomes of married men working in industry, building trades, and trucking, has lessened the necessity for married women to work in the fields for hire, although almost all declare themselves to be *braccianti agricoli*, and pay their own minimum benefit contributions. The *caporale* interviewed said that only 6 or 7 percent of the women he employed are married, and that this has dropped over recent decades. Married women may, however, seek employment from neighbors during the grape harvest, especially if it is possible to accumulate some days to log toward social welfare benefits. It is, and informants testify that it always has been, an ideal that married women perform agricultural labor mostly on household lands.

Before 1940 a person wishing *bracciante* benefits went to a notary with 4 witnesses and declared how many days a year he or she worked.[4] With the law of September 24, 1940, in 28 provinces in the south, including Bari, each municipality established an *elenco anagrafico*, a registration list of those who were agricultural workers, which divided them into 5 categories according to the number of days per year they worked. A municipal commission established these lists, guessing somewhat haphazardly about the number of days each worker was employed. Employers were to pay workers' benefit contributions according to compulsory estimates of their labor needs. Those on the lists were automatically entitled to benefits during the fascist era (the lists were retroactive to 1929), and after the war.[5]

On June 27, 1962, as farm workers in the Province of Bari began a 72 hour strike for higher wages, the Constitutional Court, lobbied by several Apulian land barons, abolished the lists, declaring them unconstitutional because there was no secure way of verifying the actual number of days worked, or, indeed, whether or not the individuals carried on them were really agricultural laborers (Gramegna, 1976: 202).[6] The abolition of the lists threatened cancellation of benefits for thousands of farm workers, and this heated up and prolonged the strike, inducing even the CISL (DC labor union) to unite with the leftist unions in their struggle. "The Great Strike," as it was called, lasted 12 days and eventually resulted in a victory for labor which won a new contract specifying higher wages.[7]

Although the registration lists remained abolished, as a result of worker agitation, laws were enacted which extended them for five years, but blocked the addition of further names. Since that time the "blocked" lists have been extended periodically, and those carried on them have been entitled to benefits without demonstrating the number of days a year they actually work. When an individual goes on pension, his or her name is subtracted from the list, which the government assumes will simply disappear with time. While the lists were open, inclusion on them, or exclusion from them, could be used politically, and once blocked, the carrying over of individuals who no longer worked as agricultural laborers could be similarly used. The lists were, in local parlance, "dirty." Informants (of various political colors, including DC) most often laid manipulation of these lists at the feet of the local Christian Democratic union, but some reliable DC informants intimated that the leftist union, the CGIL, had also indulged. Verification of such assertions, as in so many instances having to do with political controversy, would virtually require police powers of investigation. This, of course, also complicates the collection of accurate data about pensions, occupations, and incomes.

Even given the complications of data collection, pensions and other benefits provide a significant part of household income in Locorotondo. In total, 57.5 percent of the households in the 1982 rural samply survey collected some forms of pension income. Most of these pensions were old-age pensions of one kind or another. However, 15 percent of male heads of household who were not retired, and 12.3 percent of wives of heads (or their widows), enjoyed income from disability pensions, theoretically awarded to people with impaired earning ability. Little is necessary to secure such a pension beyond a willing doctor's signature on the paperwork, and false declarations of disability are understood to be widespread in both urban and rural Locorotondo as spoils in patron–client networks. This situation is no different from that in other places in Southern Italy, and in fact may even be less pronounced in Locorotondo.

The pension situation has been an enormous drain on the Italian economy, especially in the agricultural sector where contributions have not balanced disbursements. Some scholars have argued positively that major subsidies to agriculture have come through the transfer of funds from the social security contributions of other categories of worker to the agricultural sector.[8] Local DC politicians make this argument as well. The aging population has thrown a higher proportion of people into the pensionable retirement category, and, especially in the south, disability pensions have been widely used during the post-Second World War era as political spoils. Clark notes that in 1977 five-and-a-quarter-million Italians received disability pensions of one sort or another; this is one million more than received old-age pensions (1984: 353). In the 1982 rural sample survey there were 74 disability pensions for every 100 old-age pensions. (Of course, informants may have concealed unwarranted disability pensions in response to questions.) This is not outrageously high for the south where in certain provinces, the ratio for *coltivatori diretti* sometimes reaches as much as 10,000 disability pensions per 100 old-age pensions! In the northern Province of Mantua, in contrast, the ratio in 1973 was 53 disability pensions for every 100 old-age pensions (Sassoon, 1986: 57). Although it is difficult to determine to what degree the Locorotondese ratio represents a higher number of pensions than warranted by disabilities, there were certainly observable cases of pensioners who carried out agricultural work without health complaints. Further, there are instances of individuals who are not agricultural workers now, or in some cases ever, who receive the benefits of the category, including disability pensions, because of inclusion on the blocked registration lists.

The town institutions most closely related to the welfare systems are the *patronati*, the arms of the nationally organized labor unions which act locally to mediate between individual workers and bureaucracies of various kinds. The unions make little attempt to organize workers for any sort of labor struggle in Locorotondo. The two most important *patronati* in Locorotondo are those run by the CISL, the DC labor union, and that sponsored by the leftist union, the CGIL. Locals refer to the former office by its union initials, and call the latter the *Camera di Lavoro*, or Labor Hall. Since so few Locorotondese country people declare themselves to be *coltivatori diretti*, the *Coldiretti*, the *patronato* which serves that population elsewhere, has been of negligible importance even though there is a local office. Similarly, the ACLI (Catholic Workers' Association), and UIL, the social democratic labor union, although present during the post-Second World War era, have also been of little local importance. Artisans who do not adhere to the CGIL are served by the ACAI, the Catholic artisans' association. CISNAL, the right wing party union, enjoyed a certain importance during the late 1940s and early 1950s, but was eclipsed through the cooptation of its leader by DC interests.

Both major *patronati* (and the ACAI) have been led by father and son dynasties, and all three are linked to local electoral politics, although, the CISL, because of its DC affiliation, has had far greater power than the CGIL, and therefore larger membership over the years. The son of its leader has been mayor of Locorotondo and is a local DC power broker and faction leader. Control of CISL provides a large block of DC votes. The membership of CGIL is considerably smaller, but this *patronato* does not require official union membership of those to whom it supplies help with bureaucratic matters. Its leader (like his father), is a retired rural postman, and as such has gained wide respect among country people for the advice and help he supplied during his mail delivery rounds. Most country people turn to the Labor Hall out of trust and respect for this well-known town figure, but their doing so has never led to much political gain for the left.

Having carried out a bit of stage setting, it is now possible to examine the processes through which newly rising elite men in Locorotondo were able to capture and maintain power among the peasantry in the atmosphere of increased democratization of the post-Second World War era.[9] The war's aftermath saw the rise of several new political currents. The Communist Party swiftly reorganized among a portion of the town artisans and re-established itself in the Labor Hall. Individuals who had belonged to the fascist administration mostly gravitated toward the newly forming DC party, as did younger town men whose formation had been in Catholic Action groups.[10] Intellectual elite political players, including Don Sigismondo Calella, the founder of the cooperative winery, reorganized the Socialist Party. A notary, who, as will become apparent, brilliantly found a way to coopt peasant support, led the Liberal Party. In addition, the evanescent and anti-fascist Party of Action existed for a short while. A Liberation Committee, which was a coalition of anti-fascist parties, formed, and after some irregularities, sent its nomination of a member of the Party of Action for the post of mayor to the prefect in Bari (see Lisi, n.d.: 52–53).

The immediate post-war era was not without a measure of political violence in Locorotondo and in a few of the surrounding towns. This was directed at the emerging Communist forces, and consisted of squadrist attacks perpetrated by disgruntled fascists and other right wing individuals against Labor Halls and Communist Party offices. In 1944 reactionaries burned the Communist offices in nearby Turi and men from Locorotondo and other surrounding towns converged there seeking revenge. Allied occupational troops diffused this effort. In Locorotondo in November of 1945 a squad of ex-fascists who had mobilized a mob of peasants, interfered in a Communist political rally and then proceeded to sack the party office, burn its contents in the street, and beat several members. Cardone notes that the peasant crowd which participated, among which were some angry veterans of the brutal Russian front, had been stirred up by the leaders who told them that the Communists were pro-Soviet. General sentiments of peasant hatred toward the artisan constituency of Locorotondo's Communist Party also amplified the crowd's rancor (1972: 119). Such sentiments kept animosities toward Leftist party politics high among the peasantry. A group of armed Communists from Martina Franca descended upon Locorotondo that evening, but the police dissuaded them from violence with promises that the perpetrators of the sacking would be arrested. They were, but there was never a trial

(Lisi, n.d.: 57). Peasant animosity toward the left ran so high that one of the Communist leaders – a rural postman – had to deliver the mail armed with a revolver (Lisi, n.d.: 59). There was little worry on the part of the emerging DC political establishment that the peasantry would be captured by the left, and these violent episodes frightened men away from the Communist Party, for a time reducing its membership from over 100 to a low of 22.

The capture of peasant votes was, of course, crucial to political success, and the distribution of the peasantry over the countryside made that capture a challenge. Now suffrage included all over the age of 21, including women. Although there was some religious confraternity membership among peasant men, the general mood in the Locorotondese countryside was one of anti-clericalism. Peasant religious tradition consisted of magical beliefs and wonderful tales and miraculous beliefs about saints, and, to the chagrin of the local priesthood, little respect for church authority. Therefore, the DC had little appeal for the peasantry merely out of Catholic sentiment. In fact a substantial block of peasant voters adhered to the Liberal Party. A certain individual who manipulated unemployment office procedures to frighten peasant clients had helped gather these votes through threat and coercion. Thus the DC position was not necessarily secure during the early years of the Republic, although until 1952, that party controlled the town hall. The DC organized a network of informers throughout the countryside to keep tabs on political sentiment, and gather votes through selective withdrawal and reward with welfare benefits of various kinds. Chief weapon in the establishment party's arsenal was threat of cancellation from the *elenchi anagrafici*.[11] Party informers were well rewarded with jobs, disability pensions, and various favors for their efforts, but other peasants distrusted them. Some did double duty as police informers.

In 1952 a local political figure captured the office of mayor running as a Monarchist, with the cooperation of the neo-fascist Italian Social Movement (MSI) party. This right-wing coalition captured 20 out of 30 seats on the municipal council. His strategy was clever and simple; he obtained the peasant vote. He had been a Liberal, and as such had good contacts in the countryside. The strategy was to court the wealthier and more successful peasant small proprietors, knowing that they had a great deal of prestige among the peasantry in general because of their prosperity attained through hard work, and that they could, in turn, influence their kin and neighbors to vote for his party. The Christian Democrats had not courted such men. Party higher ups designated these influential individuals as *capi di contrada*, "hamlet bosses," and placed some of them on the Monarchist Party list. A few served as municipal councilors, although their party superiors expected them to keep their mouths shut during meetings. In essence, such men became legitimized party representatives in the rural hamlets, and once the Monarchist mayor and his coalition had captured office they functioned at the grass-roots level of the patron–client system, mediating between the needs of country clients and the communal administration. In campaigning he also skillfully played upon peasant values by promising rural improvements, railing against the DC spy system, focusing upon peasant animosity toward townsmen, and accusing the church hierarchy of scandalous activity. Even his switch from the Liberal to the Monarchist Party, its symbolism associated with order and tradition, was a stroke of genius. Country people remember the four years of his administration with regard.

The DC countered the threat to its power forcefully and the party recaptured the mayoralty in 1956, thereafter to relinquish power only briefly during the 1960s to a centauric coalition of the Liberal, Communist and Fascist parties. They brought the peasantry back under control through the application of all the coercive means available, often exercised through the CISL *patronato*. The DC established its own *capocontrada* system (which in part coincided with the existing spy network), but since the Monarchist Party had already recruited most of the respected peasant entrepreneurs, its members could exert little influence through esteem. Monarchist supporters disappeared from the *elenchi anagrafici* and then mysteriously reappeared if they changed affiliation and signed up with CISL. The opposition harassed the mayor with trifling prosecutions, and unknown persons exploded a threatening bomb on the balcony of his house.

After the defeat of the Monarchist administration in Locorotondo, power lay securely in the hands of the Christian Democratic Party which had gained control of all significant public institutions in town: the *Ente Pro Loco* (the tourism office), the hospital, the schools, and the commission for planning town festivals. During the 1950s and 1960s, the control of local health facilities, as Clark (1984: 337) notes for Southern Italy in general, was a primary source of spoils in the form of jobs which could be used to reward relatives and supporters. Similarly, control of school administration provides opportunities for the distribution of spoils, particularly in the form of hall-porter jobs. A leftist municipal councilor claimed that 2 percent of the local work force occupied such positions in the elementary and middle schools and the local agricultural technical institute. Judging from the observed population of the halls of such institutions, he may have been correct. Since in local elections the preferential votes of a handful of individuals can carry candidates into positions of municipal councilor, the ability to favor even a small number of relatives and friends can be politically useful.[12] Some country people have been favored with such jobs, but this was not a widespread phenomenon. Rather, after the DC consolidated its power in Locorotondo, its major rural vote-gathering strength was expressed through CISL.

After the final defeat of the Monarchist led right wing coalition, in the countryside only a mild threat to DC power has come from the Liberal Party (PLI). The local PLI has as its head a local doctor who is the son of a prosperous country family and who maintains an ambulatory in a particular zone of the countryside, from whence come the bulk of his preferential votes. This doctor is head of the cooperative winery, and numbers among the leaders of several other important local institutions. He is widely esteemed by country people, especially since he will make house calls day or night, and does not expect gifts in kind for his services. He is, however, the kind of patron people turn to for influence – *raccomandazione* – in certain circumstances. Also he has presented little threat to the DC power structure in terms of political opposition in the municipal council.

More recent DC politicians have captured rural loyalties in several ways besides those having to do with social security benefits, although the importance of this basis for votes continues to be underlined by the fact that the politician most connected with the CISL served as mayor during the second half of the 1970s, and in the next election took the highest number of preferential votes. However, the 1970s saw the completion of rural electrification, significant extension of Apulia aqueduct water into country hamlets, and the paving of most of the roads in the rural transportation network. As country dwellers left the status of full-time peasant to take other sorts of jobs, Locorotondo's countryside began to assume the identity of a semi-rural suburban bedroom community, and its inhabitants began to demand urban style services and amenities. These are accomplishments which would have been difficult for the other parties because they simply lack the regional and national connections and the political experience to secure the necessary funding from outside. Also, as individual men of peasant origin became economic successes as contractors, some of them chose political directions. One wealthy country dwelling individual in particular took the second highest number of preferential votes in the 1980 election and became vice-mayor. These votes came from his rural constituency and were based upon the esteem with which he is held for his success through hard work, and his willingness to help people out by loaning them money. He is part of the basis of power for the reform movement of the DC, inspired by the social upheaval of 1968 in Italy, which captured the municipality during the first half of the 1970s and then again in 1980.

Seen from the standpoint of country dwellers, another factor maintains loyalty to the established powers in the municipality. A law in 1968 required all Italian municipalities to adopt plans for housing and industrial development and zoning laws. The matter is very complex politically, but during the 1970s, plans and regulations were developed for Locorotondo which ended up limiting the volume of construction permissible in rural areas to 100 cubic meters of human living space for each 3,000 square meters of available land. The DC reluctantly accepted this task, which was a threat to its rural electoral base because the post-peasant population saw these rural zoning laws as a negation of traditional rights to construct for children's marriage settlements on parental land. Also, zoning laws operated little in the interests of the local construction industry which, as noted above, formed a significant power base within the party. Further, because the law imposed constraints which were externally defined, the DC had less local political flexibility. The Liberal Party, with its peasant constituency, held out that there should be no zoning, and the Socialists and Communists proposed various compromises which little appealed to rural constituencies. Although the plan was supposed to be ready by 1975, it was not adopted until 1980 – several DC administrations, for political reasons which are understandable, dragged their feet.

Throughout the 1970s and 1980s considerable amounts of abusive construction went on in the countryside to which administrators who wished to assure themselves rural votes had to shut an eye. For instance, a man might build a house for one of his children in which the supposed living space meets the law, but tack on large rooms which have been declared as farm enterprise space, which can be constructed at a higher ratio. These are connected to the declared living space by doors which are loosely filled and plastered over, and which will be opened and finished after building inspection. In 1982, about 300 cases of abusive rural construction had been denounced to the municipal hall, mostly by observant and vindictive neighbors. Such denunciations begin an administrative process which involves an on-site inspection and the communication of the charge of abusive construction to a higher-level magistrate (*pretore*), who acts immediately to bring the case to trial. There is usually a five day suspended jail sentence, and a small fine exacted of the abusive builder, but also something is supposed to be done about the building itself. The law allows the municipality to expropriate the building, or even to bulldoze it and charge the builder a fine which is double its worth, but neither measure has been adopted in Locorotondo. What happens is that the mayor delays further paper work as long as he can and attempts to patch together cures for cases in which it is possible. For instance, if a house has been built without an architect's plan (to save money), the abuser is admonished to have one drawn, even if after the fact, and, if the building is otherwise legal, the case can be written off. Sometimes variances are sought in the municipal council for individual clients by politicians. But as one astute local political observer put it, "sooner or later the knots will become tangled in the comb," because mayors risk being charged with the crime of omission of official acts if they do not follow up on building-abuse cases. In short, the law is well enough defined in this situation that it handicaps the flexible exercise of local options for the purposes of patron–client relationships.

Of course, whenever a person in authority closes an eye to illegalities, there is always the possibility that the eye might open. The potential threat that one's house could be bulldozed is a great one, and works to create dependencies between the postpeasant population and the administration, even if unintended by the latter. Since abusive construction is widespread, country dwellers see the municipal administration, and especially the town policemen, who handle such cases, as figures who can cause them much trouble if they are crossed. It is safer to cast one's preferential votes in the direction of those who might cause one trouble, or who, indeed, might help if a nosy neighbor went to the police about one's overly large house.

New wealth and power on the part of successful men in contracting, who identify with the countryside, has already begun to shift the political scene a bit toward that section of the municipality, and as country people gain more education they are less likely to be manipulated by the town party power structure. In the early 1980s rural demands for better roads and Apulian aqueduct water were being met by the municipality, and both townspeople and post-peasants felt that things were equalizing between town and country. Some country people were even taking a certain vindictive pleasure in constructing houses that rivaled the gentlemen's residences on the *masserie* in luxury.

A countryman's political history

To understand the post-Second World War town and country political process on a personal basis, consider the experience of a country individual who felt party efforts to control his peasant political loyalties directly. Giorgio (a pseudonym, of course) was a *bracciante agricolo*, who, before he left for military service in the early 1950s during the Monarchist administration, was convinced by the *capocontrada* in his rural area to join CISNAL, the right-wing *patronato* which at that time had about 400 local members because of the influence of the local administration. The local CISNAL office was run by an individual who, upon the promise of a municipal job, was enticed away from that *patronato* and the associated Monarchist/Fascist party coalition. Those who had belonged to CISNAL were mostly swallowed up by CISL, but Giorgio was of age for military service and departed for the north. Also he could not afford the membership dues in the DC union. Having served his military obligation he worked for a few months in Lombardy and then returned to Locorotondo to resume his life as a small proprietor/ *bracciante*.

Upon his return in 1957 he felt that he needed to belong to a union, and since he had heard that the CGIL was more interested in the needs of workers than the DC union, he signed up at the Labor Hall. By this time, the DC had recaptured the local government from the right-wing coalition, and was firmly entrenched. Soon after he found that his name no longer appeared in the *elenchi anagrafici*, and that he was no longer eligible for social security; evidently the CISL/DC network of informers had caught wind of his decision to join the CGIL. He thinks that, because he had not followed the other dispossessed CISNAL members into the DC union and had instead opted for the leftist alternative, the local power structure decided to make an example of him. He asked the advice of the local CGIL functionary who told him that the official procedures to gain reinstatement on the *elenco anagrafico* would take two years, and a friend advised him that he would be smarter just to walk over to the CISL office and take out a membership. He took that walk, explained to the CISL functionary about the cancellation of his name from the lists, and asked whether he would be helped if he became a member of the union. He was told not to worry, and before long his name indeed reappeared and once more he became entitled to benefits.

Self-admittedly, Giorgio was naive about politics and political ideology – he had no more education or experience than was the norm for country men. In fact, although one might suspect differently, he claimed that his short exposure to the more militantly unionized northern work situation, had not particularly raised his consciousness. His decision to join the CGIL was made naively on the basis of vague understandings that it operated more in the interest of true workers. He remained with the CISL/DC until the mid-1960s, serving as union *capocontrada* for his zone by acting as an intermediary between the *patronato* office and his neighbors. Around that time, higher ups in the DC began to talk about rural improvements in Giorgio's sector of the municipality. He felt that they had made a commitment, but at a meeting it became apparent to him that resources were going to be directed elsewhere, and he and the politician who he thought had made promises came to harsh words. The latter called Giorgio a communist, perhaps in reference to his former membership in the CGIL, and Giorgio recalls responding that it didn't matter whether one was a communist or a demochristian, when it came to the rights of his *contrada*. These words led to a scuffle in which others at the meeting defended his adversary. A couple of days later Giorgio walked into the CISL office and those present told him they could denounce him to the *carabinieri* because they had evidence that he had been armed with a knife on the night of the altercation. This was not true, he asserts; they said this to intimidate him. Giorgio decided that if they were going to call him a communist, and if even the leadership of CISL thought so, he might as well go over to that side.

Soon after, Giorgio signed up once again with the CGIL, and since he was a defector, the local communist party took him under its wing and even ran him in the party list for election to the municipal council. By the mid-1960s cancellation from the *elenchi anagrafici* was no longer used as a controlling technique by the party in power – the lists became "blocked" in 1962 (see above), and the DC had so consolidated its clientelistic power base as to be free from serious challenge. Thus, they took no action against him for defecting. He started to become more ideologically aware and read Communist Party literature including the daily *L'Unità*. The number of *braccianti* who were communists was (and is) small, especially in Giorgio's zone of the countryside. Giorgio, as a communist, felt criticism from his neighbors, but he felt committed until the late 1970s, when he became disillusioned with discussions in the party assembly about the implementation of the town's new zoning plan, which he and many others from the countryside saw as putting peasant parents at a distinct disadvantage with respect to the area of building that could be constructed on a given amount of land. He spoke out forcefully at a party meeting – especially in opposition to the insulting assertion by a town comrade that people with less than two hectares of land were not "true peasants." His words resulted in his expulsion from the zoning committee of the party, and he left the communists giving up politics altogether out of disillusionment.

Giorgio's experience was a bit unusual for his involvement with a leftist party, but it is instructive because it provides an example of how individuals in the peasant population have been co-opted into the town political networks and used for the extension of party political power without having their needs and opinions taken seriously. Only now that the countryside has begun to produce more highly educated people and self-made construction entrepreneurs with political clout based upon wealth has there begun to be an equalization in power between town and country in Locorotondo. Before, living far from the church bells meant living far from political power as well.

Chapter 10

SOME COMPARISONS

To gain broader perspective this chapter will compare and contrast Locorotondo with several other Italian settings. First it is useful to understand that the small proprietor based, rurally dispersed, peasant population which typifies Locorotondo, while relatively infrequent in the *mezzogiorno*, is not unique, and in fact probably belongs to a roughly definable type to which other locales can be ascribed as well. Second, the chapter will emphasize the point that Locorotondo's peasant population shaped itself and the local landscape it continues to occupy through strategic choices. Contrasts will be drawn with several other Italian places which share certain characteristics with Locorotondo and neighboring towns, but where peasant choice-making behaviors and strategic abilities were severely limited by the choices and strategies of dominating landowners. Locorotondo's development emerged instead from landowner *and peasant* strategies, and the particular nature of the settlement pattern and landscape it produced depended more heavily upon peasant choices than upon those of the local agrarian middle class, which in certain ways were more constrained by both local historical experience and by the nature of the landscape.

LOCOROTONDO AND TYPES OF PEASANTRY IN THE 'MEZZOGIORNO'

To grasp the nature of Locorotondese peasant sociocultural patterns it is useful to draw contrasts with other zones in the Italian south. Arlacchi has contributed a broad study of three distinctive Calabrian areas, each described for the late nineteenth- to early twentieth-century period, which helps do just that (1980). He asserts that these zones differ strikingly in terms of land tenure, economic conditions, and social organization, and argues against trying to generalize labels such as "the traditional Southern Italian family," as if there were a common set of family relations found over the entire *mezzogiorno*. Arlacchi reiterates that varieties of peasant family cohesion, internal relationships, and other aspects of social organization are likely to covary with the kinds of economic opportunities and constraints faced during specific historical moments. The case of Locorotondo resonates with his description of a Calabrian small proprietor dispersed peasantry, and this suggests that it may be heuristically useful to extend this and possibly his other two Calabrian types to other cases in the Italian south. To do so in much detail is far beyond the scope of this book, but it is worth considering his cases at least with respect to Locorotondo.

The areas Arlacchi describes are the Crotonese, the Piana di Gioia Tauro, and the Cosentino. In the Crotonese located at the point where the boot's sole meets its instep, there were agrotowns and a *latifundia* system in which almost all wealth was concentrated in the hands of a few large absentee landowners who employed managers. The local population consisted mostly of poverty stricken, landless rural proletarians. There are certainly several kinds of *latifondismo* found in the *mezzogiorno*, but it is possible to identify the Crotonese with certain other large areas, such as the northerly parts of Apulia described by Snowden (1986), and perhaps the zone around Matera studied by Tentori (1971, 1976), where directly managed large estates and peasant proletariats also prevailed. Arlacchi characterizes the Crotonese peasant proletarian family as having "scarce internal cohesion" (1980: 214). It tended to fly apart because family members earned day laborer incomes independently of one another. Parents became isolated after children left home; siblings drifted apart. Since there was little or no property involved in the formation of new households, couples entered upon marriage less ceremoniously and at a younger age than in the other two areas, and considered it "a formality which tended to be brought about as rapidly and as simply as possible" (215). His description of family brittleness in this area brings to mind Tentori's discussion of family in Matera in Basilicata (see below), and his discussion of marriage and courtship recalls that of Pitkin for Stilo in Calabria, also a peasant proletarian town (1985: 19–22).

Arlacchi calls the zone of the Piana di Gioia Tauro, near Italy's toe, the "zone of permanent transition" because its economy was based upon medium-sized farm enterprises which produced export crops, particularly olive oil, and were therefore readily subject to market fluctuations. Economic instability, as well as a degree of opportunity, reigned here. Most peasant families did not possess enough resources to guarantee self-sufficiency, and could be thrown into crisis by market shifts. This produced a population of highly competitive peasant entrepreneurs whose contests sometimes left the economic arena and gave rise to blood feuding. Mafia-like organizations which ruthlessly took advantage of constantly shifting economic opportunities also characterized the area. There are parallels to be drawn between this zone and the classic Western Sicilian mafia zones with respect to competition over entrepreneurial opportunities, although there are also some sharp contrasts especially in that Western Sicily remained in large estates. In the Piani di Gioia Tauro, Arlacchi describes a family life dominated by rigid and defensive patriarchal authority – a masculine overcompensation for the relative insecurity of the economic situation. Rather than being based upon respect and management necessities as in the Cosentino (see below), male authority in this zone was based upon defense of the family. Arlacchi's image of relationships between nuclear families is Hobbesian in that he sees them pitted against each other, vying for resources in contests characterized by negative reciprocity, as well as by ostentatious spending based upon temporary good fortune. In this zone codes of honor and self-help counted heavily.

Finally, in contrast to these areas, the Cosentino, located in the vamp of the Italian boot, contained a population of peasant small proprietors who farmed integrated family landholdings mostly for subsistence (also see Dickinson, 1956: 293). Their labor for others supplemented family land income, as well as income gained through sharecropping the medium-sized properties of town professionals. Here the population lived dispersed in the countryside to a degree comparable to that of the Murgia dei Trulli, and there was a high degree of peasant independence. However, early in this century "overproduction" of people with respect to available land or the resources needed to acquire it, was siphoned off through migration. In the Cosentino Arlacchi describes a nuclear family structure in which there was strong paternal authority, and membership solidarity focused around respect for the role of manager of the family enterprise. He claims that family life was rigidly circumscribed by role expectations and rules, particularly surrounding questions of marriage and inheritance (also see Piselli, 1981: 19–61). Relationships with kinsmen outside the nuclear family and with non-kin were given continuity by frequent balanced reciprocity, and among peasants there were strong sentiments against ostentation.

Arlacchi's scheme might be oversimplified, but used heuristically it helps place the peasant social structure of Locorotondo in broader perspective, and vice versa, the present discussion of Locorotondo's small proprietor, rurally dispersed, peasantry helps lend greater validity to Arlacchi's Cosentino peasantry as a useful category. Common between this Calabrian peasantry and that of Locorotondo were small proprietorship, dispersed settlement, emphasis on paternal management authority, tightly rule-circumscribed family life, rigidly controlled marriage formation, balanced reciprocity among non-kinsmen, and frugality. In his brief study of types of dispersed settlement in Southern Italy, Dickinson highlights the Murgia dei Trulli and the Cosentino, but also mentions interior lowland zones near Avellino and Benevento, as members of the same type (his type 5), which on his map of rural settlement also includes a large area of the Abruzzi centering on Pescara (1956: 288; figure 3). These areas remain little known ethnographically. Therefore, there are some other potentially similar areas in Southern Italy, and it is not unreasonable to hypothesize that where dispersed settlement accompanies a long-term family stake in land and subsistence on it, families with characteristics resembling those of Locorotondo and the Cosentino have existed.

There are, however, some important differences between the Locorotondo and Cosenza peasantries which should not be overlooked. As Arlacchi describes them, Cosentino small proprietors were self-sufficient farmers who were minimally tied into wider markets. Since Locorotondese peasants were grape growers they were directly tied into export markets, and increasingly so during the nineteenth century, but the ideal was also to operate small but integrated family enterprises which supplied most family subsistence needs. Enough families realized this ideal that there was also some degree of insulation from the vicissitudes of the market, and households rode out the profound economic crises of the late nineteenth and early twentieth centuries, as well as the attack of phylloxera. It also appears from his description, and from that of Piselli (1981), that the peasants of the Cosenza area depended more heavily than those of Locorotondo upon emigration to siphon off excess population. The permanent emigration of some children seems to have been a regular family expectation. Although, emigration was a factor in Locorotondo, the continual transfer of land from estates into peasant hands over the nineteenth and early twentieth centuries kept rates low for the area, and when people undertook emigration it was often with the intention of gaining the wherewithal to participate in that transfer after returning home.

Of course, Arlacchi's three areas, here made into an ideal-type model, do not exhaust the kinds of peasant economic and social relationships to be found in the south of Italy. Douglass, for instance, has contributed a study of a Molisano town in which the ideal was the extended family among both peasants and artisans (1984). What emerges, however, from a consideration of Arlacchi's study, is the idea that Southern Italian social structures and relations are historically specific developments having to do with particular economic experiences. There are some patterns, and a limited number of rough types could probably be worked out for the *mezzogiorno*. The Cosentino and Locorotondese peasantries suggest that an independent subsistence-oriented small proprietor category, which shares characteristics having to do with family enterprise structure, reproduction and internal relationships is definable.

PEASANT STRATEGIES

This analysis began with a quote from Antonio Genovesi, the eighteenth-century doyen of *meridionalismo*. In it he recommended a strategy for the gentleman, or churchman, unable or unwilling to undertake direct control and farm rationally. This comprised cession of land in emphyteusis, and its passage to greater peasant control, as a solution for what he saw as the agricultural problems of his times. Having such control, said Genovesi, peasants would work hard to provide well for themselves and for their children. This would increase production, provide a steady rent to landlords, and promote prosperity. It would also prevent the peasantry from becoming unruly by providing them with a secure subsistence base. For Locorotondo he was right in part, considering prosperity strictly on the local level, and as constituting such things as relatively better health and economic security for peasants than elsewhere in Apulia or Southern Italy in general. It remains in this chapter to consider the degree of choice and the freedom to create adaptive strategies which accrued to the Locorotondese peasantry. Again, this can best be done in contrast to several other areas in the *mezzogiorno*.

First, a glance at some of the conditions under which rural populations elsewhere in the south lived supports the contention that Locorotondese peasants led more comfortable lives. For instance, Snowden (1986: 57) talks of the "lethal social conditions" in the towns in Foggia Province, and the interior of Bari Province during the years of the peasant leagues around the turn of the century; he writes:

Crime, like disease, thrived in the crowded urban slums. Poverty, hunger, unemployment, broken families, and overcrowding provided the natural conditions for its growth. The tensions of a deeply oppressive society found an outlet in aggression. (1986: 61)

Or one can consider Tentori's characterization of the treatment of old people in mid-twentieth-century Matera, in neighboring Basilicata, as virtual abandonment by their impoverished offspring. He ascribes the attitudes of the latter to brutal subjection to parental will without affection. Marriage represented escape from the family of socialization. Retiring parents depended more upon benevolent neighbors than children for care, and in Matera the old-age home arose as an institution to deal with the abandonment of elderly people (Tentori, 1976: 283; 1971: 113–114). In general, it has been well-documented that the rural proletarians of the agrotowns of the *mezzogiorno* led hard lives characterized by frequent exposure to violence, hunger, disease (in crowded unsanitary conditions), and insecurity about employment.

Locorotondo did not have a rich peasantry, but neither was that peasantry characterized by the eternal hopelessness, the often-described *miseria*, of many other Southern Italian rural populations (cf. Friedman, 1953). Diversification between growing grapes and producing wine for the market, and subsistence cropping in conjunction with the employment of family members, especially the unmarried, as agricultural laborers, gave this peasantry a degree of flexibility which allowed survival through hard times. Contrary to descriptions of peasant attitudes in other southern locales, this South Italian peasantry saw work as a value, not as a necessary evil. Rural settlement meant daily living conditions which were more healthful than the crowded and cramped one-room quarters, often shared with livestock, of so many Southern Italian peasantries living in agrotowns. Locorotondese peasants knew some crime, often because they were likely victims for thieves. They knew some disease, but, in fact, outlived their town cousins, the artisans. They knew occasional hunger, especially in bad economic times such as the depression, and the Second World War and its aftermath, but hunger was not endemic. And they knew the hardships of old age, especially the ravages of spine-curving physical labor, but they could reasonably hope for security and care from their children in their waning years.

Throughout, this work has invoked the concept of adaptive strategy. A change for a population, especially a subordinate one, can be considered to have truly resulted from a strategy only if that population had some range of choice and a sense of control at the outset. One asks where, in the case of Locorotondo, local developments toward small proprietorship and a dispersed settlement pattern came from. Did elite estate owners who, of course, initiated emphyteusis contracts during the late eighteenth and the whole of the nineteenth centuries, set the pattern for their own advantage and capture the peasantry's labor with a strategy which kept the latter well enough fed and harboring an illusion of independence so as not to become unruly? Or did local agricultural patterns come from the peasants themselves, through their own adaptive strategies, which especially involved the idea of moving outside the town walls?

It should be clear by now that the peculiarities of Locorotondo emerged from strategic decisions made by both elite landowners and peasants in response to particular economic and ecological conditions, such as poor land and the ready availability of a market for grapes. Each group adopted a series of strategies thought best at the time for maximizing individual and family interests. While an emergent phenomenon, the unusual patterns found in Locorotondo do not necessarily represent a long-term symbiosis between those diverging interests and strategies. Indeed, in 1827 Locorotondese *galantuomini*, apparently recognizing that emerging developments were contrary to their interests as a class, tried in vain to reverse the changing settlement pattern by attempting to force the peasantry back more securely under their control inside the walls. By then it was simply too late for them to exert such power. Strategies adopted by individuals reacting to the conditions they experienced at particular historic moments and set on course, so to speak, by long-term contractual relationships such as emphyteusis, did not always continue to yield the advantages which were perceived initially, as *galantuomini*, whose emphyteutical incomes eroded with inflation, found over the longer span. Emphyteusis variously and at different times worked to both the advantage and disadvantage of peasant and *galantuomo*. Herein lies part of the usefulness of Bennett's concept. To say that something is an *adaptive strategy* is not necessarily to say that it is *adaptive*, especially over the long run.

One cannot say that the elite landowners of Locorotondo managed to control the situation totally and exert a hegemony over the peasantry, leaving them no choices. The emphyteusis strategy to a great extent divorced the landed from the productive process, the possibility of enfranchisement even meant the risk of total loss of property, once the contract had been entered, especially after 1861. Rents payable in cash introduced the danger of erosion by inflation. Most importantly, the contracts specified nothing whatsoever about peasant residence. The choice to live far from the church bells, in other words the choice of settlement pattern, was that of peasants, not their emphyteutical landlords, although it was certainly a choice conditioned by the exigencies of land transformation defined in the contract. The peasantry of Locorotondo, not the *galantuomini* or their contracts, *made* the local rural landscape.

To understand this more fully it is useful to contrast the Locorotondo system with several others containing similar elements. In the more common Italian dispersed settlement system based upon so-called "classic" *mezzadria*, found in the north and center, the owners exerted a high degree of direct control over the use of their land, and this degree of control was expressed directly in the contract. Living on the farmstead was an important stipulation of the relationship, and the owner could dictate much about the nature of the household through his control of the number of people in residency. He could even regulate such events as marriage. In essence, the settlement pattern under the classical *mezzadria* pattern, and even aspects of household size and composition, were not peasant strategies; rather they were integral parts of the owner's strategy. The owner also exerted direct control over farming decisions. The power exerted by owners under this system is perhaps illustrated by the persistence of feudal customs involving small tributes in kind to be paid annually by the sharecroppers. Owners relinquished very little of their control over the means of production in the *mezzadria* relationship and protected themselves from the ravages of inflation by collecting their rents in kind not cash. In general then, upper Italian *mezzadria* landlords exerted a much stronger hegemony over their tenants and far more severely limited their strategical choices contractually than did landlords in Locorotondo (Silverman, 1975: 55–62; Kertzer, 1984: 26–38).

Another comparison, this one closer at hand to the Murgia dei Trulli, is instructive because, although it does not involve a rural dwelling peasantry, it does involve viticultural development. During the 1870s and 1880s, in response to the attacks of phylloxera in France, and to the declining market for Apulian wheat, large scale owners, especially the Pavoncelli family, in the upper reaches of the Barese interior (from Cerignola to Bitonto), adapted the strategy of planting vineyards. Labor for this intensive operation was recruited not through emphyteusis, but through improvement contracts. These had a duration of between 25 and 29 years and were never renewed. After the period ended all improvements reverted to the landlord; the peasant found himself landless once again and returned to the town-square labor market. The owners used the improvement contract to entice propertiless day laborers onto a small piece of land to plant and cultivate vineyards and, after the document had run its span, continued to cultivate the vines with hired laborers. Tenants were closely overseen on all phases of land improvement and cultivation to assure uniform quality in the grapes which would be harvested for the owner's winery. If they departed from instructions, the labor was performed at their expense by hired workers under the direct supervision of the owner's overseer. This was a tightly rationalized system in which the peasants granted contracts were even required to sell their product to the landlord's winery on dates, and in quantities, specified beforehand (Snowden, 1986: 35–40). There was no room or time for growers to develop even a marketing strategy, or for a peasant class of wine buyers to develop as it did in Locorotondo. Here one can scarcely talk about peasant agricultural strategies, except in that they elected to take on the contracts in the first place. *Braccianti* accepted the harsh terms of these improvement contracts because doing so meant a little more security than relying totally upon the daily labor market in the *piazza* before dawn, and it meant that they could vaunt some of the qualities of peasant small proprietors, even if temporarily. Little actual control accrued to them.

This system developed after Southern Italy had become well integrated into international agricultural markets. The owners involved were also highly sophisticated, capitalistic entrepreneurs, sometimes of foreign origin. By that time the development of Locorotondo's dispersed settlement pattern and small proprietorship had been fully accomplished, and although viticulture expanded there, as elsewhere in Apulia, as a result of expanding international demand, it was already mostly in the hands of small proprietors. However, during the same period harsher contracts involving non-perpetual leases, initial entrance payments to contracts, and tighter control, also began to develop in some towns of the Murgia dei Trulli which neighbored Locorotondo, but lagged somewhat behind it in viticultural development (see Chapter 7).

Underlying peasant and elite adaptive strategies in Locorotondo was another important set of considerations which can best be grasped in a comparative light. Differential development in Locorotondo also came from the initially impoverished agricultural environment. This is perhaps surprising, because one might expect the development of a relatively comfortable peasant society in a more favored landscape, not in an area such as this, where soils were thin and water drained away underground. But, in fact, the general environmental impoverishment of the area served to curb the possibilities of large landowners and forced certain strategic choices upon them.

This perhaps ironic situation on the Murgia dei Trulli can be cast into relief through a brief comparison with another large South Italian area in which emphyteusis contracts were widespread at one time, but in which peasant control of land *did not* persist. Under the old order noblemen often adapted emphyteusis, and other kinds of contracts under which they offered peasants favorable terms over the long run, to bring population to underpopulated or depopulated feudal estates. For instance, Mack Smith notes that wealthy Sicilian noble families used this strategy widely during the period between 1500 and 1650 to settle their sparsely populated estates. This helped meet the demand for wheat generated by expanding population. The founding of new villages also lent such Sicilian barons prestige by bringing them seats in the baronial house of parliament. Settlers on these Sicilian estates were often foreigners gathered across the Adriatic Sea (Mack Smith, 1968a: 195–198). In Genuardo, the pseudonymous town Blok describes, landowners conceded fields to Greek islander colonists in the seventeenth century. There was a second wave of emphyteutical leasing in 1720. After this, as the large estate pattern took hold, there were no further concessions (1974: 31–32). In Sicily many of these small peasant gains were lost at mid-eighteenth century, when, especially in the western half of the island, landowners connived to repossess control over their lands because they began to see the advantages of planting extensive cereal fields and feel the disadvantages of long-term leasing. In 1752 the Sicilian emphyteusis contracts of the sixteenth through early eighteenth centuries were officially and arbitrarily abrogated by the king, who responded to baronial pressure (Mack Smith, 1968b: 278–279).

In Sicily, noble magnates perceived a better strategy for themselves, because the land, although not nearly as productive as, for instance, the Po Valley, would produce adequate incomes from cereal production without great capital investment. Emphyteusis in early modern Sicily had been a tool for getting people to the estate to farm cereals, not for getting people to invest massive amounts of labor into transforming poor land to make it productive, as was the case in Locorotondo. Once the labor was mobilized in Sicily, and a population was established and growing in the rural countryside, the relinquishment of control implied in the emphyteusis contract reduced the landowner's flexibility to respond to markets, and such landlord/renter relationships lost their appeal. Baronial levels of power under the old order overcame this inconvenience.

In Locorotondo, on the other hand, the strategy of letting land to be developed into vineyards created a productive system in a poor environment with little short-term risk to the landowners, but also a system which could not easily be reabsorbed under their direct control, because viticulture was labor intensive and therefore too costly for all but a few *galantuomo* families to carry on with wage laborers. This became particularly true during the years of transoceanic migration when labor in Apulia became scarce and more expensive (Presutti, 1909: 147). There was little possibility for landowners to attempt the land's recapture as had been done in Sicily. The land was initially very poor; only peasant motivation, in conjunction with markets, could make it produce in the absence of large amounts of capital, hence at the heart of the relative prosperity of Locorotondese rural society were the thin plateau soils and the karst landscape, although clearly not in a deterministic way. For the peasants of Locorotondo the hope to "eat a piece of bread" far from the church bells depended also upon a local middle class of only middling wealth, and for the most part, mild entrepreneurial ambitions at least in comparison to the agribusinessmen of the more northerly regions of Apulia. But above all, it depended upon, and fed, their extraordinary motivation to work until their bones ached so as to make a step ahead for their children.

Appendix I Pronouncing Locorotondese dialect

Since it is often pleasant to have a sense of the sound of foreign words included in a text, there follows a short guide to the pronunciation of Locorotondese dialect. Most readers who will wish to have such a sense will have some familiarity with Italian, and the book uses an orthography based upon that of standard Italian and French.

Consonants in Locorotondese have approximately the same values they have in the national language, although certain combinations (*ng*, or *mb*, for instance) can occur initially, without following a vowel. This is a characteristic of many southern dialects. The little used "j" of archaically spelled Italian has been adopted herein with its value close to the English "y" sound, as in "yes."

Similarly, simple vowels in dialect have the same sounds, more or less, as those in Italian. Locorotondese, however, makes much use of the unaccented "schwa" sound. This has approximately the sound of the "e" in French "*de*" (of) and may occur alone, or combined with other vowels to produce a series of diphthongs which gives the dialect, particularly as spoken in the countryside, a characteristic sound. I have chosen to represent this schwa vowel with an unaccented "e," and to use accent marks to indicate open and closed "e's," according to the usages of French spelling. Thus "é" represents a closed "e" and "è" the open version. Diphthongs using schwa vowel are "eu," "eo," "ei," "eé," and "euo." Some examples: "teu" (you); "u teore" (the bull); "u veceine" (the neighbor); *Curdunneés* (Locorotondese); and *u crestiène de feuore* (the man from outside – i.e. a peasant).

Aspects of grammar are beyond the scope of this short note, but a sense of how the plural is formed will be useful. With most nouns number is indicated simply by context or with an accompanying article: *u teore* (the bull), *i teore* (the bulls); *a mamme* (the mother); *i mamme* (the mothers). Certain irregular nouns, however, form the plural by adding the suffix *-ere*. Much encountered in the text will be *u jazzeile* (the hamlet), *i jazzèlere* (the hamlets).

Appendix II Glossary of Italian and dialect terms

Abbreviations: dial., dialect; Arch. It., Archaic Italian; So. It., Southern Italian usage; It., Standard Italian.

borgo (It.) An extramural, but town as opposed to country, neighborhood.

bracciale (Arch. It.) In the eighteenth century, the term used for peasant small proprietors with few animals.

bracciante agricolo (It.) Modern term for agricultural worker.

capocontrada (It.) Either a locally recognized and esteemed country hamlet leader and/or an informal rural political party representative.

caporale (It.) A farm labor recruiter.

casèdde (dial.) A *trullo* dwelling.

caseddère (dial.) A mason who specializes in *trullo* construction.

casella (Arch. It.) Archaic Italianization of both *casidde* and *casèdde*.

casidde (dial.) A field hut built in *trullo* style used for storage, or as a stall.

chiusura (Arch. It.) In the eighteenth century an enclosed piece of land.

contadino (It.) A peasant.

contrada (It.) A rural subdivision of a municipality.

decurionato (It.) Under the Kingdoms of Naples and Two Sicilies, the town council.

Don (It.) Title applied to landowners, priests, and professionals.

elenco anagrafico (It.) List kept between 1940 and 1962 of individuals entitled to agricultural worker employee benefits. Cancellation from these lists was used widely as a political weapon.

foglio d'ingaggio (It.) The paperwork which must be filed when employers of agricultural workers hire people and pay contributions towards their benefits.

galantuomini   (It.) Term used to refer to the elite classes in the south of Italy, especially to elite landowners.

jasteime   (dial.) A curse.

jazzeile   (dial.) A rural hamlet in which the space and facilities between dwellings are communally owned. (pl. *jazzèlere*.)

jeuse   (dial.) A one-room dwelling owned by peasants in the town of Locorotondo for use during visits to the center for Mass or business. Often rented to artisans during the day.

mantenemènte   (dial.) The allowance in foodstuffs provided equally by offspring for their retired parents.

mascière   (dial.) Local witch or sorceror, usually a male, whose power emanates from knowing how to use a magic book obtained from the Devil.

massaro   (So. It.) In the eighteenth century a peasant with a larger integrated operation involving animals, who may or may not have taken on estate land as well. More recently either the salaried manager of a landowner (*massaro da campo*), or the sharecropper of a large estate.

masseria   (It.) A medium to large estate in Locorotondo, and by extension the buildings forming its headquarters.

'mbasciateure   (dial.) A middleman. Someone who negotiates labor or the sale or leasing in emphyteusis of land.

meridionalista   (It.) A scholar or politician concerned with the problems of Southern Italy.

mési mési   (dial.) The practice of rotating the living arrangements of an old and feeble parent among siblings.

mezzano (menzano)   (Arch. It.) In Apulia during the old order, land set aside for grazing animals of traction. In Locorotondo in the eighteenth century, for all intents, high quality pasture.

mezzogiorno   (It.) Southern Italy.

palma   (So. It.) 1. Local measure of length equivalent to 25 centimeters. 2. An olive branch blessed in church on Palm Sunday and exchanged among people.

palmento   (It.) A concrete or stone floor for crushing grapes.

patronato   (It.) The local branch of one of the labor unions which mostly functions to help people solve bureaucratic problems.

quartiero   (Arch. It.) The local measure of vineyards used during the eighteenth and early nineteenth century. Contained 625 vines. Equivalent, more or less to a *stoppello* (which see).

serrata (Arch. It). An enclosed piece of land during the eighteenth century, perhaps securable with a gate.

servetutene (dial.) Adoption of a relative or non-relative by someone without an heir in return for care. Often involved provision of a marriage settlement.

signorotti (So. It.) Local term used by working classes to describe the elite classes.

stoppello (So. It.) Local measure of land which is equivalent to 1,074 square meters.

tomolo (So. It.) Local measure which is equivalent to 8 *stoppelli* (which see).

trullo (It.) A building typical of the Murgia dei Trulli, constructed with a corbelled, cone-shaped dome surmounted by a whitewashed finial.

vetedurante (dial.) The right of use until death, particularly of a dwelling, provided to a parent after a child has received a marriage settlement.

Notes

1 Introduction

1 *Ce ui mangé u pen, sté lunten dé campen.* See the appendix for an explanation of the pronunciation of Locorotondo's dialect.

2 My studies of Pantelleria constitute another specific look at small proprietor peasants in the *mezzogiorno* from an anthropological perspective (Galt, 1979, 1980; Galt and Smith, 1979, among others). However, the Pantescans are an island folk, and this strongly influences their cultural system. Locorotondo presented a mainland small proprietor situation which might be more typical of others in the area. Douglass' portrayals of Agnone in the Molise, near the Abruzzese border, also concern a peasant population which lives, at least in part, dispersed in the countryside (1980: 343–347, 1984). However, in neither publication does Douglass go into much detail about the nature of land tenure, or about relative proportions of peasants living in given settlement patterns.

3 Major historical anthropological analyses have been carried out in Italy by Blok (1974), Schneider and Schneider (1976), Kertzer (1984), Douglass (1984), and Holmes (1989). Eloquent cases for historical studies in the context of the analysis of institutions in complex society also have been made by Silverman (1979) in her analysis of the Sienese Palio, and by Davis (1977: 5–7) in his comparative review of Mediterraneanist social anthropology. Historical work has now become almost paradigmatic in the anthropological analysis of Italian communities. The document-rich archives of Italy present marvelous opportunities for examining the pasts of communities in which anthropologists interest themselves and for tracing social change in them.

4 All translations from Italian or Locorotondese dialect, unless otherwise indicated, are the author's.

2 Work and the crowded countryside

1 There is a sizeable illustrated literature in English and other languages on this form of "architecture without architects", so detailed descriptions are unnecessary here (see especially, Allen, 1969; Berteaux, 1899; Battaglia, 1952; and Wilstach, 1930).

2 The origin and function of these signs is the subject of a small literature. The most recent and most comprehensive contribution is that of M. L. Troccoli Verardi (1972). Her study notes that inhabitants of *trulli* rarely have a clear

sense of the meaning or even function of the signs on roof cones and interviewing for the present study confirms this, and suggests that their origin is perhaps that upon building a *trullo*, the inhabitants consulted a local witch/curer, or *mascière*, for a sign. The *mascière* gained his magical status through the possession of a magical book called a "command book" (*u livère de cummande*) which may have been some kind of almanac with zodiacal symbols in it. This would parallel other attempts to secure protection and cures which are directed at this figure in rural society. No one interviewed remembered how roof symbols were chosen, not even the octogenarian *trullo* builder consulted. Since no informant made any secret of other magical beliefs, it seems that active beliefs about the efficacy of the roof symbols have passed out of memory. Old photographs of the area show them to have been much more frequent in the first decades of the twentieth century than now (see in particular, Wilstach, 1930).

3 This practice is discussed in Presutti, 1909: 140. According to his discussion, emphyteusis contracts only allowed planting grain on the ridges during the first years, and this probably served as a means for the peasant to grow some subsistence crops while waiting for the vines to reach full bearing age.

4 *U Boss*, "the boss," was the nickname of a man who emigrated to work in mining in Century, West Virginia, early in this century. He was a work leader, hence the nickname.

3 Inside Locorotondo

1 See Allen, 1969, for photographs of the historical center of Cisternino.

2 A photo of such a livestock fair held on the feast of San Cosimo and Damiano in the neighboring town of Alberobello will be found in Wilstach, 1930.

3 The means are easily significantly different at the 0.01 level using a one-tailed test. T = − 3.31 with 47 degrees of freedom.

4 An excellent recent discussion of patron–client relationships and politics in a nearby Apulian town is Resta, 1984.

4 Settlement and economy

1 The mid-eighteenth century (1756) map mentioned survives in an early nineteenth-century (1810) copy in the possession of Professor Luigi De Michele of Locorotondo (ALM, 1810), but also published in a facsimile edition by the lawyer Vito Mitrano. This map is very detailed and contains many place names as well as accurate, if not properly proportioned, indications of the road network. Figure 4.1 reconstructs that network and the territory defined in 1566 by superimposing them on the modern territory of Locorotondo.

2 In one case (which also appears on the aforementioned map), the property of two related men named Fumarola was divided such that the *casella* (*trullo*) of one ends up in Martina Franca, and the *domus* (house) of the other lies in Locorotondo (Chirulli, 1982: 226). Here the notary clearly distinguished the

Latin word for house from the local word for *trullo*, probably indicating that the latter was not a dwelling, but rather a storage building or a stall. The Italianized, or in this case Latinized, version of the local dialect words for *trulli* always present problems of interpretation. In local dialect a *casèdde* is a corbel domed dwelling (a *trullo*) and a *casidde* is a field hut not meant as a permanent dwelling. In Italian documents both words become collapsed into *casella* or *casetta* (the former being strictly correct Italianization of *casèdde*). Therefore it is always doubtful whether one is reading a description of a dwelling or merely of a field hut. In the 1566 document, however, the author has made the distinction. No other *domus* happens to fall near the boundary line, although a number of *caselle* do. The question then becomes: was this house the house of a small proprietor peasant, or the headquarters of a landowner's estate, and was it an inhabited *trullo*?

3 Baccaro erroneously dates this *trullo* to 1559 (1968: 55). More likely, on the basis of a personal field reconnaissance, the date reads 1599, although a reading of 1509 is within the realm of possibility.

4 See Villari, 1977 for a thorough discussion of the variety of differing customs for concession of commons in a selection of communes in the vicinity of Salerno.

5 Manuscript copies of the *onciario* for Locorotondo remain in the National Archives in Naples, and in the Provincial Archive in Bari. Both were consulted for this study. The copy in Bari, microfilmed for analysis in the United States, bears marginal notations indicating changes in property ownership between 1749 and 1765, while the document was kept in the town hall.

6 Omissions of ages for 146 people (of which 48 priests) and undercounting of small children, noted above, make it only approximate. The former at least partially explains the imbalance between males and females at middle age, and the latter problem explains the narrowed younger cohorts.

7 The word *chiazzile* is a semi-Italianization of the dialect term *jazzeile*. Documents also refer to *piazzile* – the full Italianization of the term.

8 Few studies of the *catasto onciario* or of eighteenth-century peasant culture in South Italy contain any mention of inheritance of houses at marriage. A notable exception is a recent study by Giacomini which uses the *onciario* and notarial records to reconstruct marriage patterns in Belmonte on the Tyrrhenian coast of Calabria (Giacomini, 1981). In Belmonte there was a tendency toward patrilocal extended families and males, instead of females, inherited houses.

9 The reader should consult Galt, 1991, for a more thorough discussion and explanation of changes in marital assigns in Locorotondo, especially those having to do with the bestowal of houses.

10 A comparable calculation has been made for only one other town using the cadastral data and this is Calopezzati in Calabria (Assante, 1964) where the Gini coefficient, adjusting for landless hearths, equals 0.87. Calopezzati had a slightly higher degree of landlessness; 20 percent of households had nothing. No other data exists in print with which to compare Locorotondo's distribution of landed *wealth*. De Meo (1935: 393) reports Gini coefficients for distribution of *income* for Bari (0.771), Foggia (0.757), Castellamare di

Stabia (0.74), and Barletta (0.677), but not for land. A comparable income distribution cooefficient for Locorotondo is 0.72.

11 An emphyteusis contract dating to 1801 contains a surveyor's report which defines an ideal *quartiero* as a square 25 by 25 vines (ASN-AN, 1777–1808: Nov. 1, 1801). The mid-nineteenth-century minutes of a session of the town council, which respond to a query from provincial level about local weights and measures, show that a *quartiero* at 1,098 square meters was a bit larger than a *stoppello*, which measured 1,074 square meters. These can be considered equivalent for the purposes of analyzing the *catasto onciario* which was compiled from declarations of land surface area rather than accurate surveying.

12 Each year some of the must is mixed with concentrated grape syrup before vinification so that it develops more alcohol. This wine (*cotto*) resists hot weather better than wine made from simple must. The syrup is concentrated in a cauldron outdoors over a fire. The burners mentioned in eighteenth-century documents were for this purpose.

13 It is also possibly the case that not all Locorotondese notarial acts are represented in the provincial archive, because until the nineteenth century, no law required the registration or deposition of contracts outside the notary's office (Dibenedetto, 1976: 195–196).

14 The cadaster records enclosed fields for only 15.9 percent of hearths, and they total 8.1 percent of the total agricultural surface area. The 49 priests owned the biggest proportion of enclosures (36.4 percent). *Massari* follow with 24.1 percent, and then come the landowning families with 14.8 percent. The entire portion owned by *bracciali* totaled only 23 percent.

5 Society and terminal feudalism

1 In the records there is no mention of *pesi*, "burdens," owed to the baron for particular fields (as it is for fields within the territories of the church organizations of the coastal plain) except for land which was distinctly held in emphyteusis from him. It may not have been necessary to mention this because the *vigesima* did not apply to particular fields so much as to all production of foodstuffs within the territory, and the burden may have been understood without being made explicit in contracts and the *cadaster*.

2 Several leases granted later in the century survive (ACMF, 1797: Busta CM-54-2; ASN-CO, 1749: *Atti preliminari*, Vol. 8697, *Foglio* 16).

3 To better comprehend social class within Locorotondo the author conducted a cluster analysis on two 20 percent samples of the hearths in the *catasto onciario* which represented households (some "hearths" were religious institutions), using measures of estimated taxable income from land, animals, loans, stores or workshops, and house rents, combined with a measure of indebtedness. This procedure produced a tree diagram which grouped households according to wealth and indebtedness. These groupings and the individual households which fell into them were analyzed to understand their characteristics. This analysis, alongside readings of the notarial acts, formed the basis for inferences about the nature of the local stratificational system

described in this chapter. The full details of this cluster analysis are available elsewhere (Galt, 1986). The present discussion of eighteenth-century social stratification reports only the results of the procedure, trusting that the methodologically interested reader will refer to the original article.

4 The source is Dr. Giuseppe Petrelli, to whom gratitude is extended for an informative interview.

5 See Galt, 1991, a, for details on the content of typical settlements and trousseaus during the eighteenth century.

6 The 1811 Napoleonic Census (ACL-SP, 1810–1811) lists most peasant women as *filatrici*, spinners (see Chapter 6).

6 Rural settlement in the nineteenth century

1 The first step in compilation involved dividing the communal territory into lettered sections. Fields, rural buildings, and other properties were assigned numbers and described within the sections. Land was classified by quality as first, second, and third class and use was designated. The section of the cadaster known as the *Stato di Sezione* listed all landed properties in this way, along with an estimated annual net income equal to the value of hypothetical or real rent minus expenses, with one-fourth ascribed to depreciation. The preparatory papers to the cadaster contain detailed lists of land rents compiled from the notarial protocols for several decades before. (Houses and other buildings were taxed according to their areas.) Compilers similarly described and numbered town property and then included the records in the cadaster proper which listed properties by owner. They produced two copies of this; one was sent to the provincial tax office (and ended up in the provincial archives – ASB-CP, 1816) and the other, which was to be modified as property eventually changed hands, was kept in the municipal hall (ACL-CP, 1823–1930). The author has consulted both documents during this study, and reduced the Stato di Sezione for Locorotondo conserved at Bari to computer readable code. Officials took care in compiling the Stato di Sezione and during the rectifications and corrections of the cadaster which took place between 1815 and 1817, a surveyor measured the large estates of the zone. Initial compilation was carried out by a local commission, but a *controllore*, an inspector, from elsewhere reviewed and rectified their work. In Locorotondo this also involved a new definition of the communal boundaries and a map was produced which showed both the sections, which were divided from one another by major roads radiating from the town center, and the shape of the commune, which has remained essentially the same since (ASB-LRCP, 1815–1817: busta 6, fascicolo 51, and published in Carlone, 1981: 57).

2 The author's friend and colleague Giorgio Cardone deserves special mention for his discovery of this document in 1986. His work with the document, without the benefit of a computer, laid the groundwork for this analysis.

3 It is usually possible to infer relationships from the patterns of naming in families.

4 It was hoped that it would be possible to pair individual entries in this document with the entries in the *catasto provvisorio*, which dates 5 years

later, and form a data set partially analogous to the *catasto onciario* for comparative purposes. Unfortunately this has not been possible because for the town dwellers, patronymics were not often recorded, and it is not possible to precisely assign the many duplicated names – Francesco Palmisano, for example – to entries in the cadaster. For country dwellers, patronymics were usually recorded and it has been possible to create a data set of probable country dwelling property owners from the *catasto provvisorio* data. This is not comparable, however, to the *catasto onciario* because there is no indication in the 1749 document of domicile.

5 Although, no specific references to the era of construction of these extramural, but town, neighborhoods, consisting of buildings with pitched (*cummerse*), or flat terraced roofs, have seen the light, from their absence on the sketch of Locorotondo on the map dating to 1756 (ALM, 1810), and the distinct presence of a row of extramural buildings on a similar sketch of the town on maps detailing the Duke's properties in 1796 (ACMF, 1797), it is likely that the *borghi* date to the latter decades of the waning century and possibly to the beginning of the nineteenth.

6 There is a discrepancy between this population figure and that derived from the census of 1811 of some 200 people. Demarco's figure is that reported in the *catasto provvisorio* itself, which like all figures in that document was supposed to refer to 1806. The cadaster was completed, however, in 1816 and this population figure may refer to that date instead. In making the comparisons which follow, the population and cadastral figures Demarco reports have been adopted for consistency. The figures he used come from the summarizing tables of the documents themselves and are of course subject to whatever computational errors the compilers made.

7 However, attempts to link the Census of 1811 and the *catasto provvisorio* show that, at least for the country, all property brought to a marriage was ascribed to the male head of household. Therefore this difficulty of comparison between the two cadasters may be mitigated.

8 It was possible to identify a rural population of households formed in the decade before the 1811 census through a comparison of that document with marriage contracts. For this population of 59 households there were few cases (about 24 percent) in which members of the parental generation which produced the brides and grooms involved in the contract could be indicated as even possibly living in the countryside at the time of census. (Problems arising from the compiler's lack of care in recording father's names for the town population make identification of individuals with similar names who were not country dwellers very difficult.) Unfortunately, this seeming discontinuity cannot be taken as supportive of the idea of a recent wave of settlement in the countryside. Because of simple demographic factors such as a life expectancy, which probably fell in a person's fifties (cf. Douglass, 1980: 349–350), and the expectation of marriage in the middle, or perhaps, late twenties, many men would have neared death as even their eldest children married. (It is difficult to exactly estimate age at marriage by comparing marriage contracts to the census, because there is no way of knowing, in most cases, how much time passed between the drawing up of a contract and the marriage which followed.)

9 Unfortunately documents about this case do not appear among the cases preserved in the State Archive in Trani, site of the Gran Corte Criminale.

10 What can be reconstructed of peasant life in rural Locorotondo much depends on interpreting scant evidence from various sorts of documents, in particular notarial contracts and judicial records. Police interrogations of witnesses in criminal cases yield considerable insight into some of the details of country life and into some of the kinds of stresses and strains in Locorotondese rural culture.

11 The *catasto provvisorio* of Fasano (ASB-CP, 1807) shows that Laureto which surrounds the main road from the coast just as it crests on the plateau, was planted completely with vineyards and dotted with *trulli*, as were the Fasanese halves of two other Locorotondese contrade – Lamie di Olimpia and Pantaleo. The other major plateau zone of Fasano, Selva, which is a short distance from Locorotondo's borders, showed a similar pattern.

12 Again the reader is referred to Galt, 1991, for a more thorough description of these marriage contracts and the patterns reflected in them.

13 This is the zone in which the author and his family resided during both field seasons in Locorotondo. Walks in the countryside between Lamie di Olimpia and Serralta helped confirm the presence of many recognizably old *trulli*, most of which are now abandoned, at least as full-time residences, and which are used either as summer cottages or rented to tourists.

14 Information on Martino Tarì and Giorgio Palmisano and his gang will be found in ASB-CD, 1864. Contained in the documentation on the Palmisano case are confessions dictated by both Palmisano and Tarì.

7 How peasants populated the countryside

1 These estimates assume a population of about 5,200, an average household size of 4 people projected forward from the 1811 census, and that about 50 percent of the population remained in town.

2 The figures reported by Assante (1974: 205–211) refer to prices and salaries in the coastal towns of Molfetta, Barletta, and Trani, all to the north of Bari itself, and therefore at some distance from Locorotondo but there is no reason to suppose that such general trends would have been untrue of the Murgia dei Trulli area. Fortunately, reports on climatic conditions and agricultural outcomes sent to the Intendant by a local dilettante at meteorology survive for these years (ASB-PI, 1822–1844).

3 Calella reports such strategies in his twentieth-century description of rural settlement in Locorotondo, and he notes that many olive orchards at the time of his writing were, during the nineteenth century, originally vineyards (1941: 90).

4 Currently grape growers rarely transform fields into vineyards because of the uneconomical nature of viticulture, and the high costs of labor and mechanized means involved. The author had hoped to be able to observe this process in the field, but could not for these reasons. Furthermore, current methods involve the use of explosives and earthmoving equipment, such as backhoes, and differ greatly from the traditional methods used by peasants throughout the nineteenth and early twentieth centuries. It was possible,

however, to carry out careful interviews with peasant men who had engaged in the process in the past to check the figures reported in the literature, and to amplify understandings of the work processes involved. A very detailed account of the process of transformation of fields into vineyards on the Murgia dei Trulli, specifically in the countryside of Martina Franca, is Liuzzi, 1986.

5 For example, the town of Alberobello was founded by the Count of Conversano in about 1480 through emphyteusis (Marraffa, 1960: 13), and a feudal lord settled Serbian peasants in the town of Sammichele under a larval emphyteusis contract in 1615 (published in Ricchioni, 1952: 39–42).

6 There is, however, a contract about the demolition of a house in town in 1803 in which the unskilled manual laborer who would do the job was to receive 20 ducats to take the house apart and move the usable stones inside the Church of San Giorgio, then under construction (ASB-CB, 1798–1807: Sept. 25, 1803). If a *bracciale* was to receive such a sum for the unskilled job of demolishing a house, one can imagine that considerably more would have to be paid a skilled mason and his apprentices to put one up.

7 These differences are apparent from an examination of buildings in the area and can be observed in the photographs and plans of *trulli* and Cisternino town houses (especially similar to those in Locorotondo) in chapters 4 and 5 of Allen, 1969.

8 Oral historical accounts suggest that the peasantry of rural Locorotondo had a long experience with attempts to evade taxes on, and the confiscation of, foodstuffs, particularly during the Second World War years. Many households knew ways of hiding stores of grain and other staples where investigating authorities could not find them, and there is no reason to suppose that these means were improvised for the occasion.

8 Rural social structure

1 Alongside the *jazzeile* described, two others were the object of complete interviews and genealogical study, and more fragmentary observations were made about several others. This one was chosen because its history is both reasonably typical of what went on in the others, and because that history presented a full variety of inheritance processes.

2 This narrative has now come close to the present and, to respect the anonymity of those who related the vicissitudes of families which dwelled in this hamlet, the description reveals neither its name nor the true names of the families. To avoid stilted prose which labels families and peoples with letters or numbers, the narrative uses nicknames which are authentic to Locorotondo's countryside, but chosen specifically because they are *not* used in the vicinity of this *jazzeile*. Readers from Locorotondo may find that this device lacks verisimilitude, but maintaining the anonymity of consultants was paramount.

3 Some examples include: *Malèrve* (Weed), *Fradiaue* (Brother devil, probably after the infamous early nineteenth-century bandit Fra Diavolo), *Farfalle*

(Butterfly), *Chéepetunne* (Round head), and *Scimmie* (Monkey). There are many more.

4 Severe storms are such a problem on the Murgia dei Trulli that magic was performed to prevent them, and more recently (1969) a consortium of peasant weather observers was formed to provide early warning and tracking of threatening storms. At time of fieldwork there were more than 1,000 members involved in a large territory, extending into Basilicata from the Murgia dei Trulli. Anti-hail rockets are fired from 160 launching pads operated by the membership. The consortium was founded by a Locoroton-dese agricultural entrepreneur of peasant origin, also known locally for other agricultural innovations such as planting large cherry orchards, and introduc-ing grapes grown overhead on high wires.

5 Fiancé murders in the nineteenth century are to be found in ASB-CD, 1889, and ASB-CD, 1894.

6 The tale collected was told by Maria Luigia Curri, Contrada Pentamone. Like several other tales of saints collected in rural Locorotondo the statue of the saint becomes an object to explain. In this case, what is explained is why statues of St. Lucy both hold the saint's eyes in a dish and have eyes in their heads. The folk have projected upon this contradiction a simple tale which emphasizes family values.

7 Dowries brought by women to marriages differed in the early twentieth century rather little from those recorded in the eighteenth and nineteenth centuries in marriage contracts drawn up by notaries. The major difference was in the number of each item brought. Typical for peasant families during the years at mid-century was a six-item dowry (*panni sei*). This included dresses, handkerchiefs, scarves, underwear, stockings, shoes, sheets, bed-spread, mattress (a large sack stuffed with lamb's wool), the iron bed supports, and the bed boards, a bedwarmer, a cauldron for cheese making, a breadboard, a cheese grater, chains to hang pots in the hearth, several tripods for the hearth, and a chest of drawers. Aside from land and a house, men were likely to bring a chest which was decorated and had cushions on top for seating (*a casce turche*), a table and 6 chairs, and some framed prints for the walls.

8 The 69 women represent those of median age and above who were in the parental generation in the households sampled in the Locorotondo Sample Survey. Their ages ranged from 47 to 84 with a mean of 59.1 and a standard deviation of 9.6. Unfortunately the circumstances of data collection dictated that interviews had to be done anonymously without recording names, surnames, or patronymics. This means that it was impossible to control for sisters in the sample. This probably skews the number of children reported for the generation of mothers above the sample of 69 toward slightly higher numbers. Since the sample was collected in a wide range of locales, however, there is no strong likelihood that more than a handful of pairs of sisters have been included.

9 The data for this calculation come from municipal sources. Records of births survive beginning only in 1936, and close records of causes of death survive only from a few years in the mid-1930s.

10 In those articles the severe limitation of births on the Island of Pantelleria was accomplished in an environment of limited land resources (an island) without recourse to mechanical or chemical means of birth control, and strictly through an exercise of will. The statistical analysis showed that successful small proprietor viticulturalists maximized for small families so as not to overly divide the limited amounts of land they had among too many children. On Pantelleria, the limits of the system – the shores of the island – are ever present; in Locorotondo, from the peasant point of view, land became available from the division of estates, and the limits of the system were flexible enough that the limitation of births was not inspired.

11 Curses consist of harmful wishes directed at individuals who have wronged the curser. The texts of curses include such things as: "May he have problems like a mouse in a cat's jaws!" "May he spend all the money on medicine!" (In reference to a victim cursing a thief.) "May he die during the night!" "Lord, may he get worms!" "May he have a stroke!" Another dialect word for the curse is *a sentènse*, the "sentence," in the sense of a judicial sentence pronounced by the wronged individual.

12 However during the World Wars, women left behind in Locorotondo to run family enterprises had to carry out all agricultural tasks, and it is not unusual to find peasant wives and daughters who have had to plow, or wield the heavy hoe to turn the soil. The deaths or disabling of fathers and husbands in war, or otherwise, could also throw the heaviest of agricultural work on to the backs of women.

13 Exceptions to this rule occurred when addressing elite individuals, who were given the third person of the verb, and addressed with the pronoun *signuri* coupled with the title *Don*.

14 The observations in this section, unless distinctly marked, refer to the postpeasant current situation as experienced in the field as well as to the peasant past. However, in keeping with the tenses used in the rest of this chapter the narrative will remain in the past tense.

9 *Town and country*

1 Unfortunately, space considerations dictated that the story of the rise of Locorotondo's elite landowning and professional classes could not be told in this work. However, the connection to which the passage alludes is documented in the papers relating to the murder of Don Martino Nardelli in 1816, which was carried out by one of Ciro Annichiarico's men and contracted for by other elite families in Locorotondo. See ASB-RUAPP, 1816–1822. For a less than accurate account of the affair see Church, 1895.

2 Such generalizations come from the author's complete investigation of such documents for the nineteenth and early twentieth century. In particular that investigation involved a thorough leafing of correspondence with, and about, mayors of Locorotondo which reached the attention of the prefect of the Province of Bari (ASB-GSP, 1872–1902; ASB-GSPS, 1914–1915). The results of that research on factions and factionalism will form the basis for other publications.

3 This brief sketch of artisan labor history in Locorotondo is largely based on Archangelo Lisi's autobiography (Lisi, n.d.). Lisi was a local socialist and labor union leader.

4 Giuseppe Campanella, ex-DC mayor of Locorotondo, merits appreciation for an informative interview in which he precisely described the *elenchi anagrafici*, and their history.

5 See Clark, 1977: 6–8 for a discussion of the lists.

6 Laws needed only the impetus of a single judge to be referred to the Constitutional Court for testing, and small pieces of legislation could be passed easily with lobbying, given the Italian parliamentary commission system, which meant that legislative proposals could be adopted without going through parliament (Clark, 1984: 334, 340).

7 The post-war Apulian farm-workers movement was a very active one which had national repercussions. Gramegna (1977) chronicles it. However, because the left in Locorotondo continued to be an organization composed primarily of artisans, this movement by-passed the town to a great extent.

8 See Clark, 1977 for a general discussion of pensions and Italian agriculture.

9 The following discussion leans heavily upon Cardone, 1972 for information, as well as upon interview materials collected in the field.

10 Catholic Action groups disappeared from the local scene in the late 1960s, probably as part of general trends toward secularization.

11 Cancellation from the *elenchi anagrafici* was used elsewhere in Apulia by DC/CISL interests, but mostly against CGIL farm labor organizations. Cf. Gramegna, 1976: 170.

12 In municipal elections, as at other levels, a system of preferential voting is used by which the voters must cast their votes for a single party list, but then may vote for up to 4 individuals on the list preferentially. Since the preferential vote is not obligatory, many simply choose to vote for the party list, and therefore the electorate involved in choosing individuals for seats on the municipal council is smaller than the total number of people on the election rolls.

Bibliography

Note: Document listings precede those of published works.

Documents

ACL-ABF (Archivio Comunale di Locorotondo. Agricoltura, Bosche, Foreste.) (1816). *Stato nominativo di tutti gli operari, che travagliano nelle masserie del Tenimento di Cotesto comune, e di tutti i pastori che son adetti alla custodia degli animali piccoli e grandi, che nella presente stagione sogliono venire in questa provincia.* Categoria XI. Busta 1, 1.

(1856a). *Statistica per la coltivazione degli ulivi e delle viti, e del prodotto che se ne ottiene.* Categoria XI. Busta 1, 13.

(1856b). *Statistica riguardante la produzione di cereali, con stati riguardanti la estensione delle terre messe a colture, ecc.* Categoria XI. Busta 1, 14.

ACL-CP (Archivio Comunale di Locorotondo. Catasto Provvisorio.) (1823–1930). *Catasto Provvisorio di Locorotondo.*

ACL-SP (Archivio Comunale di Locorotondo. Statistica Popolazione.) (1810–1811). *Statistica della popolazione del comune di Locorotondo formata in esecuzione degli ordini di S. E. il Signor Intendente.* Busta 71, Fascicolo 450.

ACMF (Archivio Caracciolo-De Sangro Martina Franca) (1699). *Testimento di Madama Pelligrini Castelli. 4 Maggio.* Busta CM 55–4.

(1711). *Monte Frumentario – atti di fondazione.* Busta CM 55–4.

(1757). *Luogorotondo Entrate.* Busta CM 53–2.

(1796). *Scrittura di Affitti.* Busta CM 55–18.

(1797). *Commissione feudale.* Busta CM 54–2.

(1817). *Perito del Parco del Vaglio.* Busta CM 55–15.

ALM (Personal archive of Dott. Luigi de Michele, Locorotondo.) (1810). Map of Locorotondo (copy of original dating to 1756).

ASB-ACA (Archivio di Stato di Bari. Amministrazione Comunale Antica.) (1827). Correspondence relating to removal of peasants from the Locorotondo countryside and their relocation in the town. Opere pubbliche, Busta 29, Fascicolo 375.

ASB-AD (Archivio di Stato di Bari. Atti Demaniali.) (1809). Various reports on the status of commons in Fasano, Cisternino, and Locorotondo. Busta 69, Fascicolo 843.

(1810). *Locorotondo: Sentenza della Commissione Feudale, 30 Novembre 1810.*

ASB-AIC (Archivio di Stato di Bari. Agricoltura, Industria e Commercio) (1866). Communal council minutes concerning changing market day. Busta 61.

(1871). *Relazione sullo stato delle campagne.* Busta 120, Fascicolo 121.

ASB-AN (Archivio di Stato di Bari. Notarial Acts.)

(1683–1729). Acts of Not. G. Aprile.

(1729–1780). Acts of Not. P. Aprile.

(1734–1784). Acts of Not. G. Chialà.

(1761–1796). Acts of Not. A. G. Chialà d'Aprile.

(1777–1808). Acts of Not. F. G. Aprile.

(1780–1838). Acts of Not. Giuseppe Convertini.

(1819–1867). Acts of Not. F. Musaio.

ASB-CB (Archivio di Stato di Bari. Corte Baronale.) (1798–1807). *Obligationes penes acta della Corte Baronale di Locorotondo.*

ASB-CD (Archivio di Stato di Bari. Corte d'Assise.)

(1864). Trial of Giorgio Palmisano *et al.* Seconda versamento, Busta 28, 29.

(1878). Trial of Vincenzo Partipilo *et al.* Seconda versamento, Busta 149, Fascicolo 79.

(1881). Trial of Paolo Donato Barbarito. Seconda versamento. Busta 167.

(1889). Trial of Elisabetta Ferrini. Seconda Versamento. Busta 239.

(1894). Trial of Anna Maria Minno and parents. Prima versamento. Busta 34.

ASB-CO (Archivio di Stato di Bari. Catasto Onciario.)

(1749). *Locorotondo.*

ASB-CP (Archivio di Stato di Bari. Catasto Provvisorio.)

(1807). *Catasto Provvisorio di Fasano – Stato di Sezione.*

(1816). *Catasto Provvisorio di Locorotondo.*

ASB-GBP (Archivio di Stato di Bari. Gabinetto della Prefettura.) (1872–1902). *Personale dei sindaci di Locorotondo.* Busta 35, Fascicolo 17, 18, and 19; Busta 72, Fascicolo 4.

ASB-GSPS (Archivio di Stato di Bari. Gabinetto della Prefettura, Seconda Versamento) (1914–1915). *Personale dei sindaci di Locorotondo.* Busta 101, Fascicolo 29.

ASB-ICO (Archivio di Stato di Bari. Intendenza – Consiglio Generale degli Ospizii, Amministrazione.) (1809). *Rappresentanza per lo Monte di Montanaro del Comune di Luocorotondo.* Busta 110, Fascicolo 1954.

ASB-LRCP (Lavori, rettifiche, e revisione dei catasti provvisori, volume per l'operazione del catasto provvisorio) (1815–1817). *Locorotondo Anno 1815, Topografia del Terreno di detta Comune.* Busta 6, Fascicolo 51.

ASB-OP (Archivio di Stato di Bari. Opere Pie.) (1855). Letter from Intendente to Presidente of the Consiglio Generale degli Ospizii about lack of churches in countryside in Locorotondo. Busta 108, Fascicolo 1932.

ASB-PA (Archivio di Stato di Bari. Intendenza, Polizia Antica.) (1812). Case concerning indemnities to be paid to peasants robbed of all their possessions by brigands, Nov. 1812. Busta 15, Fascicolo 549.

ASB-PI (Archivio di Stato di Bari. Intendenza – Pubblica Istruzione.) (1822–1844). Correspondence about choice of Maestro and Maestra primario(a), Meteorological reports 1836–1837. Busta 19.

ASB-PSP (Archivio di Stato di Bari – Pretura, Sentenze Penali.) (1819–1857). Proceedings of minor criminal cases in Locorotondo.
ASB-RUAPP (Sacra Regia Udienza – Antichi Tribunali – Processi Penali.) (1816–1822). Trial for the murder of Don Martino Nardelli. Busta 13.
ASN-CO (Archivio di Stato di Napoli. Catasto Onciario.) (1749). *Locorotondo.*

Published Sources

Alberti, Leandro (1551). *Descrittione di Tutta Italia.* Venice, Pietro dei Nicolini da Sabbio.
Aleffi, Michele (1983). Il lupo. *Umanesimo della Pietra, numero unico,* July 1983.
Allen, Edward (1969). *Stone Shelters.* Cambridge, Mass., M.I.T. Press.
Ancona, Sante (1988). La lunga notte di Tetè e Tutuccio. *Locorotondo,* 3, 113–127.
Arlacchi, Pino (1980). *Mafia, Contadini, e Latifondo nella Calabria Tradizionale.* Bologna, Il Mulino.
  (1983). *Mafia, Peasants, and Great Estates: Society in Traditional Calabria.* New York, Cambridge University Press.
Assante, Franca (1964). *Calopezzati: Proprietà Fondiaria e Classi Rurali in un Comune della Calabria (1740–1886).* Naples, Edizioni Scientifiche.
  (1974). *Città e Campagne nella Puglia del Secolo XIX: L'Evoluzione Demografica.* Geneva, Librairie Droz.
Aymard, Maurice (1982). From feudalism to capitalism in Italy: the case that doesn't fit. *Review,* 6, 131–208.
Baccaro, Giuseppe (1968). *Memorie Storiche di Locorotondo.* Locorotondo, Biblioteca del Lavoratore.
Barbagli, Marzio (1984). *Sotto lo Stesso Tetto: Mutamenti della Famiglia in Italia dal XV al XX Secolo.* Bologna, Il Mulino.
Battaglia, Raffaele (1952). Osservazioni sulla distribuzione e sulla forma dei trulli pugliesi. *Archivio Storico Pugliese,* 5, 34–44.
Belmonte, Thomas (1979). *The Broken Fountain.* New York, Columbia University Press.
Bennett, John (1969). *The Northern Plainsmen: Adaptive Strategy and Agrarian Life.* Chicago, Aldine.
  (1976). *The Ecological Transition: Cultural Anthropology and Human Adaptation.* New York, Pergamon.
Berteaux, E. (1899). Etude d'un type d'habitation primitive. Trulli, caselle et specchie des Pouille. *Annales de Geographie,* 8, 207–230.
Biassutti, Renato (1932). Ricerche sui tipi di insediamenti rurali in Italia. *Memorie della Reale Società Geografica Italiana,* 27, 5–25.
Blok, Anton (1966). Land reform in a west Sicilian latifondo village: the persistence of a feudal structure. *Anthropological Quarterly,* 39, 1–16.
  (1969). South Italian agro-towns. *Comparative Studies in Society and History,* 11, 121–135.
  (1974). *The Mafia of a Sicilian Village. 1860 to 1960.* Oxford, Blackwell.
Boso, Pietro (1969). *Martina Franca nel 1755.* Taranto, Grafiche Cressati.

Brettell, Caroline (1986). *Men Who Migrate, Women Who Wait: Population and History in a Portuguese Parish*. Princeton, N.J., Princeton University Press.

Calella, Sigismondo (1941). *Colonizzazione e Ruralizzazione. Un Modello: Il Territorio di Locorotondo*. Martina Franca, Aquaro e Dragonetti.

Cardone, Giorgio (1972). *Marginalità e Dipendenza: Primi Appunti per una Ricerca Sociologia su Locorotondo*. Thesis in Lettere e Filosofia, Università degli Studi di Bari.

  (1980). I balli di campagna. *Commerse*, numero speciale [July], 40–43.

Carlone, Giuseppe, ed. (1981). *L'Immagine e il Progetto*. Monopoli, Grafiche Colucci.

Chayanov, A. V. (1966). *The Theory of Peasant Economy*. Homewood, Ill., American Economic Association.

Chirulli, D. Isidoro (1982 [orig. 1752]). *Istoria Cronologica della Franca Martina cogli Avvenimenti più Notabili del Regno di Napoli*. Tomo II. Martina Franca, Edizioni Umanesimo della Pietra.

Church, E. M. (1895). *Chapters in an Adventurous Life: Sir Richard Church in Italy and Greece*. Edinburgh and London, W. Blackwood and Sons.

Clark, M. Gardner (1977). *Agricultural Social Security and Rural Exodus in Italy*. Ithaca, New York, Western Societies Program Occasional Paper No. 7, Center for International Studies, Cornell University.

Clark, Martin (1984). *Modern Italy 1971–1982*. London and New York, Longman.

Cofano, Antonio (1977). *Storia Antifeudale della Franca Martina*. Fasano, Schena editore.

Cormio, Aldo (1974). Strutture feudali ed equilibri sociali in Terra di Bari nei secoli XVIII e XIX. In P. Villani, ed., *Economia e Classi Sociali nella Puglia Moderna*. Naples, Guida editore.

Cornelisen, Ann (1969). *Torregreca: a World in Southern Italy*. London, Macmillan.

  (1976). *Women of the Shadows*. New York, Random House.

Cronon, William (1983). *Changes in the Land: Indians, Colonists, and the Ecology of New England*. New York, Hill and Wang.

Dal Pane, Luigi (1936). *Studi sui Catasti Onciari del Regno di Napoli. I – Minervino Murge*. Bari, Macri.

Davis, John (1973). *Land and Family in Pisticci*. London, Athlone Press.

  (1977). *People of the Mediterranean: an Essay in Comparative Social Anthropology*. London, Routledge and Kegan Paul.

De Felice, Franco (1971). *L'Agricoltura in Terra di Bari dal 1880 al 1914*. Milan, Banca Commerciale Italiana.

Delille, Gérard (1988). *Famiglia e Proprietà nel Regno di Napoli*. Turin, Giulio Einaudi editore.

Demarco, Domenico (1970). La proprietà fondiaria in provincia di Bari al tramonto del secole XVIII. In, Various authors *Terra di Bari all'Aurora del Risorgimento*. Bari, Laterza.

De Meo, G. (1935). Caratteristiche demografiche di classi economicamente e socialmente differenziate in una città italiana del secolo XVIII. *Genus*, 1, 359–409.

De Michele, Vittorio (1986). *Locorotondo: Rinvenimenti Archeologici in Contrada Grofoleo: Origini di un Centro Abitato della Valle d'Itria*. Martina Franca, Nuova Editrice Apulia.

Dibenedetto, Giuseppe (1976). *Gli Archivi di Stato di Terra di Bari*. Roma, Centro di Ricerca Editore.

Dickenson, Robert E. (1956). Dispersed settlement in southern Italy. *Erdekunde*, 10, 282–297.

Direzione Generale della Statistica e del Lavoro (1903–1918). *Statistica della Emigrazione Italiana per l'Estero*. Rome, Ministero di Agricultura, Industria, e Commercio.

Dolci, Danilo (1959). *Report from Palermo*. New York, Viking Press.

Douglass, William A. (1980). The south Italian family: a critique. *Journal of Family History*, 5, 338–359.

  (1984). *Emigration in a South Italian Town: An Anthropological History*. New Brunswick, N.J., Rutgers University Press.

Dovring, Folke (1965). *Land and Labor in Europe in the Twentieth Century: a Comparative Study in Recent Agrarian History*. The Hague, Martinus Nijhoff.

Fiore, Tommaso (1978). *Un Popolo di Formiche*. Bari, Laterza.

Foster, George (1961). The dyadic contract: a model for the social structure of a Mexican village. *American Anthropologist*, 63, 1173–1192.

Friedmann, F. G. (1953). The world of 'la miseria.' *Partisan Review*, 20, 218–231.

Galanti, Giuseppe Maria (1969 [orig. 1793–1794]). *Della Descrizione Geografica e Politica delle Sicilie*. F. Assante and D. Demarco eds., Naples, Edizioni Scientifiche Italiane.

Galt, Anthony H. (1979). Exploring the cultural ecology of field fragmentation and scattering in south Italy. *Journal of Anthropological Research*, 35, 93–108.

  (1980). Structure and process in social stratification on the Island of Pantelleria, Sicily. *Ethnology*, 19, 405–425.

  (1986). Social class in a mid-eighteenth-century Apulian town: indications from the catasto onciario. *Ethnohistory*, 33, 419–447.

  (1991). Marital property and allied issues in an Apulian town during the eighteenth and early nineteenth centuries. In Saller, Richard and David Kertzer, eds., The Family in Italy; from Antiquity to the Present. New Haven, Yale University Press.

  (forthcoming). Emphyteusis and indigenous agricultural development: the case of Locorotondo, Italy. In Richard Herr, ed., *Themes in the Rural History of the Western World*. Ames, Iowa, Iowa State University Press.

Galt, Anthony and Larry J. Smith (1979). Fertility on Pantelleria: an interdisciplinary perspective. *Population Studies*, 33, 223–238.

Garofalo, Salvatore (1974). La dimensione storica nell'analisi delle strutture agrarie: La Murgia dei Trulli. *Economia e Storia*, 21, 330–59.

Geertz, Clifford (1963). *Agricultural Involution: The Processes of Ecological Change in Indonesia*. Berkeley, University of California Press.

Genovesi, Antonio (1978 [orig. pub. 1769]). Il problema della terra. In Rosario Villari, ed. *Il Sud nella Storia d'Italia*. Bari, Laterza.

Giacomini, Mariuccia (1981). *Sposi a Belmonte nel Settecento: Famiglia e Matrimonio in un Borgo Rurale Calabrese*. Milan, Giuffrè Editore.

Giustiniani, Lorenzo (1802). *Dizionario Geografico-ragionato del Regno di Napoli*. Naples, publisher unknown.

Gramegna, Giuseppe (1976). *Braccianti e Popolo in Puglia 1944–1971: Cronache di un Protagonista*. Bari, De Donato Editore.

Guarella, Giuseppe (1983). *La Chiesa della Greca in Locorotondo*. Locorotondo, Cassa Rurale e Artigiana.

(1985). *La storia di Locorotondo nel Manoscritto di Angelo Convertini*. Locorotondo, Amministrazione Comunale di Locorotondo.

Hobsbawm, Eric J. (1959). *Primitive Rebels: Studies in Archaic Forms of Social Movements in the 19th and 20th Centuries*. New York, W. W. Norton and Co.

Holmes, Douglas R. (1989). *Cultural Disenchantments: Worker Peasantries in Northeast Italy*. Princeton, N. J., Princeton University Press.

ISTAT (Istituto Centrale di Statistica) (1933). *Catasto Agrario (1929–VIII. Compartimento delle Puglie. Provincia di Bari*. Fascicolo 71, Rome, Instituto Poligrafico dello Stato.

(1972). *Secondo Censimento Generale dell'Agricoltura*. Rome, Istituto Centrale di Statistica.

(1983). *Dodicesimo Censimento Generale della Popolazione, 25 Ottobre*. 1981. Volume II – Dati sulle Caratteristiche Strutturali della Popolazione e delle Abitazioni. Rome, Istituto Centrale di Statistica.

Kertzer, David (1984). *Family Life in Central Italy 1880–1910: Sharecropping, Wage Labor, and Coresidence*. New Brunswick, Rutgers University Press.

Leone, Vittorio and Felice Vita (1983). Aspetti della vegetazione e problemi di tutela. *Umanesimo della Pietra, numero unico*, July 1983.

Lisi, Arcangelo (n.d.). *Storia del Movimento Operaio di Locorotondo*. Locorotondo, Arti Grafiche Angelini e Pacc.

Liuzzi, Achille (1981). *La Murgia dei Trulli: Lineamenti Caratteristiche, Sviluppo Economico e Civile*. Martina Franca, Nettuno.

(1983). Piogge e altre meteore a Martina. *Umanesimo della Pietra, numero unico*, July 1983.

(1986). L'Antica arte del mettere il pastino. *Umananesimo e la Pietra, numero unico*, July 1986.

Lopreato, Joseph (1967). *Peasants No More*. San Francisco, Chandler Pub Company.

Mack Smith, Denis (1968a). *Medieval Sicily 800–1713*. London, Chatto and Windus.

(1968b). *Modern Sicily, after 1713*. London, Chatto and Windus.

Maranelli, C. (1946 [orig. 1908]). La Murgia dei Trulli; un'oasi di popolazione sparsa nel mezzogiorno. In C. Maranelli, ed., *Considerazioni Geografiche sulla Questione Meridionale*. Bari, Laterza.

Marraffa, M. (1960). *I trulli di Alberobello*. Alberobello, Editrice Tipografica Adriana.

Martinelli, Flavia (1985). Public policy and industrial development in southern Italy: anatomy of a dependent industry. *International Journal of Urban and Regional Research*, 9, 47–81.

Masella, Luigi (1979). Economia e Società nel Periodo Spagnolo. In G. Musca, ed., *Storia della Puglia*, vol. II. Bari, Adda editore.

Masi, Giovanni (1962). I monti frumentari e pecuniari in Provincia di Bari. In, Various authors *Studi in Onore di Amintore Fanfani*. Milan, Dott. A. Giuffrè Editore.

(1966). *Strutture e Società nella Puglia Barese del Secondo Settecento*. Matera, Montemurro.

(1968). *La Crisi dell'Antico Regime in Terra di Bari (1791–1814)*. Matera, Montemurro.

Massafra, Angelo (1979a). Economia e sociatà nel settecento. In G. Musca, ed., *Storia della Puglia*, Vol. I. Bari, Mario Adda editore.

(1979b). Dal Decennio Francese all'Unità. In G. Musca, ed., *Storia della Puglia*, vol. II. Bari, Adda editore.

(1983). Murgia dei Trulli: trasformazione del paesaggio agrario dai primi dell'ottocento ai giorni nostri. *Umanesimo della Pietra, Numero unico*, July, 1983.

Mele, Domenico (1883). *Annuario Storico-Statistico-Commerciale di Bari e Provincia*. Bari, Stabilimento Tipografico F. Petruzzelli e Figli.

Mennella, C. (1957). Sulle disponibilità idriche stagionali in Puglia in rapporto alle precipitazioni. *Atti del XVII Congresso Geografico Italiano*, 17, 268–278.

Molfese, Franco (1964). *Storia del Brigantaggio dopo l'Unità*. Milan, Feltrinelli.

Moss, Leonard and Stephen Cappannari (1960). Patterns of kinship, *comparaggio*, and community in a south Italian village. *Anthropological Quarterly*. 33, 24–32.

Palasciano, Italo (1986). Locorotondo: viticoltura anni trenta; primi anni di vita della cantina sociale. *Umanesimo della Pietra, numero unico*, 29–40.

Palmisano, Nicola (1986). *Anche il Fragno Fiorisce: Don Francesco Convertini Missionario Salesiano*. Locorotondo, Comunità Civica ed Ecclesiale di Locorotondo.

Pastore, Martino (1960). *La Cantina Sociale di Locorotondo*. Graduate thesis, University of Bari.

Pinto Minerva, Franca *et al.* (1983). *Le Condizioni di Vita degli Anziani nel Comune di Locorotondo: Rapporto di Ricerca*. Locorotondo, Città di Locorotondo.

Piselli, Fortunata (1981). *Parentela ed Emigrazione: Mutamenti e Continuità in una Comunità Calabrese*. Turin, Giulio Einaudi editore.

Poli, Giuseppe (1981). Appunti per una tipologia dei contratti agrari nella fascia costiera di Terra di Bari nel cinquecento. In Angelo Massafra, ed., *Problemi di Storia delle Campagne Meridionali nell'Età Moderna e Contemporanea*. Bari, Dedalo Libri.

Presutti, Errico (1909). *Puglie. Vol. I. Relazione del Delegato Tecnico. In Inchiesta Parlamentare sulle Condizioni dei Contadini nelle Provincie Meridionali e nella Sicilia.* Rome, Tipografia Nazionale di Giovanni Bertero.

Resta, Patrizia (1984). *Democrazia e Particolarismo: Conflitto e Mediazione nella Macchina Politica Meridionale.* Lecce, Edizioni Milella.

Ricchioni, Vincenzo (1952). *Studi Storici di Economia dell'Agricoltura Meridionale.* Florence, Macri Editore.

   (1958). Miracoli del Lavoro contadino; i vigneti della Murgia dei "Trulli." *Annali della Facoltà di Agraria dell'Università di Bari,* 14, 347-381.

   (1959). Sopravvivenza dell'enfiteusi nel mezzogiorno. *Rivista di Economia Agraria,* 14, 13–23.

Rochefort, Renée (1961). *Le Travail en Sicile.* Paris, Presses Universitaires de France.

Rosa, Mario (1974). Sviluppo e crisi della proprietà ecclesiastica: Terra di Bari e Terra d'Otranto nel Settecento. In P. Villani, ed., *Economia e Classi Sociali nella Puglia Moderna.* Naples, Guida Editori.

   (1979). Politica e amministrazione nel settecento. *In* G. Musca, ed., *Storia della Puglia,* vol. II. Bari, Adda editore.

Salvemini, Biagio (1982). Quadri territoriali e mercato internazionale: Terra di Bari nell'età della restaurazione. *Società e Storia,* 18, 831–876.

Sampietro, Giuseppe (1922). *Fasano: Indagini Storiche.* Fasano, Schena editore.

Sassoon, Donald (1986). *Contemporary Italy: Politics Economy and Society since 1945.* London and New York, Longman.

Schneider, Jane and Peter Schneider (1976). *Culture and Political Economy in Western Sicily.* New York, Academic Press.

Silverman, Sydel (1975). *The Three Bells of Civilization.* New York, Columbia University Press.

   (1979). On the uses of history in anthropology: the Palio of Siena. *American Ethnologist,* 6, 413–436.

Snowden, Frank M. (1986). *Violence and Great Estates in the South of Italy: Apulia. 1900–1922.* Cambridge, Cambridge University Press.

Tentori, Tullio (1971). Il sistema della vita della comunità Materana. In Tullio Tentori, ed., *Scritti Antropologici.* Vol. III. Rome, Edizioni Ricerche.

   (1976). Social classes and family in a Southern Italian town: Matera. In John G. Peristiany, ed., *Mediterranean Family Structures.* Cambridge, Cambridge University Press.

Tragni, Bianca (1985). *I Nomadi del Pentagramma: le Bande Musicali in Puglia.* Giovinazzo, Edizioni Libreria Peucetia.

Troccoli Verardi, M. L. (1972). *I Misteriosi Simboli dei Trulli.* Bari, editore Adda.

Villani, Pasquale (1968). *Feudalità, Riforme, Capitalismo Agrario. Panorama di Storia Sociale tra Sette e Ottocento.* Bari, Laterza.

   (1972). Numerazioni dei fuochi e problemi demografici del mezzogiorno nell'eta del Viceregno. *Rassegna Economica,* 36, 1627–1650.

Villari, Rosario (1977). *Mezzogiorno e Contadini nell'Età Moderna.* Bari, Laterza.

(1978). *Il Sud nella Storia D'Italia: Antologia della Questione Meridionale.* Bari, Laterza.

(1985). Masaniello: contemporary and recent interpretations. *Past and Present,* 108, 117–132.

Wilstach, Paul (1930). The stone beehive homes of the Italian heel. *National Geographic Magazine,* 57, 228–260.

Index